"Why Does My Social Life Pick Up When I Leave the Country?"

And other (mostly) whimsical essays

by
Saul Schachter

"Why Does My Social Life Pick Up When I Leave the Country?" and other (mostly) whimsical essays

Copyright © Saul Schachter, 2019

Quantity Sales available.
For details contact the author at the email address above.
Printed in the United States of America

ISBN-13: 978-1-7326927-3-2
"Why Does My Social Life Pick Up
When I Leave the Country?"
And other (mostly) whimsical essays

Author: Saul Schachter

Library of Congress
ID: Case #: 1-7531827541
March 2019
101 Independence Avenue
Washington, DC 20559-6000

Cover design and interior layout
by Kevin C. Horton
Tender Fire Books

Illustrations by Iwan Yasin Agustin

"Why Does My Social Life Pick Up When I Leave the Country?"

And other (mostly) whimsical essays

by Saul Schachter

Tender Fire Books

Index of Articles

To my mother, Vivian Schachter, whose kindness to others, warmth, and humor have inspired me to be as wonderful as she is. I hope someday to come close!

Introduction

When I was growing up, I wanted to be a journalist. I got my first typewriter at 8 and began "publishing" newspapers for my classmates using the school's ditto machine (My fingers were always blue, but my spirits weren't!). When I reached Junior High, I joined the newspaper staff and continued on in High School where I was the Sports and Features Editor. My friends called me, "Scoop," for two reasons: I wrote for the school paper and I worked at our local Baskin-Robbins ice cream parlor. I was all set on making journalism my career, until I volunteered to help out in Fran Lawrence's 6th grade class at Glen Head School and discovered how much I enjoyed working with children. During my Senior year in high school, I received *The Long Island Press'* John Greene Award for "excellence in journalism" and this further complicated my plans!

What to do? Despite my love of writing, I majored in education and American History in college, while writing for the school paper. I received an internship to Newsday, loved the experience there, but as graduation loomed, I had to make a decision: Journalism or teaching? I loved writing, but I loved teaching more. I decided to become a teacher and subbed for a year in the North Shore School district, my alma mater, and was subsequently hired to teach 3rd and 4th graders at Friends Academy on Long Island. The following year, I moved on to 6th graders at North Merrick, New York, until I found my dream job: Returning to North Shore to teach Social Studies---where I remained for 33 happy years.

But, I never gave up my love of writing.

I decided to become a freelancer. I wrote my first story about returning to North Shore to sub and sent it out to newspapers and magazines. Twelve rejection letters later, I decided to try *The New York Times*. Why not, I thought. If they turned me down, I could frame a rejection letter from the world's greatest newspaper. But, they threw me off-balance by accepting it! My first published essay---in *The New York Times*! From there, I went on to write other essays for the *Times*, plus *The Boston Globe, The Chicago Tribune, The Philadelphia Inquirer, The Pittsburgh Post-Gazette, The Miami Herald, Newsday, The Denver Post, The New York Post, The New York Daily News, The Christian Science Monitor, The Toronto Globe & Mail, Family Circle*, and *Newsweek*. In 1980, *The Washington Post* began a travel section and I began submitting manuscripts. Instead of writing about the canals of Venice or the fjords of Norway, mine were humor essays such as, "The Joys of Jet Lag" (the chores I happily do at 4 a.m. when I can't sleep) and the title piece, "Why Does My Social Life Pick Up When I Leave the Country?"

I retired from teaching in 2014, but I am still writing, mostly for *Newsday* where I have had 60 published essays. Overall, 138 pieces have appeared in newspapers and magazines and occasionally I've appeared in a new outlet: on-line. And, now, I've gathered these essays for this book. Not all of them are appearing here, but my favorites are. I hope you enjoy them!

1.

A Substitute's Lot Is Not An Easy One: How One Survived

The New York Times, November 16, 1980

There is perhaps no more maligned human being in the world than the substitute teacher. Each morning these kamikaze pilots of the education system enter the classroom battlefield and risk life, limb and sanity to carry on the education process to pick up $35 a day. Few survive intact.

Frequently one hears a report that a sub staggered off at lunch and never returned. The subs come in all ages, sizes and shapes, but usually fit into one of three categories:

•The young enthusiastic teacher trying to break into the school system with hopes of landing a full-time job.

•The person who enjoys being with children, but does not want all the responsibilities that go with being a full-time teacher.

•The older teacher who wants to ease his or her way into retirement, but still enjoys the sounds and activity of the classroom.

I fall into the first category.

Unable to find a full-time teaching job, I was hired by my old school system, North Shore Schools, in Glen Head, Long Island, as a substitute teacher. Returning to North Shore after five years was like a scene out of "Welcome Back, Kotter." I was subbing for teachers I had as a student and teaching students whom I had in Little League, who were neighbors of mine or who were brothers and sisters of my old classmates.

I can unabashedly say I loved it. I became practically a full-time substitute, being called on to teach junior high and senior high subjects ranging from mathematics to Latin, from English to shop. One day I discussed journalism in an English class and the next day I found myself discoursing on the causes of the French Revolution in a social studies class. By substituting, I began observing other teachers' techniques and incorporated their ideas and style into my own.

The most crucial moments for a substitute teacher are the first few minutes after he enters a classroom. The students size him up as if he's the new kid on the block. During this introductory period a substitute establishes the rules and sets the tone for the day. If the class rowdy mutters to his buddy, "Hey, he's cool," then you're in. If the teacher finds that for some mysterious reason the filmstrip projector doesn't work (it's been unplugged), or that his chalk has suddenly disappeared, he begins to pray for snow. Once settled, the students develop a rarely-seen camaraderie. As the substitute teacher takes attendance, Jeffrey will ceremoniously raise his hand when Johnny's name is called. Jennifer will do likewise for Rebecca. All of a sudden, the students are a model of decorum, until Fred answers to Sally. "My parents always wanted a girl," he says, sheepishly. If the teachers goes along with the game and says, "Thank you, Sally," he'll likely earn a few points with the class.

The students try other ways to test a substitute. Upon seeing a substitute enter a room they might devise a way of getting out of the room; like the "S. Lee" caper. One week, I was besieged by students waving passes signed by their teachers, "S. Lee," authorizing them to get out of class. I grew suspicious. I knew Sandra Lee was an English teacher, but why did she want to see students from my class? I refused to let them go and tried during the week to track down Mrs. Lee.

Near the end of the week I found Mrs. Lee and she confirmed my thoughts: No, she never signed those passes, and furthermore, she didn't even know those students. Later I collared some of them, and they insisted that Mrs. Lee had signed those passes.

A week passed, and the incident was almost forgotten when a 10th-grader thrust a pass in my hand signed by guess who? I looked at her thoughtfully and said, "Robin, I'd like to let you go, but I really can't."

"Why, not?" she demanded.

"Well," I replied, "Mrs. Lee is absent today." The girl turned ashen and returned to her seat. The "S. Lee Caper" was over.

I was in so often that teachers and students alike shortened the question of "Who are you in for?" to "Who are you today?" In the junior high, teachers stopped addressing me as "Saul" but would cheerfully call me by the first name of the teacher for who I was subbing. In one week I was addressed as "Gladys," "Vicki," "June," "Lydia" and "Diane."

Some teachers cajoled me into adopting the mannerisms and disposition of the teacher. I became alternately gruff and cheerful, arrogant and sincere. Once, while subbing for a gregarious social studies teacher, I threw my arm around a young female math teacher at lunch and whispered, "Good morning, Debbie." She looked at me blandly and said, "Oh, you must be Gabe today."

But the real joy was in working with the students. When I entered the high school a group of freshmen girls would inevitably be waiting at my homeroom regardless of where I was teaching that day. It seemed that they would arrive at school early and check in the office to see whom I was covering for. Still others would drop in on their free periods or between classes to chat or to give me the latest news on their brother and sister.

Over the months, I watched with avuncular pride as they matured, made new friends, teased and laughed with one another. I watched gawky, uncomfortable girls develop poise and confidence and freshmen boys combing strands of hair down to their earlobe so that they, too, could have sideburns.

Teaching a wide range of subjects was particularly gratifying because, I too, gained knowledge. I was worried, though, when I was called on to lecture on photosynthesis for four eighth-grade classes. I knew less about photosynthesis than I did about organic chemistry (which I had "taught" the previous week). Fortunately, the teacher had left me copious notes and I was able to answer most questions tossed my way. By the end of the day I felt drained, if not relieved.

The next day I was in for my old Latin teacher. A student asked a question about the dative case, and I was stumped. I hemmed and hawed, quickly scanned my Latin textbook, but came up with nothing. Finally a voice piped up from the back, "Oh, come on John, give Mr. Schachter a break, He still hasn't recovered from photosynthesis!" While the class roared with laughter, I thanked my friend in the back.

My stay at North Shore came to an abrupt end last year. I no longer teach French, algebra, organic chemistry, shop and not even photosynthesis. One morning I was interviewed and hired the same day as a third- and fourth grade teacher at a private school nearby. My happy days as a pinch-hitter had ended.

2.

A Taste Of Broadway In The School Auditorium

Newsday, September 20, 1981

I was not prepared for this.

As a new teacher I felt well-equipped to handle a sixth-grade class. After all, I had completed four years of college where I studied various teaching techniques, became an expert on behavior modification, and knew Piaget better than even Mrs. Piaget. I passed the interview, was handed a plan-book, and was told, "Your class play goes on in six weeks."

A class play? Scenery? Costumes? Oh, no! The memories of my own class plays were too painful. In first grade, we had put on a "Fashion Show." Each "model" was to walk through an arch, say, "My name is _____, and I'm wearing a blue shirt, black pants, brown shoes," twirl a few times and walk back properly through the arch and sit down.

This took seven weeks of rehearsal. Obviously, I needed more time. I went through the routine smoothly until it came time for me to walk majestically through the arch. Instead, I saw my buddy across the stage, sauntered over to him and sat down. For this indiscretion, I was persona non grata for three weeks.

In second grade, we did *Spring* and I was cast as a raindrop. There were six other raindrops and none of us were too happy about having to wear yellow leotards. On the day of the performance, five of us stayed home, and rain received very little stage time.

Third through sixth grade remains a blur to me, although I seemed to be cast year after year as a policeman who would confront a hysterical girl with, "How big was the monster, miss?"

With that inauspicious background, I set out to find a suitable play. It was no easy task I curled up one weekend with more than 40 scripts from a publication that specializes in children's plays.

I had to find a play that would interest all ages, that had a cast of at least 20 characters and that would last between 30 and 40 minutes.

I found history, science fiction, satire, adventure stories, and even *Spring* – my old second grade play. I finally decided on *Robin Hood Outwits the Sheriff*. A charming play with adventure and comedy.

When I announced the selection to my students, I was greeted with stares and groans. "Robin Hood? Why Robin Hood?"

I think if I had announced that we were doing,*My Fair Lady* and that we were flying to England for rehearsals, it would have met with the same response.

Nevertheless, the students grudgingly went along and after several readings, auditions were held and a cast assembled. To enliven the production, four rewritten contemporary songs were added. Instead of "Our Kind of Town, Chicago Is" the students sang, "Our Kind of Woods, Sherwood Forest Is." And for the piece de resistance, I added two dancing numbers, which I adapted from my adult education classes.

Initially, the response was underwhelming. The songs were "dumb" and only a handful of the girls showed any enthusiasm for the dances. But I was undaunted.

In due time, the show began to take shape. Some students who didn't have parts were given new lines that we added to the script. One boy, Andrew Braun, became "Brawny Andrew" and, paying homage to the original production, we called two actors "Flinn Errol" and "Hale Alan."

Many students had trouble with the English dialogue, but

that was left intact. Other parts were updated, however. When Robin Hood addressed his cohorts with, "Well, my merry men..." a chorus would scream out "people!" to which a beleaguered Robin would throw up his hands and sign, "my merry *people*."

Romantic scenes generated no enthusiasm. Robin's "No, my love" to the beautiful Maid Marion was greeted with revulsion by both characters. The offending line was thus deleted, though in the years to come Robin will probably regret that move.

The songs and dances fared a little better, and then, suddenly, it was Friday – show time!

When the curtain at last opened, I sat nervously in the front row, cupping my ears so that the actors would speak louder and smiling foolishly when they looked morose. My fears were unfounded. The acting was impeccable, the songs loud and clear, and even the dancing was terrific. There was applause not only after the songs, but after many scenes as well. And the "merry people" line nearly brought down the house.

Still there were moments... One actor uttered lines that he was supposed to say five pages later, and I thought, "Oh, no, now the rest are going to follow suit and the play will be over in 10 minutes." Fortunately, Robin stepped in and guided the group.

Then, there was the time the music teacher inexplicably began playing one song five lines early and I wondered what would happen when the song ended. Would the person who lost his lines return to deliver them or would the person scheduled to speak after the song jump in? It was a very long three-minute song. But, happily, the displaced actor spoke his lines and again the rest followed smoothly.

And, then, just as I began dreaming of Broadway, it was all over. The principal congratulated the cast on the marvelous production, and Brawny Andrew, on behalf of his classmates, presented me with a small gift.

The following week, another class performed in turn, with one student telling a beaming teacher before the entire school, "We want to thank you for your help and aggravation." Fortunately, when it had been my turn, Brawny did not make a speech.

3

Returning To Teach At My Alma Mater: "Welcome Back, Saul!"

Newsday, August 15, 1982

Seven years after I graduated from North Shore High School in 1974, I returned to my alma mater. Unlike classmates who come back to see old teachers and friends, I came prepared for an extended stay: I returned as a teacher.

What was so surprising about returning to North Shore was how little things have changed. On my first day as a 9th grade Social Studies teacher, I scanned my class roster and was startled to see the names – Wollenberger, Stevenson, Anderson, Milano – all names of my old classmates! A further check revealed that about 30 percent of these students were neighbors or former players from my Little League teams. There was even a Schachter at North Shore – my younger sister, Louise, fortunately a 10th grader, who two days into the term informed me that I was to address her as "Louise" in the halls and that "Weezie," "Little Lou" and "Cupcake" would simply not be tolerated.

After overcoming that hurdle, I next had to deal with my relationship with the teachers. My old teachers were now my colleagues. It was difficult to get used to. "Call me Bill," said my old science teacher, Mr. Brown. "Hey, look, it's Marion," urged Mrs. Razler, my old journalism teacher. Gradually, my uneasiness yielded and I was calling everyone by their first name. Well, not quite. I just couldn't address the hall monitors, many of whom were mothers of my friends, as "Rosemary" or "Dotty." It was fine to call the chairman of the Science Department "Ira," but "Rosemary" and "Dotty" were consigned to the box that contained "Cupcake" and "Weezie."

Nevertheless, what made my transition easier than most who are suddenly thrust into a teacher's role after being on the other side of the desk for many years is the warm, sincere relationship I've been able to maintain over the years with my teachers. Periodically, my old English teacher, Dick Eustis, will enter the class to check out the progress of my rapidly receding hairline, whereupon I'll offer an appropriate comment on his plaid pants ("I remember when I was in school and those pants were in style") or his age ("I enjoyed having Mr. Eustis as my teacher – and so did my father, and his father…").

I've often kidded him and others in my department about age, but it's remarkable how youthful they look in a profession where I believe everyone turns prematurely gray. One of my colleagues, whom I had in the 7th grade, looks younger today than I do! Still it makes me feel good when I am the recipient of age jokes:

"Saul," said my Chairman, Bill Hartman, "if you take the Honors Class next year..."

"Saul should *be* in the Honors Class next year," corrected colleague Don Parker.

When it comes to age, I'm a lot nearer those of my students than of my colleagues. At 15, they seem to be less different than the freshmen of my youth. True, they're probably more involved in experimenting with drugs and drinking, and sadly, more of them are living with grandparents, but on the whole, very little seems to have changed. The boys and girls seem to notice each other at an earlier age, but weekends are still usually spent with members of the same sex at a friend's house, going to movies or roller skating.

In the classroom, the differences are more apparent. Students are not as bright as they were before. More students are coming who speak little English, their desire to become proficient in their new language and to excel in other subjects has encouraged even the most reluctant student who frequently has all but given up. In my "general" class, Max, a boy from Italy with six months of English training behind him, read a passage about Africa (after some prodding from his classmates) that left his peers numb with joy until they erupted with cheers as he finished.

There are others who have left their mark on our class:

There's Joe, who frequently begins his essays with lines such as, "Josef Stalin, like all of us, had his good points and his bad points."

Then there's Tara, the skinny little girl who at the snap of a finger will do her shrieking imitation of a gorilla (to which someone will respond, "Is it live or is it Memorex?")

Take Carl, the mischievous kid whom most believe will be voted in his senior year as "Most likely to be beaten up."

And Danny, whose half-comatose state in class prompts me to advise him, "Try to keep your enthusiasm down."

Or Hank, the 200-pounder whose favorite phrase seems to be, "Do you want to go outside and settle this?"

Finally, there are students who, judging by their conversations with their peers, appear to have no first name: Minsky, Alberti, Carmichael.

They are a group that genuinely seems to like each other. They are extremely active on sports teams (the girls participating much more than when I was at North Shore), theater and musical groups, and various other clubs. They are less active politically than those of my generation, but there doesn't seem to be as many pressing issues as there were then.

They are a group that knows how to have fun without being malicious. One day I remarked that the room was getting messy and the next day I arrived to see all the desks and chairs piled high to the ceiling. On another occasion I entered the class to find a picture pasted to the blackboard of a beautiful, bikini-clad girl with the notation, "Mr. Schachter's wife." To which I replied, without skipping a beat, "Marie, you look wonderful!"

Needless to say, it's nice to be back.

4

Traveling Alone Doesn't Mean You'll Get Lonely

The Graduate, 1982

I never expected to travel alone. I thought a young traveler needed the security of friends and companionship. It's reassuring to be among familiar faces and to huddle with someone who can read a map, get you on the right bus, and provide conversation during the slow spells that occasionally crop up during extended periods of travel. Thus, I was both scared and worried when I discovered that my friends were not going to show up for our long-planned tour of Europe. When I realized that I was alone and unloved in Copenhagen, I did what any seasoned traveler would do: I looked for the first train home.

Ultimately, I decided to stick it out, but those first three weeks found me depressed and lonely. It was a frightening feeling. It was an understatement to say I was intimidated by the prospect of being alone in Europe for two and a half months.

Until then, I'd never been in a position in which I had total responsibility for taking care of myself. At the beginning of my stay I rented rooms with families, but I saw my hosts only at mealtime, I didn't meet anyone, and I became even more discouraged and lonely. It wasn't until I began staying in hostels with other travelers my ages that my fortunes turned around.

Hostel living provided me with the dorm life I'd missed out on as a commuter student in the States. Most of my roommates at the hostels were young, adventurous, and good-natured. I've stayed in touch with many of them.

I realized that being alone doesn't necessarily mean that you have to be lonely. I met more people traveling by myself than I would have had I been in a group. And if I had the chance to do the trip again, I'd go solo.

In a group you tend to cling to your companion – feeling obligated to stay with him, frequently arguing over the most trivial matters, and never getting out on your own. I've seen friendships disintegrate following shared vacations, and I'm glad it's never happened to me. I was happier alone.

After touring all day by myself, I was eager to get back to the hostel and swap stories about my adventures with my room-mates. Sometimes, my roommates provided me with the adventures.

In Rome, I stayed in a hostel room containing four beds. One morning my three American roomies left, and four beautiful Scandinavian women arrived. I graciously offered to give up my bed and move across the hall so the four friends would not have to split up. Gathering my belongings, I shuffled across the hall, reminding the girls that my name is Saul Schachter – SAUL SCHACHTER.

All was serene until later that evening when I was dressing to go out. I discovered that the shirt I needed was hanging on the line outside the ladies' window. I knocked on the door, and one girl called, "Come in." Although it was only 9 p.m., the room was dark and the women were in bed. One whispered to me that they had had a long train ride and were exhausted. I apologized for barging in and explained softly, "I just want to get my shirt. I left it outside your window."

"Don't worry," she replied, "I'll get it." She rose from her bed stark naked and calmly walked over to the window to retrieve my shirt. I was delirious. So delirious that I left a pair of socks on the line for the next day.

Walking tours were another way to meet people, though my fondest remembrance is of an elderly gentleman who wasn't a member of the tour.

One evening I went on a walking tour through an old section of Stockholm. As we approached one courtyard, an elderly man beckoned to me from his balcony. "Come, take a picture from up here!"

I ran up the winding staircase to his small, well-kept apartment. The old man was a sculptor who lived alone, and much of his work graced the courtyard below.

I took some pictures from his balcony and followed him back into the living room. "I don't do much work anymore," he said sadly. "I'm getting old."

"Oh no you're not," I replied.

"Take a guess how old I am," he said.

He looked to be around 80, so I said, "About 75?"

"Sixty-six" he said sharply.

Taking this as a cue to leave, I shook his hand and left, stopping once more in the courtyard to take a final photo of him waving from the balcony. It was a nice experience, and I didn't bother to look for my long-departed walking tour.

Mealtime might seem lonely for the solo, traveler, but I made eating out a game. I would stride confidently through a restaurant, eyeing all the other diners who were eating alone. Smiling and appearing relaxed, I would choose a dinner partner and ask if I could join him or her for the meal. An enlightening evening invariably followed, and I learned more about Europeans over crepes, spaghetti or bratwurst than I ever could have learned from a textbook. When I revealed that I was from New York City, people were amazed that I had never been mugged or assaulted. By the end of the meal, we usually swapped addresses before heading our separate ways.

Organization played a major part in the success of my trip I planned my itinerary one or two cities in advance, and bearing in mind that I couldn't see everything, I confined my sightseeing to the major cities.

In the summertime, these cities were literally overrun with backpackers. There were many Europeans, but I was continually amazed by the number of Americans I met. If I'd returned to the

U.S. early, I'm convinced the place would have been empty.

Three to five days were sufficient to cover a city, and my schedule was flexible enough so that I could stay an extra day or two if the town was particularly appealing.

My best trip companions proved to be my guidebooks, Arthur Frommer's *Europe on $20 a Day* and the Harvard Student Agencies' *Let's Go: Europe*. The Frommer book covers budget hotels in the major cities and lists inexpensive restaurants and sights, train schedules, foreign exchange rates, and –my favorite feature – menu translations.

The authors of *Let's Go: Europe* did a thorough job of researching student hostels. Although Frommer's book is more complete, *Let's Go: Europe* covers smaller cities for the more intrepid traveler. Both are invaluable guides.

Still, the popular guidebooks can create some problems. After arriving in beautiful but hot and humid Florence, I trudged off to a hostel highly recommended by *Europe on $20 a Day*. It was 2:30 in the afternoon, and all I wanted was a cool drink and a place to set down my bags. I turned up the street and was startled to see dozens of fellow backpackers. To my chagrin, they were all carrying the same guidebook, and they, too, were heeding the book's recommendation. The hostel was full, and from that point on I began consulting fellow travelers for their recommendations of places to stay.

I learned to take night trains for trips between large cities that were more than 10 hours apart. The reasons for doing so were simple:

•Sleeping on a train eliminated the cost of a bed in a hostel or student hotel.

•Getting a good night's sleep while in transit eliminated the boredom inherent in a long train ride.

•Traveling at night kept the days free for sightseeing, and my train companions often became hostel roommates when we reached our destination.

It didn't take me long to adapt to the life of the solo traveler. And then, just as I was relishing the confidence and independence

I'd developed on my travels, it was time to return home. It was a wonderful experience, this traveling alone. Rarely was I lonely, because future companions waited in every hostel, restaurant and train. Returning home brought immediate pleasure – warm showers and clean clothes every day! But after a few days, I started to collect guidebooks, maps, addresses, and everything else I would need to hit the road – alone again.

S

Different Rules For Foreigners: Student Life In China

Transitions, Fall 1982

Being a student in China involves more than studying Chinese:

•It's watching the stout Chinese woman who walked up and down the hall every 45 minutes clanging a cow bell signaling the end of each period.

•It's observing the Chinese school officials who encouraged friendship between ourselves and the Chinese students studying English on campus, but not *too* much friendship.

•It's observing how we Americans circumvented their instruction.

•Finally, being a student offers the chance to learn something of Chinese culture and build and nurture friendships.

When Hofstra University offered a six-week China study program (with five weeks of instructional Chinese in Shanghai), I signed up for the trip. I had always wanted to see China, but not through a bus window. In five weeks I became immersed in city life, learned my way around Shanghai, and picked up enough Chinese to feel that I accomplished something – even if only a handful of people could understand me.

Shanghai's Huadong Shida (East China Normal University) was the home of 154 foreign students from West Germany, Canada, and the United States. We were sequestered in two dormitories a few hundred yards from the dorms of the Chinese students. If you overlook the fact that we lacked toilets (we had troughs instead), a football team, and that we couldn't send out for pizza, we were just like any other college kids away at school. Our rooms were clean, large enough for two, and the electric fans the school provided helped us through many a sweltering day. Each student had a desk, a lamp and a mat covering a quite comfortable bed. At the end of the halls were the showers, sinks, and the troughs, It wasn't Harvard, but for our needs it was quite sufficient.

Soon after arriving on campus, we settled into a fairly steady routine. Each of us awoke promptly at 5 a.m., but this was not of our own choosing. Military music came blaring through the loudspeakers coaxing even the deepest sleepers out of bed. The more vigorous students hustled downstairs to engage in sessions of tai chi – Chinese exercise – while I opted for a jog around the track. I'd return to my dorm to shower, study my Chinese, have breakfast at 7:15 and be in class by 8. By 11 a.m. I was ready to go back to sleep.

By the third week, the military music had disappeared, and we all began sleeping until six. The more vigorous students had all but given up on tai chi, and I relegated my jogging sessions to the evenings which were cooler and easier on my body.

Before we began our studies, each of us was required to take a placement test to determine which of four classes we'd be admitted to. Having had no previous experience with Chinese, my exam was over quite quickly.

My classmates included give other Americans ranging in age from 18-year old Ted to 69-year old Manny. Our instructor, Wu Laoshi (Mr. Wu or Teacher Wu,) was a trim, 45-year old man who bicycled to school wearing his white shirt, gray shorts and sandals. Wu Laoshi smiled easily and often, and like the other teachers on campus, spoke no English. Inbetween our four 45-minute weekday sessions, Wu Laoshi would huddle with his Chinese-English dictionary.

Wu Laoshi taught from a textbook which was thankfully free of political propaganda. Chinese was learned primarily by rote. If we had any questions, we'd relay them to comrade Ted (who knew the best Chinese) to pass on to Wu Laoshi. The Chinese language eventually began to sink in once we mastered the tones and other nuances of the language.

Surprisingly, despite all the strict rules they imposed on their own students, the Chinese were quite easy on the foreigners. As the weeks went on, classes would be skipped. It was easy to blame the heat for the declining attendance, but student irresponsibility was a more likely reason.

If the language barrier was occasionally frustrating, it was nothing compared to what was going on next door. There, my roommate Jay, sat among Germans and Americans who were instructed by a German-speaking Chinese teacher. Jay moaned that he had to listen to Chinese (which was hard to follow) being translated into German (which was even harder to follow) and wait, patiently, as one of the more confident Germans tried to translate this into bits of English that he knew. I'm glad I was in the other room.

Still, classes were fun and we grew to love our teacher. As with the other teachers, Wu Laoshi was available for 90 minutes of tutoring time in the afternoons and 90 minutes in the evenings. I confined my tutoring sessions to the evenings after dinner because of the intense heat.

Our teachers filled other capacities as well. They accompanied us on weekend tours of other Chinese cities and served as "nurses" when we were ill, bringing meals to our rooms and offering good cheer.

The Chinese students on campus were very resilient. They lived in a separate more crowded dormitory (eight people shared a room with no fans), ate in an inferior dining hall, and wore down the authorities who wanted the students to practice English with the foreigners, but who didn't want too much contact. They were not allowed in our dorms.

The Chinese I encountered were polite, gracious, and studied all day long. Because of the growing unemployment, students are not permitted to hold jobs, even part-time positions. Classes are not held during the summer; nevertheless Chinese students were rarely seen without a book in their hands.

My afternoons were primarily spent in Shanghai where I mastered the bus system and felt no restraints on the places I visited or the people I spoke to. Many Chinese were eager to try out their newly-learned but limited English, and I happily obliged them in conversation.

I soon discovered that there is no such thing as taking a solitary walk around Shanghai. In a city of 11 million, it's difficult to find a quiet street. Moreover, a foreigner is a curiosity and the Chinese stare, unabashedly, at foreigners. And stare. And stare. I usually responded by smiling back, staring back, or since I had such a captive audience, I'd deliver a speech. Before crowds of twenty to a hundred people, I'd rail against Yankee owner George Steinbrenner, applaud the variety of Chinese dress (they all seemed to be wearing white shirts and gray shorts), or blame by declining basketball skills on the Cultural Revolution. All of which, of course, they didn't understand.

When I wasn't studying, socializing or exploring, I was usually eating. All meals were heavy on the rice with vegetables, pork, chicken or fish as the main dish. No cake, bread or orange juice were ever seen. By the third week, word spread that the Jin Jiang Hotel in Shanghai offered Chinese and Western meals to foreign students for $2 and seats became more available at our dining hall.

We concluded our stay in China with a one-week tour of northern China: Peking, Luoyong, and Xian, before returning to Huadong Shida.

The Chinese threw a wonderful banquet for us with everyone delivering speeches in Chinese. We received diplomas and report cards (I received a "B") and spent the evening toasting China, America, model Cheryl Tiegs, Deng Xiaoping – anyone who came to mind.

As we exchanged addresses and hugs, we promised that someday we'd reunite, perhaps not at Huadong Shida, but somewhere in China. It was a promise I hope to keep.

6

Why Does My Social Life Pick Up When I Leave the Country?

The Washington Post, May 22, 1983

One of the innumerable pleasures that travel brings a young, single person is that your social life picks up immeasurably. Granted, it's more expensive than a blind date, but it's frequently cheaper than a computer dating service. And, you don't have to resemble Robert Redford to be successful.

These foreign encounters can't be planned. Visit a local museum or see the sights of a city and you meet interesting women. They are courteous, cheerful, and they love foreign accents. A favorite pastime is to guess your hometown, and although they've usually been off by a continent or two, I've never felt it incumbent upon me to correct them.

"You must be from Australia," a pretty young woman said to me once. "Yes, Melbourne," I replied without hesitation. And, a delightful evening followed.

Not surprisingly, I've begun to travel more and more. Whenever I return home, my address book is inevitably thicker than my suitcase. When the customs agent at the airport asks, "Do you have anything to declare?" I usually sigh, "I'm in love."

All of this unnerves my mother who asks, "Why can't you meet a girl who doesn't live 3,000 miles away?"

But, really, I tell her, I don't travel to meet women. I don't go to bars, rarely frequent discos, and I can't converse in any language, save English. I travel to see the world, visit exotic places, and if I meet a woman, well, that's nice too.

Why does it happen? I travel alone and thus am susceptible to foreign encounters. I get lost easily and must summon help frequently. A map, even if it's in English, is foreign to me. I don't have a watch. I take lots of public transportation. Which is how I met Polly.

Riding through Hong Kong, I gazed out of the bus window to watch the scenery go by. Out of the corner of my eye, I detected a young Chinese woman smiling at me. I smiled back. She giggled and asked, "You, American?" I beamed, "Me, American." From then on, it was terrific. A real chatterbox, Polly was particularly interesting because she knew more English four-letter words than three-, five-, six- or seven- letter words. The more she talked, the more I knew that here was a girl that you did not bring home to mother – and, definitely, not to father.

Still, her giggle was infectious, and we went out to dinner and dancing. As we danced, she told me the names of all the other men she knew from around the world. It was a very long list. I returned a year later, and called to invite her for dinner. Again, it was a memorable evening, especially when she revealed she couldn't remember me from the year before.

I knew these women for only a few minutes. But I knew Maria even less. In fact, I never met her. When I was in Italy a few years ago, I befriended a 12-year old boy, and we began writing to each other. Enrico's letters were translated by his 20-year old teacher. Soon his teacher, whose name was Maria, began adding her own personal little tidbits at the end of Enrico's letters. As the months went by, Enrico's letters were getting shorter and Maria's were getting longer.

Soon I was receiving pictures of Maria's family, and each one of them would add their own greetings. These letters were getting very crowded. I figured that Maria was planning for a June wedding. She invited me to Rome the next time I was in the neighborhood, and I did return the following year – to see Enrico- but Maria was away. I guess I'll have to return the tuxedo and call off the reception.

There were other memorable women. There was Marina, whom I met at a synagogue in Moscow. There was Nina, whom I met in Oslo when I was lost, and Cathy, a Chinese woman I met while studying Chinese in Shanghai. All of them were very kind by my interest never went beyond friendship. That is, until I met and fell for Teresa from Dublin.

I met Teresa at the Dublin Horse Show in 1978. Teresa was sitting beside me, and since I didn't know how to keep score, I would politely ask her. Teresa had long brown hair and a delightful Irish brogue, and she spoke so soothingly that I started making plans to cancel my flight home. It started to rain, but I never noticed. I subsequently had dinner at her home, where she burned everything, and her mother made us sandwiches.

I returned to New York, and during the next year we kept the postal system busy with our frequent letters. We made plans to meet in Athens during the summer of 1979. At the appointed time and place, Teresa failed to show, but she left word with a mutual Greek friend that she was on the Island of Poros. I took the next ferry to Poros, but found no Teresa. She was on the island of Paros. It seems that with her Irish brogue and our friend's Greek accent, the vowels got lost in the translation.

I never saw her in Greece. Since she was returning to Dublin, I sent a letterhead that I'd be arriving in Ireland in one month. When I arrived, Theresa was not around. Ireland had had a terrible mail strike, and my letter never arrived. Teresa was off working 20 miles away as a nurse on the 8 p.m.-to-8 a.m. shift. During my 10 days in Ireland, I saw her three times for a total of three hours.

Faced with these frustrations, Teresa and I sensed that this relationship was not going to work out. Her letters became fewer and fewer. Nevertheless, her mother's enthusiasm for me never seemed to wane. When I hadn't heard from Teresa in a while, her mother would write to me and apologize for her daughter's negligence. She sent me birthday cards and letters telling about Teresa's activities. It got to the point where I was confiding in my friends that I hadn't heard anything lately from Teresa's mother.

We planned to meet in Hamburg the summer of 1981. Teresa was working there for the season, and I was making my second around-the-world tour. After I left China (and saying goodbye to Cathy), I went to Hong Kong (where I said hello to Polly). Then, it was on to Hamburg to see Teresa. Unfortunately, I was bumped off my flight in India, where I was stranded for a week, and flew out just when Teresa had proceeded on to another destination. We never saw each other.

In September, Teresa's indefatigable mother sent me a Jewish New Year's card, and I promptly sent her a calendar of all the Jewish holidays so she should not be remiss in her obligations to her adopted son-in-law.

Teresa is supposed to come to New York this summer. I hope I recognize her when she arrives.

7

When Parents Meet The Teacher

Newsday, August 18, 1983

With the possible exception of graduation, no school event is awaited with greater anticipation than "Meet the Teacher Night."

It's also a competition to see who can stay awake longer. In my classroom, I try to illuminate my talks by displaying pictures, hoisting the class textbook above my head, and sitting casually above a desktop. But, invariably two or three minutes into my lecture, the woman sitting in front will open her mouth wide enough to reveal last week's denture work. Taking this as my cue, I'll say, "In summing up…" and then open up the floor to questions. Most are of the usual nature:

"Why doesn't my child have more homework?"

"Why is my child getting so much homework?"

"Is my child going to take a Regents exam?"

Most of the questions are intelligent and thoughtful Of course, there are the challengers ("When you teach the French Revolution, do you consider the socioeconomic decisions of the Girondists or do you delve more deeply into the philosophical theories of Rousseau and Locke and their impact on the Revolution?"), the well-meaning ("Hey, how's that kid of mine doing?" moments after you've requested that questions about their children be saved for another day), and the simply curious. My colleagues seem to get these individuals more often. A teacher in the math department recalls the time when she was describing her course to the parents: "I was talking about linear equations, the fundamental laws of algebra, factoring, and sets and variables. I went on for about eight minutes until a woman in the front, looking very enthusiastic, raised her hand. Eager to answer the question, I recognized her, "Can you be so kind as to tell me where you bought that lovely skirt?"

I relish the encounters and situations that arise during the evening. Sometimes my mind wanders while I speak. As I look out at the multitudes before me, I can envision what my students will look like when they gather for their 30th high school reunion party. In more playful moods, I assume that they've acquired the working habits of their parents. The woman in the back chewing gum — That has to be Susan's mother. The disheveled-looking guy in the corner who can't find his pen. He has to be Rick's dad. The giggly mother in the Jordache jeans is obviously Diane's mother. And what about the burly guy talking in the back of the room? What do I do if he really becomes disruptive? Do I send him down to the principal's office? Should I call his kid and complain? Problems, problems.

Between periods I stand in the hall, watching parents make their way to their next class. During the evening, the parents will follow their children's eight-period schedule. Staring uncomprehendingly at maps, many resemble bewildered freshmen during the first day of high school. From the looks on their faces, I'm sure they will be content if they find seven out of eight classrooms.

It's nice to see familiar faces among the new ones. Some I've seen so frequently it seems as if they've sired 27 children. "Oh, no, we've got two more coming up," one told me proudly. They must own the street.

And, since I've grown up in the neighborhood and now teach at my alma mater, many parents take an avuncular pride in my work. "You gave a fine talk, Saul. I'll tell your mother."

Not all aspects of the evening are pleasant, however. Last year no parent appeared at my class for below-level students. I have 16 children in that class. Why were they absent? Was it because the baseball playoff game was on television that evening? "It's probably because they've heard bad news for so many years," volunteered one colleague. I don't know. I'm unconvinced that's the reason. I can't believe parents have given up on 14-year olds. If anything, more parents of slower students should appear than the parents of the brighter ones.

I try not to let these things bother me too much. The near-capacity crowd that poured into my seventh and final period class did much to extinguish my anger. As it is with their children, they were an animated bunch, chattering away non-stop, but in a few minutes they settled down. Notebooks open, pen in hand, they listened to my spellbinding course description of "The French Revolution to World War II." I deftly made my way through the Age of Metternich, the Industrial Revolution, the big "isms" (socialism, capitalism, Marxism, communism), and was coming down the home stretch to World Wars I and II, when an excited woman, clutching several notebooks, stumbled in, apologizing for being late. I looked at her sympathetically and said, "You must be Mrs. Williams."

She looked stunned, but pleased. "Why, how did you know?"

I returned her smile. "Aw, lucky guess," I shrugged. "Lucky guess."

Dear Students:
Come Back, Come Back,
Wherever You Are

The New York Times, August 21, 1983

I recently called a parent to discuss her child's frequent absences from school, but unfortunately the family was in the Bahamas.

A similar call to another house revealed that the child was at Roosevelt Field.

Moreover, in the days leading up to one holiday, 13 students (nearly 20 percent of my roster) had flown the coop.

Don't get me wrong, I love my job. I've been blessed in my 18 years of teaching with wonderful, cheerful students who brighten my day by their mere presence in my class. But, I'd like to see them more often.

My students go shopping, hunting, to the airport, to their siblings' class plays and to see Broadway shows (the Wednesday matinee).

Above all, my students and their families love to go to Florida. Even though we have school vacations in December, February, April, July, and August, the entire school building seems to clear out in March. "The airfares are so much lower then," a proud bargain-hunting parent once told me. I have other students who return from their vacation just when the school begins its vacation.

My students visit a lot of doctors, general-practice dentists, and orthodontists. Frequently, the parents arrive at about 10:30

a.m. to pick up their children and return just before basketball or field hockey practice begins at 3 p.m.

When I taught in the high school, my students' favorite destination during school hours was the Department of Motor Vehicles office. A colleague once suggested that we toss out all of our textbooks and replace them with the DMV's driver manual.

In December, I spoke to our band teacher and asked how the winter concert went. "Oh, it went pretty well, but it could have gone better," he said, shaking his head sadly.

"My best trumpet player didn't show. I found this morning that his parents took him to a Rangers game. "

I once had a student I'll call "Ernie." Ernie's parents owned a yacht and one year they were away 32 days with their son. "Ernie" did poorly, barely passing after racking up three D's and an F, which led him to say in an exasperated tone to me: "I've got to tell my parents that I have to be in school."

As I stare out at the empty seats before me, I can't help but think of the words Marion B. Folsom, former Secretary of Health, Education and Welfare, who once said, "Education is both a personal interest and a national asset. For education enlarges life – not only for each of us as a person, but for all of us as a nation."

We can ill-afford to ignore his wisdom.

9

Family Hopping
Around The World

The Washington Post, November 6, 1983

Armed with my around-the-world ticket, I went family-hopping recently. Thirteen families in eight cities: Seoul, Tokyo, Hong Kong, Delhi, Jaipur, Bombay, Rome and Geneva. I slept on the floor, on a bench, in a bed, and under a mosquito net. Nearly every Sunday I went to church – but with Buddhists and Sikhs.

It was like being at home – almost.

As thousands of others have discovered, nothing surpasses the excitement and authenticity of living with a family abroad. In response to this demand, many "homestay" programs have sprung up to give the traveler a taste of life with a foreign family.

I contacted one such organization, Servas, which interviewed me as a prospective "guest traveler." After passing the interview, I was given a list of host families, their addresses, ages, hobbies, occupations, languages spoken, and even directions to their houses from the airports. I purchased picture books of the United States to present to my hosts and paid only a $30 registration fee to the organization with no money going to the families ("Only friendship and learning should change hands"). Finally, I agreed to stay no more than three nights with each family.

Setting the lists before me, I felt like a computer-dating machine. What a variety of people there were: a rug weaver, a goat farmer, a chemist. I settled on families that had common interests with me, that spoke English, were accessible from the airport, and whose ages ranged from 23 to 69. For my six-day stay in Seoul, I needed to find two families. Scanning my list for potential families, I noticed that Mr. Choi, a teacher (my profession), lived at 2-Ga, Bomun-Dong, and that Mr. Uom, a calligrapher, lived at 3-Ga, Bomun-Dong. Sold! I may be circling the globe, but I certainly wasn't going to traipse across Seoul looking for Family No. 2.

After arriving in Seoul, I discovered Mr. Choi had moved six months earlier. Finally, following four phone calls, two cab rides and three patient and helpful Koreans, I found him.

Mr. Choi, a bachelor, lives in a small home with an open courtyard surrounded by railroad-car rooms, none larger than 6 ½ by 6 ½ feet. There were no carpets, windows or chairs. There was no shower, and the toilet was a hole in the ground. My room was a small, windowless cubicle with two quilts on the floor and a calendar hanging limply overhead. The Hilton, this wasn't. Nevertheless, I was comfortable.

I quickly fell into the routine of Korean life. Each morning upon leaving my room, I slid my feet into the buckets in the courtyard where I would scrub furiously for 10 minutes. Then I would join Mr. Choi cross-legged on the floor to await our heavily rice-dominated breakfast (dinner was a rerun of breakfast).

Each day, while Mr. Choi was teaching high school, I I was off exploring Seoul. We got together for meals and over dinner discussed American and Korean life. No matter where I went through the Orient, the first two questions new acquaintances would invariably ask were "How old are you?" and "Are you married?" The older locals would scold me for wearing shorts.

Most of these questions were broached as I sat contentedly in the public baths. Mr. Choi gave me the proper initiation when he escorted me to the first one. After plunking down $1, we were led into a locker room where we stripped off our clothes and were led into a steaming room where we showered and stepped gingerly into a hot tub. It was ecstasy! I told Mr. Choi that he could come back and pick me up in six months. I was content with kicking and splashing, but Mr. Choi was determined to show me proper etiquette in a tub. He, thereupon, went through a scrubbing and soaking ritual that I closely emulated. When Mr. Choi scrubbed his leg, I scrubbed my leg, When Mr. Choi caressed his elbow, I caressed my elbow. For nearly 45 minutes I scrubbed and caressed. Two days later I happily repeated the procedure.

Before I left him, Mr. Choi took me to his school where I sat in on an English class. That evening he put on an impromptu musical with his students for me and, as a gift, gave me a papier-mache mask that he made. I knew I would miss him.

My next hosts, Mr. and Mrs. Uom, were different. They couldn't speak English, but we were able to converse through his pocket computer that translated certain words from English to Korean and back again. Their home was more comfortable too. Two chairs, a radio, and television. I discovered AFKN – The American Forces Korean Network – radio and television stations for American servicemen and their families. American songs and news were on the radio and drama and comedy on television. These stations offered "helpful hints" about Korean life and customs. Occasionally, I watched Korean television – mostly dramas - but their story lines and dialogue completely eluded me.

But one night was fun. The Miss Universe Pageant was held in Seoul and the Uoms and I watched the show on a Korean station. I sat up close to the screen so I could hear hosts Bob Barker and Helen O'Connell speak English before an intrusive voice translated everything into Korean. Then, I brushed up on my lip-reading. When Miss Korea dropped out after finishing sixth, I politely applauded, and Mr. and Mrs. Uom, obviously representing the Korean people, thanked me warmly. When Miss America won, I practically leaped into Mrs. Uom's arms. To celebrate these momentous occasions, Mrs. Uom went into the kitchen and emerged with a juicy red watermelon (the only one I saw during my stay in Seoul).

Then it was on to Tokyo where I spent nine days with four families. My experiences there were less exciting, perhaps because Tokyo is a vibrant, modern city with few of the curiosities and unusual customs of the Koreans.

Two of these days were spent with the ebullient Mr. Nishi, 69, who spoke a little English, but couldn't hear so that cancelled out everything. On my first day with him, Mr. Nishi insisted on taking me around. Unfortunately, he doesn't like to walk much and we took 11 subways at an average of 80 cents per ride. It got expensive. Furthermore, he had the incredible knack of taking me to places that were either closed or off-limits to tourists. We did get to the top of the Tokyo Tower, but since the day was quite overcast we were not quite able to see over to the next building. After trekking to the Parliament Building and finding it closed, we called it a day and returned home. He wanted to take me out the next day, too, but I firmly and politely talked him out of it.

We were more successful indoors. The Nishis and I spent hours poring over the family album, and when we finished I felt like I had grown up with them. Sumo wrestling on television occupied us from 4:30 on, and I cheered for the sole American in the tournament, and the Nishis rooted for the local favorite.

My favorite, however, was the Verna family of Delhi: host Pradeep, 23, a very confident and friendly certified public accountant; his brother Nageesh, 22, also a CPA; Pradeep's uncle, and Mr. and Mrs. Verna, both in their late 40s. They all spoke English fluently. Pradeep's father owns a large accounting firm and the Vernas live very well, with five servants to manage their beautiful 1930s English-style home. Pradeep and I hit it off like college roommates.

Mealtime was quite pleasurable: Chappadi (fried bread, tastes like waffles), assorted vegetables, and dhal (lentils and spices – it resembles pea soup). Following the lead of Pradeep, I would take the chappadi and sponge up the dhal. Quite tasty. Dessert included mangoes, fruit juices and tea. Boiled, filtered water and occasionally hot milk supplemented my diet. I ate so much that the Vernas, an upper-class family, probably have now plunged into middle-class status.

One evening following dinner we saw home movies of the family. The photographer obviously felt that he was on the verge of running out of film. There's Grandma, over to Pradeep, back to

Grandma (without head), back to Mr. Verna. No feet, no heads. In focus, out of focus.

After I left Delhi, I moved on to Agra, Jaipur, Rome, Geneva, London and New York. In New York I stayed with a family that was quite accommodating: my own. There was no language barrier, trays of cakes and bagels, plenty of chairs and an honest-to-goodness toilet seat. And, what's more, they said I could stay more than three nights. It was an offer I couldn't turn down.

10

Where Have
All The Foreigners Gone?

Newsday, February 26, 1984

Why can't I ever get away from it all? Other travelers meet Italian fishermen, Dutch shoemakers, Polish steelworkers. I meet other Americans. Regardless of where I go, this invariably happens. Moreover, it seems the farther I go from home, the greater the chances are that I'll cross paths with Americans.

I have vivid memories of my stay in Hong Kong, that wonderfully chaotic city where even a basketball player could get lost in the crowds. I found an out-of-the-way, starvation-budget ($3 a night) hotel filled with transients and former transients. Told I would have to share a room, I offered no objections. My roommate, a dark-skinned, tousled –hair fellow grunted.

"Where are you from?" he asked.

"New York."

"Yeah, me too. What part?"

"Sea Cliff."

"Greetings, neighbor. I'm from Glen Cove."

We had about a dozen friends in common. I had traveled 6,000 miles to Hong Kong and I'm rooming with a guy from Glen Cove, one mile from my house.

Patty, on the other hand, was definitely a foreigner. She came from Garden City (a whole 20 minutes away). I met her in Venice … and Athens… and Geneva. I was sure she had a homing device guaranteed to find me wherever I turned up. I liked her, but I wanted to meet some Europeans. They had to be around here somewhere.

Patty and I finally went our separate ways. I traveled through Switzerland and southern France before settling down in Paris for a week. One day I was strolling through the city when I heard a voice call: "Hello, Handsome." Recognizing my name, I turned around and found my long-lost friend Patty. We spent the day walking around and I later escorted her to her train to Amsterdam.

I didn't tell her my destination. I felt it wasn't necessary; I'd probably run into her again.

When I was in Israel, I took time out from the summer heat and refreshed myself at the nearest hotel. Cradling a cup of water in my hands, I leaned back and closed my eyes near the information desk. Two girls strode by and stepped over to the telephone.

"Hello, operator. I'd like to call collect to Area Code 516, 484 ..."

516? That's Long Island! 484? That's Roslyn! Three miles from my home in Sea Cliff. An hour later the scenario was repeated with four more individuals. Was there anyone left in Roslyn?

Last summer I set the globe before me and picked out spots where I figured I would not meet Long Islanders. Antarctica sounded enticing, but I'm a budget traveler, and I couldn't find a People Express flight there.

The newspapers report that there are more than a billion people in China, but as I discovered when I toured there in 1981, four of them are from Long Island. There were probably hotel rooms in Nicaragua and Iran, but I decided to keep looking.

What about Poland? I did some research and six months later found myself ensconced with 74 Yugoslavs and assorted other indistinguishable nationalities in a student dormitory in Krakow.

Returning to my room one night, I stepped out of the elevator and heard, "Saul? Saul? Is that you?" It was me, all right, but who was calling? I started at the young woman behind me, blinking a few times. At first I didn't recognize her. Then I did. It was Jackie, Mazza, my old high school friend, who was staying at the dormitory with another group. We embraced and later I had dinner with Jackie and her friend, Tom, an Oregonian who, it turned out, was born in the same hospital I was.

That was last summer. I've been frustrated, but I'm not giving up. I've figured out how I am going to get away from it all this year. I'm going to stuff my backpack with clothes, books, a radio and an insect repellent and march off to a spot where I can pitch a tent and light a campfire. I'm staying in my backyard. Why fight it?

11

Fond Of Flying: In Defense Of The Food (And More) At 30,000 Feet

The Washington Post, June 17, 1984

I realize that I might be committed to an asylum for saying this, but I love airplane food.

Not only do I love airplane food, but I like everything about plane travel. And I wish more people would say so.

Novelist Paul Theroux writes of his train rides. William Least Heat Moon has produced a bestseller, *Blue Highways,* about his travels through America's back roads, but where are the airplane aficionados? Why is it no one ever talks about the flight? People come back and tell you Tahiti was wonderful, but how about a report on that 727 or 747 that got them there?"

As a peripatetic traveler of great distances, I would like to come out foursquare in defense of airplane travel. To me, there is nothing like it. It far surpasses the automobile or the train. For one thing, there are no stop signs when you're traveling 30,000 feet above the ground. The meals are tasty. Although I'm frequently trading the cheese for those juicy carrots or the apple pie, I have nothing but the utmost praise for the rest of the plate.

Try eating chicken, rice, string beans, cake and coffee in your Volkswagen. On train rides, I've seen food travel across the aisle onto unsuspecting passengers. I love airplane food and the snacks between meals. In fact, sometimes I force myself to skip a meal because they come so frequently. After each meal, I make sure I get up and circulate around the plane, talking with interesting people. In an automobile, you can't put the vehicle on automatic pilot and go about socializing. And, if you did, where would you go? Into the back seat? Poking around in the trunk? On a train, especially on the long rides, there are all those compartments that discourage congeniality.

My eagerness to board the plane usually prompts me to get to the airport early. I stride right up to the ticket counter to get my boarding pass, requesting an aisle seat (I walk around the plane a lot), in the no-smoking section near the door. It's not that I plan on exiting early, but this seat affords more legroom. Once I've secured my boarding pass, I race over to the door adjacent to the plane, ignoring plaintive cries from attendants, "But, sir, the plane doesn't leave for five more hours."

Then, the exalted moment occurs – the door opens and I sprint on board. My first step is the magazine rack where I scoop up my reading material. I'm not particular in my reading habits, though I concentrate on current events, politics, sports and entertainment. Sometimes I browse through a foreign magazine, comparing it with American counterparts. I later dutifully return it to the rack.

I'm probably the only one who watches the stewardess give instructions on how to use the life preserver in case we land in the Atlantic Ocean, but I feel it's important. A few years ago, I took Eastern's Unlimited Travel ticket (which enabled me to see 12 cities in 19 days) and watched the life-saving procedure so often I felt compelled to join the stewardess in giving directions. The powers-that-be refrained me from doing this, so I simply echoed the words to the annoyance of my seatmates.

And how about those stewardesses? To paraphrase Will Rogers: I never met a stewardess I didn't like. They're so helpful. Even when the plane encounters turbulence and the stewardess is strapped in across from you, there is a comforting feeling seeing her, even if she is turning blue.

There is, of course, musical entertainment. I plug in the

earphones and can listen to show tunes, classical music, Top-40 or the Ray Conniff Singers, who seem to be on every flight I've ever taken. Later on, the movie is shown, and although it's one I've invariably paid $5 to see at home, it's nice to know it's available. Later on, after the movie, I resume reading, and after I've finished a periodical from Thailand, or Brazil, I'll read the paperback I brought from home.

For those who like celebrities, there are usually a few on flights to Los Angeles. On one trip, I stood in line to use the lavatory behind David Janssen and followed Peter Graves to the magazine rack while fans behind us whistled the "Mission: Impossible" theme. I'm always amazed at how inconspicuous they try to remain by wearing dark glasses. I mean, how inconspicuous can you be if you're the only one wearing dark glasses on an airplane?

Then, there's that other free entertainment you get simply by looking out the window. From my airplane, I've seen the majestic Alps, a gurgling Mount St. Helens, the flat lands of Nebraska, and my favorite sight on returning home – the Statue of Liberty.

Finally, I enjoy flying because it's safe. I am totally at ease when I board a plane, knowing the frequency of mishaps is very low. There have been instances that have reinforced this secure feeling. Once on a flight from Delhi to Rome, I found that my section was occupied almost entirely by nuns. My seatmate, an Indian fellow, was nervous, and he acknowledged that this was his first flight. I tried to put his fears to rest. "Do you think God would let anything happen to his plane?" I asked, extending my arms toward the nuns around us.

He shook his head and smiled.

In what frequently seems like minutes, your plane starts its descent. When you reach your destination a large crowd is inevitably on hand to greet you. Hugs, kisses and tears are plentiful. Even when I enter a city where I know not a soul, I'll still wave and acknowledge the cheers of the crowd. It's all part of the joy of airplane travel. I can't wait for my next flight.

12

Dorm Trips: They're For The Young At Heart

The Miami Herald, July 1, 1984

Weary of claustrophobic and expensive guided tours, I was ready to burn my traveler's checks when I discovered dormitory trips. Exciting, yet relaxing, adventure-packed, yet inexpensive, 'Dorm Trips' are for the young or young at heart.

In essence, a 'dorm trip' is one where your group is deposited in one city around the world (in my case it's been Shanghai, Dublin and Krakow) and housed and fed in a dormitory with people from everywhere. Language lessons are available for college credit, and entertainment and guided tours are provided – if you want them. Set down your suitcase and don't pick it up for a month. Learn the bus system, recognize landmarks, and before you know it, you, too, will be giving directions to others, suggesting favorite restaurants and pubs, and amusing the locals with something resembling fragmented Polish. All this usually costs about $10 a day, airfare excluded.

Each program follows a similar routine: Language classes are offered in the morning, free time is available in the afternoon, and entertainment is provided at night. There are weekend trips to various cities where all you need are a change of clothes and a toothbrush. Your suitcase, remember, never budges. Groups tend to be large, but with such flexibility in schedules, you are able to meet a lot of different people without seeing them too often. And, what's more, dorm travelers tend to be adventurous, span the generations, and are more amenable to less-than-deluxe accommodations and services. Which reminds me of my latest trip to Poland.

On the way to Krakow by bus, our driver got sick and had to drive with his head out the window, and kept swerving off and on the road. Lovely trip. Little or no ventilation made the ride even more uncomfortable. Six hours (but only 165 miles later) we arrived at our dorm. As it turned out, we were five hours earlier than our luggage – which had started out on the bus right behind us.

After arriving, I set out to find a roommate. This is an important task because you'll be sharing the same room for anywhere from four to six weeks. But, I struck it rich with Ron Czarnetzky, a terrific fellow who loves sports and possesses a wonderful zest for life. He was a graduate student majoring in international politics and we got along splendidly.

We also had four priests and a nun in our group. Sister Jane from Michigan was a rascal who whispered to me one evening, "Do you know where the priests are sleeping?" On another occasion, she was interviewed on Polish television and told her interviewer she was from Flint, Michigan. ("I was so mad at myself," she said later, "I should have said 'Silver Spoon, Michigan,' and put it on the map.")

Every group seems to have an Ugly American. "Big Ed," 55ish, wore a VFW jacket and sported buttons that proclaimed, "Polish Power," "If you don't register and vote, don't complain," and "We Love it Here" with an arrow pointing to the state of Massachusetts. I tried to ignore him.

But, I did mingle with just about everyone else. Dorm life was fun. The building was built in 1981 and was situated about 15 minutes by tram from the city center. It's a prefab building ("Don't stay too long on the balcony," we were warned) with leaky bathrooms and bottomless garbage pails. Everyone had their favorite story. One girl took a book off her shelf and all the shelves came tumbling down. The shower flooded in our bathroom but we didn't know it until the girls on the 9th floor came up to tell us.

Elevator stories also abound. Sometimes ours moved and

sometimes it didn't. If you didn't open the door fast enough, it took off with you inside or out. On occasion it would go up one floor and stop and on others it would go to the 13th floor and come back down to the lobby without stopping.

Unlike the average Pole, we ate very well down in our dorm cafeteria. I personally thought we were getting too much pork, potatoes, tomatoes, and sauces, but the soups and vegetables were hearty, and desserts were a treat. We had to hand in meal tickets and the rules were strictly adhered to: No ticket, no food.

After breakfast, we'd walk over to our Polish language classes, where, after only a couple of days, I was already at the bottom of the class. We had mostly American and Danish students, ranging in age from 18 to 74. No one ever got bored because the rear walls were festooned with photographs of near-naked men and women for the anatomy lectures were also offered here. In addition to our language classes, the university sponsored lectures and seminars on history and culture.

In the afternoons, I would catch a tram and go downtown. Krakow is lovely. Untouched by the Germans during World War II, it is a cornucopia of 15th century churches, busy streets and ubiquitous flowers.

My evenings were occupied with movies and dances – traditional and modern. But, it was the weekend excursions that everyone eagerly awaited: a river-raft ride, a Polish barbecue, and visits to Auschwitz, Czestohova, Zakapone, and the famous Salt Mines just outside Krakow.

Unfortunately, just as I was getting used to salami for breakfast and scrambled eggs for dinner, it was time to depart. We boarded our bus, surveying for the last time our Dom Studentcki (student dormitory). Our guides, teachers, and even the waitresses came out to see us off.

13

The Pleasures And Perils Of Traveling On A Eurail Pass

Transitions, Spring 1984

If former Secretary of State Henry Kissinger had engaged in shuttle diplomacy in Europe, I'm positive he would have used a Eurail Pass. It's inexpensive, fast, and Dr. Kissinger would never have run out of people to talk to. He could hop on and off trains at will, visiting a king here, a prime minister there, all with little fuss or bother. However, Dr. Kissinger, like us lesser mortals, would have to be careful. For although the Eurail Pass is considered to be the greatest boon to European travel since the invention of the traveler's check, it does have its pitfalls.

Take a recent trip of mine, for example. My friend and I were sleeping on a train to Barcelona, when a conductor entered our compartment in the middle of the night. He asked to see our passports and I groggily rose and withdrew it from my pocket where I kept it snug against the wall. My companion was not so lucky. His was gone. In fact, nearly all of his valuables (wallet, passport, eyeglasses, plane tickets) which he kept on the table between us, were gone. Someone had entered our compartment in the middle of the night and absconded with his possessions. Fortunately, my friend was able to get a temporary passport when we reached the next destination, but he had to end his trip.

Contrary to what the travel brochures might indicate, not everyone is friendly and accommodating in Europe. Even before my friend's unfortunate incident, I've made it a point to always keep my valuables securely in my front pockets (even when I sleep on trains). I've found money pouches to be helpful, too.

Experience, it is said, is the greatest teacher. On a trip from Rome to Brindisi, I shared a compartment with what seemed like the entire population of Italy. Actually, I never reached my compartment. The boisterous mob pushed and shoved its way and I was pasted against the wall next to the bathroom. All evening long, the fattest short women elbowed their way through, making pilgrimages to the bathroom of which I was the guardian. The next morning I spoke to a conductor who encouraged me to travel during the week when there is so much room. I wished I had met him 24 hours earlier.

I thought of that conductor before I took a Saturday night train from Milano to Nice. I made certain I could get a seat and be comfortable. The train ride was smooth and we pulled into the station on a bright, Sunday morning. Sunday. Another mistake. The first stop for every organized Eurail Pass traveler is the bank at the railroad station, but I did not fall into the "organized" category yet. The banks are closed on Sunday. I soon found myself on a long line behind other chagrined travelers at the hotel banks where exorbitant exchange rates are charged. That was the last time I arrived in a foreign city on a Sunday.

I planned on catching a weekday 6:35 p.m. train that would pull into Paris at 10 o'clock the next morning. I checked out of my pensione (hotel) and nonchalantly appeared at my train at 6:25 p.m. I started to board when one of the conductors stopped me "I'm sorry. This is for first-class passengers."

"Oh," I mumbled, and walked down the line. I tried to board again, but was reproached by another conductor.

"You can't go in there. That's for passengers who have reserved couchettes (sleeping cars)." I backed down, and continued walking along the cars until I realized I had run out of cars.

No second-class compartments. What was I to do? I offered to pay for a couchette, but a conductor shook me off. I asked another conductor and yet another one. No good. Finally, a conductor pointed to a ticket window and suggested I buy one there.

I took off, bags in hand, racing the clock. I apologetically pushed my way to the front of the line screaming in English "You have to let me in, my train's about to leave." I slapped down my money and said I wanted to reserve a couchette, but the ticket agent shook her head. "You have to reserve a couchette two days in advance." I was frantic. I ran back to the train, perspiration pouring over my entire body racing from car to car, begging the conductors to let me on. "I'll pay for a couchette," I pleaded again. Finally, what seemed like the 50th conductor agreed to let me board. Thirty seconds later, the train rolled out of the station.

Heading north proved to be the tonic I needed. I avoided weekend travel, but continued to take night trains. Sleeping aboard a train, I discovered, yielded many benefits: It saved me a night's hotel costs; boredom never set in as I slept away the hours; by traveling at night I didn't lose a day of sightseeing.

When I left Italy, I took some of its currency with me, for which my throat was grateful. You see, if you want to purchase food and drink on a train you are never sure which currency is accepted. When I decided to purchase a Coke on the train to France, I discovered that the conductor only accepted Italian lire. Had I spent all of my lire in Italy, I would have gone thirsty the entire trip. Even if I hadn't spent all my lire, I could easily exchange the paper money in France or wherever my next destination would be. (The coins are not exchangeable, however.)

Nevertheless, I learned to carry some bread, fruit and a drink aboard because some trains are not equipped with dining cars. In the middle of the night or the next morning, I found that a little nourishment went a long way in relieving hunger pangs. Furthermore, these little "care packages" sustained me when my train was delayed or suffered an unforeseen breakdown.

No one expects you to speak every European language fluently, but if you can pick up a few phrases, it will serve as a great ice-breaker when you share a compartment with others.

Traveling by Eurail Pass was like participating in an all-you-can-eat buffet. In my allotted time, I not only devoured the rails free, but partook of the many free buses and ferries. Bus rides in Europe exposed me to the German countryside. Ferries between Greece and Italy and France and Ireland introduced me to civilizations thousands of years old. I took a ferry from Stockholm, Sweden to Malmo, Sweden for no other reason than that it was free – and it made an enjoyable day trip. In the course of my first two-month trip to Europe, I visited 13 countries and 18 cities. I ate exotic foods and added names of wonderful people to my address book. It was in my own small way, Shuttle Diplomacy. Henry Kissinger would have been proud.

14

Looking Up Your Aunt's Brother's Cousin Can Be An Adventure

The Washington Post, November 4, 1984

I guess it all began when the beleaguered King Louis XVI was fleeing the angry mobs of France, trying desperately to reach the safety of the Austrian border. His wife, Marie Antoinette, called out (according to reports that are unconfirmed, but suitable for this story): "When you get to Austria, look up my brother, Joseph. He's the king there, you know."

She didn't realize it at the time but Marie Antoinette started a trend. Today, hopeful friends and relatives suddenly come out of the woodwork, tearing out pages from address books and stuffing them into the hands of unsuspecting travelers with the request, "Please, when you arrive, contact my uncle (aunt, cousin, lover)." It is the ultimate move to "reach out and touch someone."

Unlike other travelers who have felt harried by such pleas, whose time abroad is precious and who have no desire to go traipsing around unfamiliar countries looking for an errant aunt or a long-since-deceased acquaintance, I relish the opportunities thrust at me.

These adventures have a treasure-hunt allure. The first thrill is actually finding the house after pessimistic direction-givers have given up hope. The second is the wonderful times – sharing a meal, a drink, a conversation – that evolve from a visit. And, finally, by passing on news from your friend and returning with news from abroad, a traveler reflects with quiet satisfaction that he's done a good deed.

Over the years I've found more people than I've lost. I've unearthed distant cousins in Madrid, located a dissident Chinese in Shanghai and tracked down a Boston Red Sox fan in Stockholm. I've had ice cream with my former social studies teacher in Barcelona and spent two delightful evenings eating moussaka with Greek acquaintances, Mr. and Mrs. Papadimitropoulous (they addressed me as "Saul," but I didn't call them anything because it took me an hour to say there name).

Families haven't been the only lucky recipients of my visits. In Sweden, I paid a visit to the Saab factory, the birthplace of my sometimes-operating car. It wasn't exactly reminiscent of the scenes from "Roots," but seeing the factory where my car was produced made me shed a tear or two.

These journeys have followed no particular pattern. Each year I set off with address book in tow, intent upon tracking down as many individuals as I can. In some cases, my New York friends will write ahead to let the other parties know they may be receiving a guest. When I left New York for a European trip a few years ago, a family friend, Ruth Harris, gave me the names of three families to look up. One was in Oslo, and another in Athens. "When you're in Copenhagen, you must call the Andersons," said Ruth. "They're terrific people."

I did. I called Mrs. Anderson and said, "Hello, this is Saul Schachter, I'm a friend of Ruth Harris. Would it be okay if I came over this afternoon for a bit?"

"Well…" Mrs. Anderson replied with some hesitation. "All right. Come over at 3 p.m."

It was an eventful afternoon. I met Mr. and Mrs. Anderson and their 17-year-old son. Mrs. Anderson served soft drinks and cakes and treated me like a king. I talked about what the Harrises were doing: Mike and Ruth were planning on going to China,

Wendy had a good job, Jane was going to Georgetown University, and Danny – would you believe? – was going to graduate from high school.

It would have been a perfect afternoon except for one thing: The Andersons had no idea who the Harrises were. Never heard of them. Didn't know Mike or Ruth and didn't give a hoot what Wendy, Jane, or Danny were doing (I found out later that the Harrises rented one of the Andersons' guest rooms a few years ago, stayed three days and have talked ever since about the Andersons as if they were bosom buddies). Well, we did have a good laugh over this (at least I did), and I soon left, I couldn't wait to meet the rest of Ruth Harris' friends.

Undaunted by this episode, I called Peter Tretzch, another Dane and friend of another friend. Yes, I could come over to visit him. Peter suggested we take a walk in the lovely parks that beautify Copenhagen, and I agreed. We spent a leisurely but unexciting afternoon until I detected something amiss: all the women in the park were topless. Tall ones, short ones, blondes and brunettes. Suddenly, I felt sensational. I walked through 27 parks that day.

With this feeling of euphoria, I later looked up Caroline, 23, a lovely Swedish woman. Stockholm's Kunstradgarden Park offers free dancing lessons at noon twice a week, and I needed a partner. Caroline had heard I was coming and agreed to join me. We made our way out to the dance floor where a colorfully garbed instructor demonstrated the Swedish "hambo" with his partner. He asked for volunteers and Caroline and I quickly jumped in.

It was fun, but I couldn't follow the directions (they were being called out in Swedish). My partner and I were quite terrible. A large crowd gathered and we soon realized that everyone was watching, guess who! The dance required that I occasionally lift my partner and swing her around. Well, when I tried to lift her, she wouldn't budge and then suddenly she would leap into the air at the same time I was landing back on earth. Our timing was off. The audience howled. At the end of the hour, the instructor waded into the group distributing buttons to the best dancers. Finally, he came over to me and proclaimed: "This one is for you – for courage!"

The crowd roared and I waved triumphantly.

I was more successful with friends of friends in English-speaking countries. When I was in Dublin, I looked up Tricia Caviston, a 22-year-old friend of an old school chum of mine. When I called Tricia, she said in a delightful Irish brogue, "Oh, Saul, I've been studying in France for the past two years and I've just returned a half-hour ago. I haven't seen my parents, friends and family for such a long time…"

Her voice trailed off, but then she offered, "Why don't you come over? After some time with my family, I'm going out to meet my friends and perhaps you'd like to join us." I accepted, hopped a bus and was at her house in minutes. Tricia and her family were delightful – I've never seen so much red hair in all my life. Tricia introduced me to her family and each member seemed a foot taller than the previous one. After tea and conversation, Tricia and I drove over to the local pub, where I met a dozen of her friends. The evening flew by. During this time, I was never actually introduced to Tricia's friends and my relationship to her was never made quite clear.

"How long have you known Trish?" a fellow on my right would ask.

"Oh, about an hour," I'd reply, and the fellow would look at me, smile and go back to his beer

The party finally came to an end at 11:30 when the pub closed, but as I was to discover, the evening was just beginning. All the participants relocated at the home of one friend, and the party resumed. This time, someone hauled in a record player, and soon American and European pop tunes filled the air. It turned out that I was the only male who could dance and I soon found myself in great demand (fortunately, no one wanted to do the Swedish hambo). Whenever I was pleading exhaustion, another hand grabbed me and it was back to dancing. The party ended about 5 a.m. primarily because most of the people had fallen asleep – although I was still on my feet, amazed at my stamina and at being the center of attention.

Tricia and I finally made our exit. As we walked through

the light rain, her arm locked in mine, I thought how nice it was that travel affords one the opportunity to meet others from around the world. I couldn't wait to add more names and addresses to my book.

15

Television Is One Way Of Getting A Feel For A Country

The Washington Post, November 11, 1984

Don't tell anyone, but when I'm overseas, I watch a lot of television.

I saw Prince Charles kiss Lady Diana in – of all places-China. I saw the Parliament elect a new government in New Zealand. I became a late-afternoon sumo wrestling addict in Japan.

Now, don't get the idea that I lock myself in a hotel when I visit foreign countries. I don't, but I have discovered that one of the best ways of getting a feel for a country is by watching its television. I watch the news, sports, dramas, comedies, and when the commercials come on, I never stray from my seat to get a croissant or a six-pack of sake. Even the weather reports are helpful, as I learn the geography of a country.

I'm most interested in the news shows, especially in countries such as England, Ireland, New Zealand and Australia, where the reporters speak my language. Coverage of world events is excellent. In small countries such as Australia, New Zealand and Ireland, there doesn't seem to be much local news except for some bickering in Parliament or a scandal or two. Instead, the programs devote a lot of time to human interest stories and sports and they do a thorough job in both areas. When I was in Australia and New Zealand, 19 ½ hours a day were devoted to the Los Angeles Summer Olympics.

Entertainment shows in these countries are often American productions, such as "Magnum P.I.," "Hart to Hart" and "Cheers." And it's obvious that many viewers are avid fans of shows like "Kojak" and "Hill Street Blues," because they're amazed to discover that a New Yorker like me has never been robbed or attacked. Still, they love these shows and never seem to get enough of "Dallas."

Travelers who get homesick for American shows would especially love Australia. Turn on the television and on any of the five channels you're sure to find a hodgepodge of old and new American shows – "Scarecrow and Mrs. King," "Falcon Crest," "I Love Lucy," "The Flying Nun," "The Munsters."

Even the shows produced in Australia have a familiar ring to them. There's an investigative "weekly newsmagazine" called "60 Minutes" (complete with ticking stopwatch). There are game shows such as "The Price Is Right" ("Ian Donovan, come oooon down!") and late-night variety shows such as "The Tonight Show with Bert Newton" ("And now, heeeere's Bert!"). Early-morning viewers can enjoy "The Today Show" and "Good Morning Australia." In the evening, after "M*A*S*H" (which is on five days a week), there is "Eyewitness News" and two other news shows that feature the same theme music as New York stations. There is a live, unfunny, "Hey, Hey, It's Saturday" that looks strikingly similar to "Saturday Night Live."

In commercials, happy Australian Toyota owners all cry, "Oh, what a feeling!" as they leap in the air and children lean close to their cereal bowls to hear their Rice Bubbles go "snap, crackle and pop." Their mothers, meanwhile, are washing out their clothes with Mr. Sheen. Beer commercials often find two ex-athletes grappling over the merits of a favorite beer.

Slightly disappointed at the dearth of Australian-produced

shows, I actually left my hotel room and went out one evening with a few Australian friends. Suddenly, around 9:45, my friends rose and pushed towards the door. "We've got to get back home to see 'Dinnestee.'" Enthusiastically I went along because I had grown tired of the American fare and was anxious to see what the Aussies could produce. We flicked on the set, sat down, and I groaned as we watched John Forsythe and Linda Evans saunter across the room. This was "Dynasty."

Occasionally, Australian television did stray from the norm. Commercials appeared not only during breaks from a show, but even when an episode was on. Blurbs appeared at the bottom of the screen as a show was in progress. Conditioned by my American viewing habits, I read these messages, thinking they were urgent news bulletins, but they were invariably pushing a soft drink or a new automobile.

This was a bit startling, but it was in other countries where my head spun. I heard John Wayne speaking in Russian. Spanish singer Carmen Miranda spoke fluent Hindi in India. In Seoul, all of the "Eight Is Enough" characters spoke in Korean. Eight was more than enough.

There were other curiosities: Every day in Egypt, I saw an elderly, bearded Muslim holy man chanting his prayers for 10 minutes, followed by a bevy of scantily-clad belly dancers.

But the most intriguing shows were the ones from the one-channel Communist countries. No "Dallas'" or "The Munsters" were shown here.

Every night in the Soviet Union, I watched the news with a few English-speaking Russian acquaintances. The show followed a set format: On a bare stage stood a stolid, humorless-looking fellow about 60 years old. The show opened with President Leonid Brezhnev (this was 1978) pinning a medal on a proud Russian officer. This happened every day for the two weeks I spent in the Soviet Union. (We Westerners knew the film had been hauled out from the vault because at this time the ailing Brezhnev hadn't been seen in public for four months). After the handshakes it was on to the disasters from the West: The Texas sniper who killed nearly a dozen people; the strikes in Italy; the violence in Northern Ireland; the unemployment lines in England. Then it was back to Russian leaders shaking hands with leaders from other Communist countries. Russian farmers taking care of the wheat (wasn't that *our* wheat?). No feature stories, no interviews, not even a funny weatherman. In 15 minutes, the news was over.

Sports, however, were handled well. I saw half a dozen hockey games between American teams and the Russian national squad. There were two commentators and the camera work was exemplary, and the Russians won every game.

In China, there were volleyball matches (China defeated Brazil, when I was there) opera, war movies (the courageous Communists defeating the nasty Nationalists), and a more upbeat news program that devoted 15 minutes of coverage to Prince Charles' wedding to Lady Diana. There was an objective report on the upcoming American elections and a diatribe against the hated Vietnamese. But the most popular show was one that came on early in the evening: English lessons. The Chinese are extremely eager to learn English and this show is of immense help.

Finally, I viewed some Polish television. In many ways it resembled Russian programming in its drabness and anti-Western propaganda, but there were two shows that caught my interest. On one, a reporter held an innocuous interview with a nun visiting from overseas. My curiosity wasn't exactly piqued until I realized that the nun was from our tour group. Sister Jane, fluent in Polish, answered all the questions ("Where are you from?" "Do you like Krakow?" etc.) with aplomb, and we all agreed, will certainly become the first American media star of Poland.

I felt that Sister Jane's performance was the highlight of my television viewing, until I reached the Warsaw Airport for my flight home. After checking my suitcases, I languidly watched a TV murder mystery where the victim lay stretched out across the floor. The detective was interrogating a guilty-looking fellow. As they were talking, a woman emerged from the bedroom wearing a smile and nothing else. Hmmm. I pulled up a chair. So did a lot of other people. Because my Polish vocabulary is limited to a handful of words (such as "Hello" and "Thank you"), I couldn't understand everything that was said, but what I saw, I understood. My flight was about to depart, but I didn't want to leave Poland. There would be, I reasoned, other flights out. Totally invigorated, I started making plans to return to Poland, to see how this episode turned out and to watch more Polish television.

Just don't tell anyone.

16

If This Is Japan, How Come I'm Speaking Spanish?

The Washington Post, May 26, 1985

I'll never forget the time I confidently approached a sales clerk overseas and asked her in Spanish, "¿Como esta usted?" She looked at me blankly – which is not surprising because I was in Poland.

It always seems to happen. When I speak a foreign language I'm always one country behind. I've brought many good conversations to a halt when I've unconsciously spoken Italian in Thailand, Spanish in Japan, and Chinese in Australia.

I can't figure out why this happens. Other people get jet lag, I get language lag. I love to travel and I love languages. Unfortunately, I've always done fine in the former but lousy in the latter.

In high school I studied Latin (which would help if I ever run into Julius Caesar). In college I studied Spanish, and overseas I've studied French, Chinese and Polish. I've always felt obligated to learn the language of my host country, even if it's only a few phrases. And it was just a few phrases that revealed to me that I was never going to be a linguist.

I was traveling through Europe trying to see as many countries in two months as my Eurail Pass could cover. It was, I astutely reasoned, silly to try to master 24 languages in 50 days. So I turned to my guidebook for assistance. In the back were capsule phrases and I thought I'd try them out one evening en route to Copenhagen.

On the train I sat opposite a cheerful looking, elderly Danish couple. I flipped to the back of the book and with an exaggerated accent tossed off a few less-than-sophisticated comments about food, the weather and bathrooms. The elderly couple smiled but said nothing. I repeated the phrases. No response. I tried other phrases. I counted my fingers and toes aloud. More smiles from the couple, but no replies. I thought of counting their fingers and toes, but my guidebook only went up to 20.

I was getting agitated. This couple didn't look so charming anymore, so I finally yelled the phrases at the old geezers. They looked petrified, but neither said anything nor called the police. Finally, I held the book up to their faces and pointed to the oft-repeated phrases. They looked at each other and shook their heads consolingly. Then they pointed to an English word at the top of the page. My Danish actually was Dutch. I was on the wrong page.

When I began spending longer periods of time in a country, I took intensive courses in the language of my hosts. My first course was Chinese, which I studied three hours a day, five days a week for five weeks. Our instructor didn't speak English, but we had a textbook that was written in English and Chinese, so we all survived. When we did well, our teacher would give us a thumbs-up gesture and exclaim, "hen hao" (very good). I was the only person to attend all 75 hours, and I made use of the language on my daily afternoon forays into downtown Shanghai. But sometimes I had the sneaking suspicion that I wasn't making myself clear.

I remember when I was seated at a banquet with a dozen or so Chinese. They were local dignitaries and I thought it would be nice to engage in a bit of small talk.

"Wo meiguoren laoshi," I said, explaining that I was an American teacher.

"Huh? What was that you said?" the fellow on my right

asked in English, appearing a bit startled.

"Wo meiguoren laoshi," I repeated with enthusiasm.

The fellow on my left looked at me. "Sir, you are going to have to speak slower and clearer," he said in English. "Many Americans study Chinese, but they make basic mistakes and get confused trying to use all the proper accents."

I spoke more slowly, more clearly, tried different phrases, but couldn't get one person at that table to understand a word I said. I was in the right country, using the right language, but the only time I could make myself understood was when I explained in English what I was trying to say in Chinese.

The next year I maintained my perfect attendance record through five weeks of Polish lessons in Krakow. But every time the teacher called on me, I would suddenly blurt out an answer in Chinese. That Chinese, which had lain dormant for a year in the States (and which, I guess, was pretty dormant in China), now came bursting forth with such rapidity that I couldn't believe what was transpiring. It was a shame I couldn't take my Polish final exams in Chinese.

Now, four years later, occasionally I unconsciously say hello to friends in Polish or Spanish and find Chinese springing out in my seventh grade classroom. When a student answers a question particularly well, I've been known to give the thumbs-up gesture and say, "Hen hao!"

None of this leaves me particularly disappointed. The locals appreciate it when a visitor strives to communicate in the language of the host country. I'm proud of my attempts to master Latin, French, Spanish, Chinese and Polish – the last language that I studied. This summer I hope to take a crack at the language my grandparents often spoke – Yiddish. I'm looking forward to hearing my Polish again!

17

An American Teacher's Adventures In China

The New York Times, January 5, 1986

There is nothing so heartwarming to a teacher as when he walks into a classroom and his students accord him a standing ovation. Unfortunately, this display of affection does not happen to me all that often, but it did when I taught English last summer in the People's Republic of China. Besides the standing ovation, I found that the hot cup of tea that a student brought me each morning before I began my lectures also wasn't hard to take. I also enjoyed the celebrity status I was given when I rode a bus ("Mr. Saul, welcome to my bus"), walked down the busy streets ("Teacher, could you give me your views on Hemingway's style and prose?") or merely entered a room to see a movie and students stood offering me their seats.

I was embarrassed by it all, but who was I to complain? It was a nice life: a clean, comfortable dormitory bed, three hot meals a day, teaching eager students, never having to deal with angry parents, no cafeteria duty, and no fire drills interrupting lessons. Unfortunately, it was all to come to an end in four weeks.

I was one of 25 American teachers who spent the summer teaching at the Liaoning Normal University, a teachers' college in Dalian, formerly known as Port Arthur, in southern Manchuria. Sponsored by the *Wisconsin Institute of International Education*, which sends teachers to several countries, we taught English, conversational English, linguistics, American literature, science and technology, and composition. Though we taught in English, it was, we were to discover, going to be a challenge. We were the first group of Americans granted permission to teach in Dalian since the Communists came to power in 1949.

In the morning of the first day we were welcomed warmly by the administrators, given a briefcase that contained stationery, pencils and a bottle of glue. Then we marched into the auditorium, where our 500 students stood and cheered. I knew from that moment that I was going to like this place. We were each introduced and speeches were given by a few American teachers and by our Chinese hosts. At 10:30, the big moment arrived: I entered my classroom and met my students.

After receiving my second standing ovation of the day-- I wondered: Would I receive one when I walked into the cafeteria? -- I introduced myself and described the program. I would be teaching three classes in the morning (the group before me now would be my Period 1 class), six days a week, for 50 minutes each. I would have tutoring sessions three afternoons a week for 90 minutes a class.

My students looked more nervous than I did. I had a total of 30 of them in my three classes, about 10 to a class, ranging in age from 22 to 55. They were all teachers of Chinese or English who left their families back home to attend the school. Most had never met an American before.

The first hurdle I had to overcome was how to address my students. Normally it would not be hard to learn 30 names, but when they are names like Xiang Qi-swong and Liu Xia-wou, it becomes a bit more difficult. I considered giving them English names, but I felt I was robbing them of their identities, and therefore I was determined to learn their names, no matter how difficult it would be. However, the Chinese students insisted on receiving American names and I gave in.

It was a difficult task. How do you name a Chinese person? I paused and considered the choices available. Playfully, I considered naming them for my favorite New York Yankees baseball players, but I couldn't imagine saddling a Chinese student with "Yogi."

I finally gave them simple names like Charlie, George and Steve. During the semester, I often marveled at the power I had: I had named my students! I had given them a new identity!

After the baptism, I set out to see how much English they knew. Unfortunately, the classes were not grouped by ability. Some students had four months of English, while others had 6 to 10 years. So I tailored my lessons to give as much individual attention as I could to each student.

Classes were fun, if a bit awkward at times. The first sign of pedagogical differences occurred when I encouraged my students to ask questions. This request was met by a blank stare. Chinese students are discouraged from asking questions. They asked not only about English, but also about life in America, music, movies, civil rights, women's liberation and American youth. I, in turn, asked them many questions.

One day, we discussed dating, a subject that drew giggles from my class. I had pointed out that most American youngsters start dating between the ages of 15 and 17. Put a group of teenagers in a room, I said, and the first thing they will probably talk about is the opposite sex. Not so in China, I learned. Most of my students did not date until their late 20's, and then often married their first boyfriend or girlfriend. Some in their 30's and 40's have never dated at all. Two women told me privately that they had never kissed anyone and that those kisses would be saved for their husbands.

They were an interesting group. Donna (her Anglicized name) was a girl who seemed to have been born in the wrong country. She loved to dance, enjoyed American and British literature, which could be found everywhere I went, was a fine cook, a terrific tennis player, a movie and theater buff and seemed to have opinions about everything. Charlie was in love with a girl he said wouldn't return his affections because she came from a family with more money. George, 29, missed his wife so much that he wrote to her every day. Don, 55, hadn't spoken English since he served as an interpreter with American troops during World War II. Now, when he spoke, American slang from the 1940's flowed from his lips. Frank, who desired to tape –record each lesson, spent most of his time trying to figure out why his recorder wouldn't work. Tom always smiled, Maria never did. Ivan rarely showed up for class, Walter never seemed to leave. Nearly all the men smoked cigarettes. They were all warm and friendly, and through our experiences inside the class and out, we became quite close.

My students emulated their American counterparts in many ways: their dress, their interests and their expressions. Unfortunately, as the year progressed, they imitated them in other ways: they started to cut class, come in late and not do their assignments.

I even caught shy Ella and honorable Henry in the act of plagiarism. They had turned in identical essays. When confronted with the evidence, they both admitted they had copied their responses from a textbook. They had acted alone. They didn't know each other. The surprising thing was that neither showed remorse or embarrassment at being caught. As Ella said simply, "Everyone does it."

I came down hard on the late-comers, the class-cutters, the assignment-avoiders. Privately I chuckled about it, because I was under the mistaken impression that the Chinese were the most diligent, conscientious students on earth. But these demonstrations proved they were human. Most of them did maintain a perfect attendance record and did write 99 percent of their assignments, but since, for reasons I never learned, no credit was offered for this course, they didn't feel compelled to their best.

The classes I enjoyed most were the afternoon tutoring sessions, actually they weren't tutoring in the way we regard the word. They were 90 minutes of pure conversation with the class discussing politics, customs, China, the United States – anything that came to mind. I was very honest with them, and my opinions were frequently quite strong. I told them why I considered Communism a failure, but I did it in a way that was not disrespectful. I voiced displeasure with President Reagan, not because I wanted to attract new members to the Democratic Party, but because I wanted to see the Chinese students' reactions to an American criticizing their leader. Those afternoons left me drained, but if I had encouraged my students to think and ask questions, then I was happy. At times I expected a Chinese official to appear at my door, hand me a plane ticket and send me home, but this never occurred.

On the days we didn't have tutoring sessions, my students turned into hosts. They took me to the beaches, the museums, the zoo and the shops. When I was alone, I'd join Chinese townspeople at long picnic tables set up in blocked-off downtown streets at noontime and enjoy a 40-cent meal of noodles and vegetables. Women cooked next to the tables and served meals to their customers. Sometimes I'd return early to campus and play tennis with students on a dirt court. Once I walked down the street to get my hair cut from the local woman barber, who charged me the fairly reasonable price of 14 cents. My students and I attended volleyball matches, soccer tournaments and acrobatic shows.

After dinner, I'd dash over to watch a videotaped movie in the university. After acknowledging the students' applause and declining their offers of the best seats, I'd settle down to enjoy the predominantly American movies that were obviously beamed in from the large satellite dish on campus. However, after a few minutes it was apparent that not all these shows were broadcast from the United States. It was the foreign commercials that gave them away. Smiling Japanese faces of a family buying a new Datsun or an Australian couple contemplating a trip to Europe filled the screen.

In addition to teaching classes, some Americans were called on to give lectures in their fields. One teacher spoke about the American space program. Another discussed the civil rights movement. I had agreed to speak on press freedoms and was given 90 minutes for my presentation. But how do you talk about freedom of the press and the public's right to know in a country where there is no freedom of the press and the public doesn't have the right to know anything? I tried not to step on anyone's toes. I had brought American magazines and newspapers and a few of my own articles. I prepared a speech tracing the history of journalism and its role in American society. I compared it with Soviet journalism (which was my mischievous way of comparing it with Chinese journalism, since its tenets are basically the same).

I was told that my talk would be for only the Chinese teachers who taught Chinese. Why the others were excluded, I don't know. I began at 9 a.m. in the basement of the university. There were about 50 students present, and extra chairs had to be fetched. Some of the students were from my own class and although they were not Chinese teachers, I didn't object. If they wanted to hear my speech, I was honored. But not everyone was happy. The chairman of the department of foreign languages stormed in and had me announce that my talk was only for Chinese teachers. I made the announcement, a few students rose and left, and I began my speech.

Soon the official returned and announced that the room was unsuitable for a speech and moved us to the third floor. There I was urged to ask those individuals who didn't teach Chinese to leave again. I complied with his request, but only a few plodded out. A few minutes later, the chairman returned and announced that my latest room was unsuitable for my lecture and off we went to another class.

After the students were resettled, the chairman summoned me out into the hall. Angrily, he told me that the lecture was only for Chinese teachers. He acted as if it was my fault and my responsibility to throw out the rascals. I again pleaded for those individuals who were not Chinese teachers to leave. Obviously, my efforts were not good enough. The chairman stormed over to individual students and started to haul them physically out of the class. Two of them were my students. One of them, George, cried out, "Saul, I apologize for my country," while Charlie, the other one, yelled, "There is no freedom here."

There were similar encounters with the Chinese officials that disrupted our otherwise tranquil experience. A female Chinese student was spotted having dinner at a local hotel with a male American teacher. She was reported, rebuked by a Chinese department head and forbidden to see the teacher socially. A beach trip that required the Americans to follow dozens of rules upset us. A dance hosted by the officials excluded the Chinese students.

These incidents caused some teachers to yearn for home. At the end of one of the six-day work weeks, someone scribbled on the dorm blackboard, "T.G.I.S.," for "Thank God It's Saturday." Some teachers began to carp over the slightest thing. Life in China, we agreed, wasn't as much fun as in the old days (four weeks earlier). Even I realized that the Schachter charm was fading. I soon found that I had to get my own cup of tea in the morning and when I entered the movie room, not on Chinese person budged to give up their seat. My V.I.P. days were over.

Eventually it was time to go. In each class, students threw parties for their venerated teachers. Gifts were exchanged. The music blared and finally American teachers danced with Chinese students. In my classroom, the students gave me beautiful porcelain vases. They brought in fruits and candy and soda. All the fruit was carefully picked and cleaned.

At our party, the mood was anything but melancholy. Frank, whose tape recorder never did record, displayed some nimble steps on the dance floor, corralling every girl that sauntered by. Harry, an urbane 55-year-old who studied Russian and fought the Americans in the Korean War, whirled his dance partner around and later gleefully whispered in my ear, "I haven't danced since 1948."

The party, which began early in the morning, was scheduled to end by 10 a.m., but it stretched into the afternoon. But when the supply of food finally ended, so did the party. There were long goodbyes and promises to write.

The American teachers were the last ones to leave the building. I joined my colleagues and walked over to the dormitories. But we never were able to finish a conversation; sobbing students would charge over and embrace us, which in turn produced tears from the Americans. In the evening, a final banquet ended with Americans and Chinese singing their national anthems.

Even after our train rolled out of the Dalian station the next morning did we discover that we were not saying our final goodbyes to the Chinese. At each station, students kept popping up in the crowd to greet us. Indeed, one girl, Monica, showed up at Shenyang, Liaoyong and Huaite. I was certain that when I returned home to New York, Monica would be there at Kennedy Airport waving and cheering. Her always-smiling face, so representative of the Chinese people we met, was one I will never forget.

I can't wait to go back.

18

Age, In Fact,
Might Make The Difference.

The Washington Post, April 27, 1986

Can a seasoned traveler be over the hill at 30?

I'm beginning to wonder.

I'm a veteran country-hopper of more than 40 nations, but as I approach my 30th birthday, I find that while my enthusiasm for travel hasn't waned, I can't – or won't – do the things I used to anymore. I find I can't sleep at Gatwick Airport when I'm down to my last British pound. No longer do I spend less money in a European city than Arthur Frommer. In the past, I thought nothing of cooking a hamburger over an open fire on my journeys out West. Now, when I travel to New Zealand, I spend $10 to watch a Maori cook a side of beef in a pit.

I haven't switched from student ID card to credit card, but it may not be long. Recently, this overseas traveler with the iron stomach who could eat anything (and did) has begun sneaking off at odd hours in search of the elusive western restaurant. Even in the People's Republic of China, I found myself stuffing granola bars into a valise.

I just can't understand what's happening to me.

On my first trip to Africa 10 years ago, I covered eight countries in 22 days (mostly by bus over unpaved roads in exhausting heat), went on safari and lost 20 pounds. One night our group was driving on a deserted road somewhere in Kenya when we were surprised by rifle-toting men who ordered us out of the bus while they rummaged through our belongings. Despite being held at gunpoint, my only reaction was: This was not in the tour brochure. It turned out the men were looking for ivory smugglers; fortunately, they found none.

Another time I arrived in Bangkok late one night, alone, hot and tired. A friend's friend was supposed to put me up; when I called her she said she'd like to help, but she lived 400 miles from the airport, it was late and … click.

These incidents didn't dampen my enthusiasm. If anything, they rekindled my desire to travel.

When I backpacked around Europe, I slept on a dozen trains with other young vagabonds, ate picnic lunches under the Eiffel Tower, jogged around the Roman Colosseum and took in the theater in London. I didn't know where I was sleeping from one country to the next, but I didn't mind. When there was a train strike in Italy, I switched over to buses. When the banks went on strike in Greece, I ate less. When I arrived with a group in Egypt and was told that we had no hotel rooms and that it would be another two or three hours before we would be able to find one, I check my bags into a locker and set out for a do-it-yourself tour of the countryside.

In all my years of traveling, I've never called home, I've never sent telegrams, and I've never worried. If my train somehow had gotten sidetracked to Iran, I'd probably have taken a walk around the place, bought a few postcards, snapped a few photographs. I wouldn't have minded.

But then a funny thing happened. I realized on my jaunts alone that I was getting lonesome. My clean, spartan dormitory rooms now looked unappealing and, by the way, who were those six shady-looking characters I was sharing a room with? Why was it that when I was sleeping on those cold airport benches, my feet would fall asleep before the rest of me did? Hey, what do you mean my room in Senegal doesn't have a color television? And eight weeks is an awfully long time to be away from home. I have a new house to take care of, bills to pay and who's going to cut the lawn? Wasn't I a bit old to be playing hockey with the boys in Moscow and roller-skating along the Great Wall? Shouldn't I have found a wife by now (preferably one who spoke English as a first language) and started to settle down?

I sat back one evening and contemplated those questions. It's difficult to admit that you're getting old. And, chronologically speaking, I am. (My generation is at the awkward age. We don't have a label. If we're in our forties we'd be considered "middle-aged." If we were 15 we'd be "teen-agers." But for those of us who remember the senior prom as if it were last weekend, 30 is nearing the crisis stage.)

But does my desire for more comfortable accommodations constitute a capitulation to my new status? I think not. In retrospect, sleeping on a train and in an airport weren't wonderful experiences. Nor was washing clothes frequently in a hotel basin. They were experiences I had to endure – usually owing to a lack of money, or to my desire for adventure.

But all of that is in the past. I have changed some of my traveling habits. I don't go to Luxor, Egypt when it's 120° F. Conversely, the next time I climb Mount Fuji in the summertime I will bring a jacket (how was I supposed to know that the temperature dips down to the 30s at night?). When I travel abroad, I now make sure a hotel room or comfortable accommodation is awaiting me. I avoid the traditional tours, but travel with groups of people who will be nearby, even if only at dinner. If I have the opportunity to fly (as opposed to taking a 24-hour train ride), I shell out the extra money and go with the airplane. I openly applaud western toilets when I see them and I've developed a strong affinity for air-conditioning when I stay in tropical countries.

But, besides that, I haven't changed much as I approach the big 3-0. I still want to see the world. Despite the protests from my family and friends, I have been checking out trips to the North Pole. I want to see South America. I would love to return to Moscow and have a hockey rematch with those Russian boys. I want to catch up with friends in Copenhagen, New Delhi, Sydney, Auckland and Shanghai.

And I want to explore the moon. I know there's already a long waiting list for the inaugural flight, but I don't care. I want to be on the first flight and I'll train to be a flight attendant, and maybe, just maybe I'll set up my sleeping bag on the launching pad the night before.

I hope my feet don't fall asleep before I do.

19

The Jet Lag Jag

The Washington Post, September 21, 1986

It's 4 a.m. and I'm wide awake. Again.

You'd think that after dozens of trips abroad, I would have kicked jet lag by now, but no.

My doctors' shots have spared me from getting smallpox in Ethiopia, yellow fever in Ghana and Cholera in India, but they haven't figured out a way to eliminate jet lag in New York. Like the common cold, there doesn't seem to be a cure.

My jet lag doesn't discriminate. Regardless of whether I've flown in from the East or the West, communist countries or democratic ones, the North Pole or the South Pole, I get it.

But, curiously, over the years, I've almost taken a liking to jet lag. It sort of grows on you – especially since you know it's a small price to pay for having a good time overseas.

I don't fight jet lag. If it's 4 a.m. and I'm wide awake, well them I'm awake. Playing soft music or pulling the covers over your head isn't going to induce sleep if your body knows it's 11 a.m. in Jerusalem. After the hard realization sets in, I turn on the lights and announce to no one in particular, "I'm up."

But being awake at 4 a.m. can pose a few problems. What do you do with yourself until the rest of civilization emerges from slumber?

Except for an occasional movie, there is virtually nothing on television. Radio is a bit of an improvement, especially since there are fewer commercials during the early hours of the morning, but sometimes these programs have a funereal air about them.

So I learned years ago to make myself useful.

I vacuum. Never a big fan of vacuuming, I find it almost pleasurable at 4 a.m. in fact, I find myself doing any number of things I deplore doing in sunlight. I dust a lot. Bookcases, desk tops, light fixtures. I can proudly look back at the work I've done in the past five years cleaning my oven, scrubbing the bathtub and scouring the sinks. I've even considered mowing the lawn – if only I could see it.

At 4:45 a.m. I call a break and sit down and reread the mail that has piled up during my absence. I respond to letters from friends and write to those I've neglected. Occasionally, and only occasionally, I've called friends overseas, because when it's 4:45 a.m. in New York, it's at least 9:45 a.m. in Europe – and the rates are lowest in the early hours.

By 5:30 a.m. I'm on a roll. I pay some bills and don't get upset by the fact that I have to pay the telephone company $20.10 even though I wasn't home to use the phone.

If it's Day 4 or Day 5 of jet lag, I frequently set up the slide projector and enjoy my trip all over again. There I am, without a care in the world, beaming in front of the Eiffel Tower or shaking hands with a guard at Buckingham Palace. If I'm really ambitious, I pull out slides from previous trips. Japan, China, Spain, South Korea. Sometimes, however, the images blur. Look at those wonderful canals in Stockholm (or is it Vienna?). What a great time we had swimming there in Greece (or is that Bermuda?). Ah, well, it brings back fond memories.

At 6:15 a.m. I pull on shorts and go for a jog. Except for a few dog walkers I have the road to myself, and although I don't require the solitude (being up and alone since 4 a.m. can give solitude a bad name), I do enjoy the crisp air of the early hours.

Suddenly it's 7.a.m. The house looks wonderful, the birds are chirping, lights are going on around the neighborhood. I shower and prepare a hearty breakfast. I set it on the tablecloth that I cleaned at 4:48a.m. and sit down to enjoy the meal.

In a half hour, I will start off for work, totally refreshed. I just hope I can stay awake until lunch.

20

Tripping Backward
In Time At Reunions

The Washington Post, January 18, 1987

Travelers are a misunderstood bunch. They have a wonderful time overseas, then when they get home, there's nobody who really wants to hear their spellbinding tales or see their breathtaking slides. They inadvertently become members of their own little private club: their fellow travelers. Who better to share the memories?

I've been to high school reunions, college reunions, but for me there's nothing as joyous as a summer trip reunion, usually just a year after the original trip. In fact, I have fonder memories of some of the trip reunions than of some of the trips themselves.

There's a camaraderie that develops among travelers who have lived together for six weeks, eaten their meals together, attended the same lectures and traipsed through the same museums, pagodas, temples, shrines, communes, synagogues, kibbutzim, churches and mosques. They've danced together, explored together, shopped and even gotten sick together. They are, in a word, survivors. (It's not unlike those World War II veterans who reunite every few years. The war may have been hell, but the friendships and fond memories endure.)

I also like trip reunions because they afford me the opportunity to travel again – this time to different places on my own continent: Maine, Wisconsin, British Columbia, California, Massachusetts and New York in recent years. But regardless of whether our journeys took us to Japan or Australia, China or Paris, the reunions back home usually follow the same, happy routine.

The guests begin arriving on an early, crisp Saturday afternoon. The weather is much cooler than it was when we parted months ago and as we embrace, nearly everyone utters the line that has been uttered since the dawn of trip reunions: "I nearly didn't recognize you with your clothes on!"

After a few minutes, everyone is talking at once and the house is abuzz with chatter. Despite the fact that we live hundreds of miles from each other, people chat as if they were next-door neighbors. How's your husband, Judy? Did Peggy get braces? Is your mother's health improved, Esther? Is Ralph doing better in science? It's amazing what we learn about each other's families in just a few weeks.

In a couple of hours, we all congregate around the dining room table for the buffet dinner (which always features a main course from the foreign country we visited), and then the entertainment portion of the program is announced: "It's time for the slides!" A cheer resounds through the room, the projector is set up, and we watch 24,567 slides go by. Even though it takes seven hours to see them all, I am never bored. (In fact, someone invariably pipes up at the end, "Let's see another carousel.")

Everyone on the screen looks so happy – and why not? No cares in the world, no bills to pay, no meals to prepare. The slides recall adventures and events we may have forgotten. There's the birthday party we threw for Barbara with a candle on a bagel. And Jeff with that banjo. And Debbie trying mightily to look as majestic, dressed as the Statue of Liberty on the Fourth of July. And Harry beaming behind the wheel of a bus, a cab, a train and a car and atop a camel.

Sometimes slides can cause confusion. A mountain will appear on the screen and 16 people will adamantly identify it by 16 different names. Every so often a scene from someone's previous trip makes an appearance before us, but no one seems to notice. Everyone is having a good time and even less-than-wonderful days are greeted with fond remembrances. My, wasn't Eilat ter-rific? (Everyone seems to forget that it was 116 degrees in Eilat and people were dropping like flies, but who's going to bring that up? It's like people who remember the Depression with fondness. You don't argue.)

And, then, what reunion would be complete without a guest of honor? The reunion always coincides with the annual visit to the States by the local guides who smiled through six weeks of flight delays, unprepared hotels and complaints about the food, weather and elevators. Now it's their turn to be pampered. They're feted, toasted and practically deified till the wee hours of the morning.

After the slides, things quiet down a bit. There's always gossip about suspected love affairs, and did you know that Silent Sue was really fluent in Hebrew and understood every word that the guides spoke? The reunion always includes a phone call from the poor chap 1,200 miles away who couldn't make the trip.

When the food, drink and conversation are running low, sleeping bags are unrolled and cots are set up. In a few hours we'll all be up again, ready to make our next voyage – home.

We always discuss future reunions, but these rarely come to pass. In fact, I've never been to a second reunion of the same group, although I do keep in touch with a few people from each trip. It's an ongoing link.

And as I embark on the next trip, I am also, of course em-barking on the next trip reunion. Bring on the slides!

21

14 Years Later: Going Out With My High School "Crush"

Albuquerque Singles Scene, June, 1987

I fell in love on October 12, 1973. That was the day I met Dorothy Fensterer. I was a high school junior and Dorothy was the most beautiful girl I had ever seen. She was the "girl next door" – although she lived a mile from my house. She had blond hair, an effervescent smile, and a shyness that made her even more endearing. Even though she was an older woman (a senior), I was in love – along with every other boy in school.

In class, my mind seemed to be elsewhere. When my science teacher asked who was responsible for the law of gravity, I'd sigh and say, "Dorothy Fensterer." I would later declare that she wrote the Declaration of Independence, developed the Pythagorean Theorem, and personally freed the slaves.

Unfortunately, she didn't know who I was. I was too shy to formally introduce myself, so I did the next best thing: I became friends with her friends. And, somehow, somewhere along the line, I was introduced to her. She was everything I'd imagined her to be. From that day on, my life was changed. At school, I'd walk halfway around the building so I could pass her in the hall and say, "Hi." When she'd emerge from her 6th period math class, we'd make small talk, laugh, and when it was time to part, I'd fall into my seat. My friend, Casey Verbert, would stand over me, fanning me, so I wouldn't hyperventilate.

Slowly, but surely, our friendship grew. I attended Dorothy's basketball games (her boyfriend even gave me rides) and in the morning I'd meet her in the cafeteria where we'd discuss life until first period began. I must admit, I was thoroughly intimidated by Dorothy Fensterer, and felt like I was spending time with royalty.

After school, she worked at the local florist, arranging flowers (of course). I would go off jogging, but inevitably my route took me to the floral shop where I circled the building 15 times before I could summon the courage to jog in. It was particularly difficult in the winter because when I finally forced myself to enter that hallowed shop, my glasses would fog up, leaving me even more discombobulated.

But, evidently, I was making progress. On the next-to-last day of school, when students left their "thanks" in the form of the Senior Class Last Will and Testament, the president stood before 1400 students and faculty members and intoned, "I, Dorothy, say to Saul, 'Thanks for all that great conversation and good times you gave me on those blue mornings when only you could cheer me up.'" The crowd roared, my buddies playfully mugged me, and my face reddened. I caught Dorothy's eye across the gym and smiled.

The next year, I rarely saw her. I went to the Senior Prom with a girl who was a friend of hers. In fact, she wore Dorothy's prom dress.

Near the end of my senior year of college, Dorothy married her boyfriend. I attended the church service and did not stand when the minister asked, "If there is anyone here who objects to these two marrying, let him now speak..." I was truly happy for her.

After the wedding, I lost track of Dorothy and it wasn't until the fall of 1984 that I ran into her at a local street festival. It was nice seeing her. She told me that she was living locally, had divorced four years earlier, and was back in college. We chatted for a while, learned that we both liked to jog, and promised to keep in touch.

A few days later, I invited her over to my house and we went jogging. Later, I cooked dinner for us both.

Soon we were spending a lot of time together, watching television, going skiing and ice-skating. And, a funny thing happened – I realized I didn't love her! I still thought she was terrific; she remained as sweet as she was in high school, but that magic wasn't there anymore.

It's funny. I care so much about her, relish the times we spend together, but I have no inclination to send out wedding invitations to my friends. And, probably because of these feelings, I am no longer intimidated. I'm not nervous around her. If anything, she occasionally seems nervous.

Sometimes I find myself laughing inwardly. I'll be curled up on the couch with her watching television and I think, "Hey, this is the girl I've always dreamed about. Fourteen years later she's here and I'm not in love!"

And, Dorothy's feelings are the same. She seems to have a dozen requests a day for dates and she frequently takes up the offers. But, Dorothy is hard to please and she frequently hurries through a date to get home to call and tell me about it. I think I'm fast becoming Dorothy's "sorority sister."

In the meantime, I'll occasionally have a date that for various reasons has disappointing results and by 11 p.m. I'm reporting in to Dorothy.

As I approach my 30th birthday, I eagerly want to get married. Dorothy wants to marry again too. But, our marriages will be to other people. Dorothy and I know each other well enough to realize that a permanent relationship would never work out between us. We have made other commitments to each other: to run the New York Marathon next year, to attend friends' weddings, and to have dinner together on Wednesday evenings.

So, even after we meet our future mates, we will continue to enjoy each other's company. In the fourteen years since we met, we've both matured and yet have maintained our giddy enthusiasm for life. I think she's still one of the loveliest girls around.

And I can finally enjoy being around Dorothy without hy-perventilating!

22

My VCR Freed Me From TV Slavery

Newsday, October 25, 1987

I had been warned about its addictive effects. It will turn your life upside down, I was told. But, I was strong. I had will-power. I would not give into temptation. Nevertheless, one day my defenses broke down, and I succumbed.

I bought a VCR.

I had always thought I would be the last one to own such a machine. After all, I don't watch much television, and I'm always the first one on line when a new movie opens at our local theater. So, why did I do it? I guess I bought the VCR for the convenience it offers. When I'm asleep, I've taped old movie classics that all seem to come on at 2 a.m. While I'm teaching school I've taped "The People's Court" for my seventh-grade law classes and "The Sinking of the Lusitania" for my World War I classes.

My weekends are culturally more enriching because of the VCR. On a recent Saturday morning while I was eating breakfast, I watched a taped "Adam's Rib" with Spencer Tracy and Katharine Hepburn. Tracy and Hepburn with my cornflakes! It was like dining with royalty. What an improvement over Woody Woodpecker!

One Sunday morning I watched "The Best Years of Our

Lives" – a wonderful movie. I received three phone calls during the viewing, but I didn't miss a thing because I was able to shut off the film. Unfortunately, every time I clicked off the VCR, the regular programming returned and there was Jerry Falwell asking me to pray for Jim and Tammy Bakker. (I didn't say the VCR was perfect).

My VCR helps me save time, too. On a Wednesday night, I watched "60 Minutes" – taped from the previous Sunday. With my remote control, I was able to race through the commercials, so I saw "60 Minutes" in 53 minutes.

And, there's more. A few times during "Adam's Rib," I missed a Tracy line and found myself emulating Katharine Hepburn ("What's that, Spensah?") and cheerfully rewound the tape and listened again. Sometimes I've watched a movie over a two- or three-day period. I once caught the previous week's "Murder, She Wrote" while I waited for the plumber to arrive.

The VCR has on occasion, however, thrown me a bit. During one taped show there was a commercial encouraging me to watch a Dustin Hoffman movie on later that evening. I stayed up for the film, but when I turned on the set, there was no Dustin. It seems that the movie was on two weeks earlier – when I had taped the show.

Still, despite the occasional mishap, I wouldn't think of giving up the VCR. My friend laments that he's spending a lot more time in front of the television screen since he purchased his model, but I don't find this to be the case with me. In fact, I'm finding I spend more time out of the house. I'm socializing more, getting more involved with other activities. Thanks to my VCR, now I don't hesitate to go ice-skating on Sunday mornings, and I've resumed my basketball playing on Thursday night.

The VCR, in fact, has even had a comforting effect on me as I sleep. One night I dreamt I was dancing cheek-to-cheek with a beautiful woman and I'm whispering in her ear, "I'm so happy. Here I am with you, the night is lovely, the music enchanting, and I'm not missing the 'Cosby Show' because I'm taping it on my Panasonic 1363."

The VCR has certainly affected my life. In a few years, I hope to get married. In the past, this might have posed a conflict because I'm a big Yankees fan and I rarely miss a game. But, now, if I get married on the day of a Yankees telecast, I can just tape the game … and watch the contest while on my honeymoon.

I hope my wife is a patient woman.

23

Telling Tales Out Of School

Newsday, December 15, 1987

The kindergartner eagerly presented his teacher with a package which contained a necklace.

"When I told him how pretty it was," the teacher, Liz Phillips of the Glen Head School, recalls, he shyly replied, "Well, it's really my mother's, but she didn't like it."

Most teachers try to discourage such offerings from students at holiday time. Some schools, for obvious reasons, forbid their staff from accepting gifts. According to my father, when he went to school in the 1930s, no one ever considered giving their teacher a gift. It was akin to sending a present to the dentist.

But things seemed to change after World War II. I'm amazed by the generosity of our students and their families. Every year they buy Christmas gifts for relatives, friends, and business associates – and somehow they always remember their teachers.

Frankly, my colleagues delight in receiving tasty homemade cookies or bright Christmas ornaments. I seem to always get a bottle of Brut. I appreciate the gesture, and it is a nice cologne, but I must have 32 bottles of the stuff by now. If I splashed it onto my face every day for the rest of my life, I figure I'll be 112 when the last bottle is empty.

My colleagues over the years have had their share of unusual gifts. A few years ago, science teacher Frank Bonosoro received a pair of pajamas. Art teacher Elaine Hendrickson was ceremoniously presented with a recently dislodged pair of horse's teeth (Her student claimed they brought good luck.) Health teacher Patti DiStefano was the recipient of gray sheer pantyhose (The boy's father worked for a hosiery company).

Among the most popular teacher gifts, according to my fellow teachers, are bottles of cheer, neckties, ballpoint pens, books and those mugs that read, "A Very Special Teacher" or "World's Best Teacher." Now in my ninth year of teaching, I have a collection of 15 such message mugs. Older colleagues have accumulated a lot more.

Vickie McQueen, who began her career in our district in 1949 as a sixth-grade teacher at the Glenwood Landing School, recalls being the recipient of "a million handkerchiefs," along with at least 25 invitations from the parents of those early postwar students. In those days, mothers rarely worked outside the home and every Christmas, the teacher was invited to each student's home for afternoon tea or even for dinner.

In return, she distributed comic books of classics such as "Treasure Island" and "Huckleberry Finn." "As long as they were reading, they'd eventually get to the good stuff and read the novels themselves," she explained.

In the late 1950s, McQueen moved up to the secondary level to teach seventh grade. The number of gift-givers declined, she says: "Seventh graders were afraid of looking too goody-goody." But in 1966, when she was pregnant with her second daughter, all of the children gave her baby presents at Christmas. "One boy was very poor and his mother crocheted a bib," she said. "I never used it. It was too good to use."

A couple of years ago, McQueen received a beautiful quilted skirt from a student whose father was a tailor. The boy's brother is coming up to the junior high next year and it looks like he'll be in my class.

Hmm… I certainly discourage my students from bringing me gifts. It is not a good practice. But I wonder if the father would consider taking a dozen bottles of Brut in exchange for a new blazer.

24

Beginning The Voyage: Reunion At A Wedding

Newsday, June 5, 1988

In 1952, my parents moved into a new development in Glen Head on Long Island. Their relatives and friends, most from Brooklyn, feared that my parents were moving to another hemisphere. Undaunted, they settled in at 71 Glen Cove Drive. Their home cost $15,000 (at 4 percent interest) and they worried about how they would make the $100-a-month payments.

In keeping with the postwar baby boom, they began building their families. I arrived in 1956, followed by my sisters, Marjie, in 1958, and Louise, in 1966. Our block resembled "Leave It to Beaver." Fathers went off to work, mothers stayed home. All the kids were in the same age bracket and there was always kickball in the street, tag or hide-and-go-seek or football in Old Man Doxey's backyard.

It was a good mix of Irish, Greeks, Jews, Italians and Poles, and we kids always got the first crack at Bud Osman's kielbasa at the New Years Eve parties and Anne Leslie's moussaka. The social event of the day was Mom's coffee klatch in our driveway.

Our block's parents were middle class, middle-of-the-road politically, and supportive of their children. For a group of about 20, we sure turned out well. Each year at graduation most of the awards for "most popular," "most well-rounded," and "most likely to succeed" went to our block.

After a while, some families moved away, but usually not too far. The Ungars moved three miles, to Glen Cove. The Costellos moved a bit farther, to upstate Saratoga. In the 17 years since, Jane Costello has sent a card for every birthday and anniversary. We call her "Mrs. Hallmark."

Recently, Chris Osman got married. Chris was born two days before I was, but we didn't always get along. The families have photos of us in a playpen, backs to each other. We patched things up on our fourth birthdays and have been friends ever since. Chris, now a CPA, met his wife, Pamela, on that most romantic of places, the Long Island Rail Road.

And now Chris was getting married. Would the old neighbors be there? Some had moved away; retirement had enabled others to travel, and illness had slowed a few.

But, of course, everyone was there. Jane and Mark Costello came from Saratoga. I stood in the doorway of the church between them, introducing myself to unsuspecting guests as their son. Soon my real parents arrived, and my mother was chattering away until she noticed the woman to my right. "Jane Costello!" she yelled. They embraced and Mom cried and cried. It was a scene to be repeated often.

We finally made our way into the church and I sat in a pew beaming at my boyhood friends. Ceal Levy, the town's feistiest 82-year-old, elbowed me in the stomach and motioned to the altar. "Does this whet your appetite?" she asked mischievously.

Later at the reception I danced with Ann Osman. Chris twirled my mom around. Finally, it was over. The bride's side had left house before, but few from Chris's side seemed eager to leave. When the cleanup crew arrived, we made our way to the parking lot.

There was talk of the next get-together and the next person to march down the aisle. Whoever's wedding is next, it should be a great affair. After all, our old neighbors will all be there.

25

What's Your Next Step In Adult Education?

Newsday, August 28, 1988

Some people contend that the most beautiful day of the year is the first day of spring. Others speak blissfully of the moment the leaves start to change colors in the fall. For me, the sun shines most brightly on the third Monday of September: that's the day my Adult Education dancing lessons begin.

For six years now, I've been a participant. In the days leading up to the first class, I begin to prepare myself. I rumba to the bathroom, waltz through the den, and hustle over to the kitchen.

I don't know what it is about dancing lessons. I have always been an Adult Ed aficionado: I've taken three cooking classes, auto mechanics, tennis, skating, swimming, and piano lessons, and I've even given three classes myself on my experiences in China. But for me, the classes that always give me an exhilarating feeling, the classes that always end too soon, are my dancing classes.

My desire to learn how to dance properly occurred during my Senior Prom. My date and I, no threat to be picked to appear on "American Bandstand," faked our way through the entire evening.

I then vowed to take lessons.

I signed up for "Social Dancing" at the North Shore High School adult-education program. Ten sessions, two hours each, the first hour included ballroom dancing, the second disco dancing. Our instructors were Vera and Santi Porcino.

When the first notes of Engelbert Humperdinck's "The Last Waltz" permeated the gymnasium, I was hooked.

For six years now, I've never missed a class. The hustle is a cinch, but the tango gives me fits. I always seem to jump a bit during the foxtrot, but that's my friend's fault: she's trying to teach me the Polka.

Friends ask me why I've taken lessons so long. Well, for one thing, it's lots of fun. The Porcinos are excellent instructors, very patient ("Saul, why are you lifting up your partner?"), and very entertaining. When they're not correcting each other (Santi: "Gentlemen, don't listen to Vera. Here's the correct way..." at which point, Vera will step in with her own pointed but good-natured comments), they are circulating throughout the gym offering encouragement to the sometimes beleaguered, but hopeful, dancers.

When I began, Vera and Santi gave lessons at North Shore, Roslyn and Syosset. But, in the past few years, they've cut back on their schedule. They first dropped North Shore, so I signed up at Roslyn. Then, they pared Roslyn from the list, so I followed them to Syosset. I feel like a Porcino groupie. I sign up each year also because, although I do the hustle often, I rarely find opportunities to do ballroom dancing, I forget the steps, and need a refresher course.

Sometimes, I've attended weddings and felt uncomfortable on the dance floor when the band played a foxtrot or a lindy. The reason: these songs were not the ones Santi and Vera played! When Frank Sinatra sings, "You Made Me Feel So Young," I can glide into a foxtrot, but what's Bing Crosby doing here? I can lindy to the Andrew Sisters but Bobby Darin wasn't played in our classes!

I've made use of my dancing steps beyond the Syosset gym walls and the occasional wedding I've attended. When I taught sixth grade, my class put on a play about Robin Hood. Not only did the Merry Men climb trees, sword-fight and kill animals with their bare hands, but they also rumbaed, fox trotted, and waltzed.

When I studied in China in 1981, I dragged my reluctant Chinese guides onto the dance floor for a few lessons. As I tangoed with a petite interpreter, she whispered in my ear, "Do Americans dance every night in the United States?"

But, back in my class not everyone is always ecstatic to be on the dance floor. My friend contends that the leading cause of divorce in America is not incompatibility or financial problems but forcing spouses to take dancing lessons. I think that's going a bit too far, but I must admit there are some amusing sights.

For one thing, in most cases it seems to be the wife who has coerced the unwitting husband to attend the classes. (In my case, I'm the pusher). The 40-50 couples seem to consist of mostly people in the 40-and-over age category with a sprinkling of newlyweds among the ambitious. Most appear to enjoy themselves, but there are moments when you feel the urge to call the cops: Mrs. Witherspoon keeps moving to the left, when Mr. Witherspoon steps back. They're never in synch. She sways, he doesn't budge. She growls at him, he stares back at her. However, a soothing word from Vera or Santi usually saves the day. The older folks usually have no problem with ballroom dancing. The tango and the foxtrot fit them like a glove. These younger couples have trouble with these steps. Conversely, the younger set moves effortlessly through the hustle, while the older veterans are always a step behind or lack the endurance for the faster dances. Occasionally, you'll see an older couple start to sneak out the back when the Pointer Sisters come on, but most manage to stick it out.

When my dancing class ended last fall, I signed up for swimming. I've been a swimmer since I was a child, but I never learned how to breathe properly. I always swallowed water. I had good form, but something was not coordinated. My instructors tired hard, my pool mates encouraged me, but nothing worked.

Growing frustrated, I finally hit upon an idea: I went to the local record store and purchased Frank Sinatra's "You Make Me

Feel So Young," and brought it to the pool. It worked! Instead of measuring steps, I measured strokes. I no longer swallowed water. I can do only a couple of laps, but for me that's great progress.

I can't help but wonder: If I ever make it to the Olympics, can I bring a record player?

26

It Was Not Love At First Byte

Newsday, October 23, 1988

I had always been the Rip Van Winkle of the electronics world.

I had slept through the years when my friends bought stereos, transistor radios, Walkmans, cassette tape recorders, and car stereos. To me, Crazy Eddie was the juvenile delinquent on "Leave It to Beaver."

The only electronic equipment I had was a radio I received as a gift in 1970 and an electric typewriter I adopted when my sister went away to college.

I guess the electronic world intimidated me. It was too big, too noisy, too complicated. What did I need a stereo for when my radio played the same records? Why purchase a Walkman when I'd rather hear the birds singing while I jog? I was a piano player in a world full of Moog Synthesizers.

But all that changed in 1987: I bought a VCR. I liked my VCR. So, in 1988, I took a bigger step: I bought a word processor.

Originally, I was going to buy a computer, but after determining what my needs were, I settled on a word processor. For months, I read ads, asked knowledgeable friends, compared prices and purchased an Amstrad PCW2512.

I'll never forget our first night together. In the evening I set it up on my desk, looking lovingly at it – as if it were my long-awaited adopted baby. I smiled, plugged it in, and promptly blew out all of my electricity.

It was definitely not love at first byte.

Things did not get much better. I had trouble deciphering the 623-page manual. I didn't understand modems, default discs, scrolling and word wraps. I looked in vain behind every conceivable hiding place for my textual movement keys.

My Amstrad was also lacking in the social graces. During my first lesson, the following message appeared: "If you continue, all of your files on the destination disc will be permanently destroyed!" I broke out in a cold sweat. This machine, I deduced, was user-unfriendly.

However, I didn't give up. I took my time and thought things through. And, finally, I was able to compose a document on the screen. But then all sorts of problems cropped up again. I decided to underline my title. I pushed a few keys, and – voila! – my title was underlined. But then I saw the second line of my document was being underlined, and then the third, and then the fourth! It was like a runaway train. I pushed the "cancel" key, the "delete" key and keys that said "alt," "eol" and "ptr." I pushed a key that said, "f7," and immediately a list of the 25 words that follow alphabetically after "raspberry" appeared on the screen. I thought of pulling the plug, but I probably would have knocked out all of the electricity in my town with that move.

Finally the frantic underling stopped. I had run out of words. I went into the bathroom and put my head in the sink.

When I returned, I tried to move my name and address from the left hand side of the document to the right. I found the menu for "right alignments" and pushed the "enter" key. Immediately, "Saul Schachter" scooted over to the right. Hooray! I did the same to "31 Altamont Avenue" but instead it jumped down to the next line. Ugh. I tried it again, and the "Altamont Avenue" slid over under "Saul Schachter" (but two lines beneath it, not directly under as I desired). And the stubborn "31" was still on the left. I pushed the "delete" and "return" keys, but only succeeded in pushing my name and address all over the screen. With my cursor, I felt like I was using a knife and futilely trying to pick up little peas that were slipping through my grasp. The screen resembled a terrible train wreck, with bodies strewn all over the place. Here's a "Saul," there's an "Altamont," and my town, "Sea Cliff," was a jumble of vowels and consonants.

Eventually (four hours later), I was able to straighten out my document. I reunited "Saul" with "Schachter" and I retrieved my address, too. It was time to print my masterpiece. I pressed all the correct keys, but nothing happened. Then something caught my eye. I had not plugged in the printer with the monitor. Silly me. It was a bit difficult to maneuver, but I was finally able to extend my body over the monitor and plug the cord from the printer into the back of the machine. I pulled myself back over and into my chair, glanced at the screen, and nearly screamed out in horror. My document was gone. In its place was a crazy quilt of optical illusionary figures. I kept waiting for Rod Sterling's voice to intone, "You have entered the 'Twilight Zone.'" This is it. I've lost it all. Goodbye, document. Hello, suicide.

I pulled myself together. I can do it, I said. I hauled out the manual, read the pertinent passages, retrieved the document, retrieved my sanity, and printed my first report.

That was a few weeks ago. Since then I've become a new person. I now read the sports section in the newspaper after I've perused the computer column. I shout out advice to the technocrats on those Wang TV commercials. In fact, for a fellow who struggles with foreign languages, I feel I'm achieving a long, elusive dream: I'm becoming bilingual. My new abilities won't help me get by in Spain or France, but it will help me succeed in the increasingly electronic world of the 1990s.

27

The Joy Of Mail Call
When Far From Home

The Chicago Tribune, April 9, 1989

Most travelers won't admit this, but one of the things they look forward to the most of all is receiving mail from home.

Because of this desire, my tour groups have raced through the Taj Mahal, scampered up and down the Pyramids, and pushed our way through Lenin's Tomb so we could meet the postman at our hotel when he delivers the mail.

What's with this need to receive mail? Did Marco Polo's mother send him aerogrammes after he left China in the 1200s? (Actually, since Marco was gone about 25 years that would have been a formidable task.) Was Christopher Columbus kept abreast by Mrs. Columbus of the gossip back home in Genoa? (Well, probably not, since Chris, in setting out for the West Indies ended up in San Salvador, and probably neglected to leave his forwarding address at the post office.)

My guess is that no matter how exciting traveling is, people do miss their loved ones.

"When you're far away and feeling lonely," says a friend, "receiving mail is like being tucked into bed at night." When travelers scribble "Wish you were here," they probably mean it. (I know I do.)

In the last 12 years I have taken about 25 domestic and foreign trips. Initially, I was hesitant about asking people to write;

today, I photocopy and distribute my out-of-town address with all the enthusiasm of a hopeful job applicant.

My friends, too, have their own techniques. Before he went to Israel, Walter Kurtzman told his friends he was leaving two weeks earlier than he actually was, so that when we arrived in Tel Aviv, his mailbox was brimming with letters.

Veteran traveler Diane Ostrand was so disappointed with her friends for their dearth of correspondences over the years, that before she went to China with our group she distributed stamped and self-addressed envelopes to them with firm instructions to write. They did.

Letter writing has strengthened friendships. On an earlier trip to China, I was living in a dormitory with American and Canadian students. The Canadians were upset because, not only was the weather hot and the food greasy, but they received no mail because of a postal strike back home. Immediately, we Americans directed our family and friends back in the States to write to the Canadians. In addition we sent postcards in China to our Canadian friends in the dorm next door. To this day, the Canadians remain eternally grateful.

Felice Katz once spent a month in Italy letter-less because the postal service was on strike. When the crisis was resolved, there was so much mail piled up that the authorities found the quickest way to dispose of it – they burned it.

George Pappas received his mail, but only after an interesting interlude. George once stayed in Indonesia for four months. He and his companions frequently wired home for money, but, curiously, there would often be a delay of weeks before he saw any of it. Later, he discovered that the fellows at the wire service were receiving the money, and then loaning it to the locals at exorbitant rates before handing the original sum over to George and his friends.

Mail can arrive at the most surprising moments and in the most unusual places. Jack Loew, who has a summer home in Puerto Morelos, Mexico, was eating at a local restaurant when the waiter handed him his menu and his mail. Jack speaks very little

Spanish, so he can't explain what happened, but he did report that his mail was infinitely more appealing than his meal.

However, most travelers, especially those who take short, whirlwind tours, don't care about receiving mail. "No news is good news," seems to be the common refrain. Others say that with a packed schedule, there is no time to write. But all agree that they always leave their itineraries and hotel names with their families back home so they can be reached in case of an emergency.

One person who doesn't shrink from admitting she likes to receive mail is Margie Legowski, a Peace Corps volunteer in Sri Lanka.

"I want all news, any news, gossip is great, but I love hearing the nitty-gritty details of day-to-day living ('Today, I bought your father a shirt...')," says this veteran traveler who has also lived and worked in Zimbabwe, Oxford and Copenhagen. "I'm not too hot about newspaper articles about Union Station, but love letters rank high on my list as do 'Hello, I miss you' telegrams and cards. 'Frequency' is the key word here."

Margie, like many overseas Americans, has had her share of frustrating times with the postal service. One letter home took two weeks to arrive, another took two months. The Peace Corps sent her indispensable VISA card via diplomatic pouch to Nepal. A letter to a friend in nearby Kandy, Sri Lanka, was returned with the message, "No such person." Margie received a letter from a friend in Poland that had been opened and censored. Sometimes letters never arrived at their destination (here and abroad) and the disappointed correspondents feel responses aren't forthcoming for a reason. "This can definitely wreak havoc on relationships," sighs Margie.

Strikes and civil wars can interfere with mail, but there was nothing more dismaying, says our Sri Lankan volunteer, than the message Margie received from her best friend, Jayne Gieger-Wyatt, back home in New Jersey: "The sign in the local post office says: 'We do not guarantee mail to Sri Lanka.'"

Here are some practical tips for Americans sending mail or packages to their family or friends overseas:

•When in doubt, send mail to American Express offices (it will be held for the recipient) or in the care of a friend in a foreign city. Addresses and names should be printed clearly. Important: Letter-writers frequently omit the name of the country. Add the country's name.

•When sending mail to poor countries, try to avoid sending letters with stamps affixed to them. The locals frequently steal them for resale. Instead, have your local post office meter-stamp our letters or send aerogrammes.

•Sending a package could cause more trouble than it's worth for the recipient. In some countries a high Customs duty is levied on incoming packages. Also, the recipient may have to travel a great distance to an obscure warehouse to fetch it.

•Tuck surprises into letters, such as M&Ms, personal items or other goodies

•If your friend is traveling to several countries, make many copies of your letter and send them to each address.

•Don't wait for an answer before you write. Mail is unreliable. And, finally, as Margie implores, "Write, write and then write again!"

28

My New Life With
An Answering Machine

Newsday, April 30, 1989

I had never wanted to get an answering machine. Too impersonal. It was, I reasoned, a machine to screen incoming calls. I kept having nightmares that I'd get arrested one night in the backwoods of Louisiana, be granted my one phone call and end up talking to an answering machine. No, it was not for me.

My friends felt otherwise. They snatched them up as soon as they went on the market. Not only did they buy the newest, snazziest machines, they also bought those "celebrity" voice tapes asking callers to leave a message.

I remember calling my friend Paul and hearing what sounded like Jimmy Cagney saying "You... dirty....rat. You shot my brother. But if you leave your name, phone and a brief message, I'll get back to you." A call to Larry's house got these pearly words from the Richard Nixon sound-a-like: "I am not a crook. But I'll consider you one unless you leave your name..."

I don't know what happened to those celebrity messages, but I guess they lost their novelty and now I hear my friends' voices instead frequently accompanied by a bit of classical music or the gurgling sounds of their baby.

Still, I wasn't interested in an answering machine until I began missing important calls. I finally gave in and bought one. And what happened? For the next 10 days I didn't receive any calls! (My buddy Pat came to the rescue and called purposely while I was at work to leave messages so I wouldn't become too distraught over my vanishing popularity). However, my lack of popularity reached outdoors, too: I didn't receive any letters.

My back luck must have been hereditary: before leaving for a one-week vacation, my cousin Gail incorrectly set the timer on her machine, and when she returned from vacation was horrified to hear: "Hi-lic-woik-rin-stip-tru-blip." It was, she said after trying to decipher the callers' identities, like playing "Name That Tune."

Still, six months after I bought my machine, I'm glad I have it. It's helped me with my job, saved me from traveling 85 miles to visit an absent friend and has bailed me out by talking to intrusive salesmen.

Some of the messages received have been joyous ("Saul, this is Mom. Come over for dinner tonight"); some *very* joyous ("Cousin Patty had a baby boy!"); and a few curious ("Can you send someone over to check my water meter?"). It turned out that Mr. Brown, my parents' elderly neighbor, accidentally dialed my number thinking I was the water company. Evidently, he was oblivious to my message ("Hello, this is Saul. I'm not here right now, but…"). I called him back, gently pointed out his mistake, and while he paused I imagined he was going to reply, "Well, can you come over and check it anyway?" Fortunately, he did no such thing. I'm just glad for him that he didn't call me and leave a message when it was 10 below zero and his oil burner had conked out.

I am astonished by what my answering machine does: It can be hooked up to a computer, call 15 people simply by touching a button, and it can switch from a pulse mode to a tone mode, which I'm sure I'll be more impressed with when I can figure out what pulse modes and tone modes are.

I never thought I'd say it, but I have indeed become a person of the '80s. Before I leave for work, I bundle up the newspapers and take them out to be picked up for recycling, prepare my VCR to tape a favorite show and set up my personal secretary, the answering machine, for its day's work.

Now, if I can only figure out how to retrieve my mail without leaving the house.

29

I Really Enjoy My Students, But I Can't Pronounce Their Names

Educational Oasis, September/October, 1989

I really enjoy my students. They're cute and innocent and leave sweet messages on my chalkboard when I'm out of the room. But, sometimes when I want to return their affection and tell them how much I enjoy them, I can't for one simple reason: I can't pronounce their names.

Haralampos Pataridis. Elena Poloukine. Yuki Takahashi. Amy Kopczynski. Prabhpal Sandhu. Angelina Cocchiola. Jimano Kwaitkowski. Whew! Every day in homeroom I feel as though I'm taking attendace at the United Nations. I'm exhausted.

During the first two weeks of school I kept calling Sunil Gandhi, "Sunnel" (rhymes with "tunnel").

"Suneeel," a chorus of students would correct me.

"Sunneel," I'd repeat obediently.

I had a much more difficult time with Aditya Mattoo. Finally, after the 47th flubbed attempt, Aditya said helpfully "Just call me, 'Dit.'" I thanked him and seated him next to Sunnel.

The girls' names are no less difficult. Jaranya Suraratana. Now, that's a mouthful. I did stun the class when I was able to say,

"Alexandra Tsakanikas" on the first try (they didn't realize that I had time to practice since I had her sister, Nicole Tsakanikas, two years earlier). The trouble is, I still can't spell Tsakanikas without looking at her name in my gradebook.

After struggling through the Poloukines, Kopzynskis, and Cocchiolas, I was delighted to see "Douglas Shore" on my list. I asked him a question, but unfortunately I couldn't make out what he said. He spoke so fast. But there was another problem. "Mr. Schachter," Neeraj Addegada said, serving as my interpreter, "Douglas is from England. He just moved here. *Nobody* understands him!"

I slumped back in my chair.

Teachers sure had it easier when I was in school. Chris Osman. Paul Cryan. Margaret Hartmann. Now, those were names that rolled off the tongue easily. But I prefer my multi-syllabic, multi-lingual group.

For one thing, they make my social studies class easier to teach. When I have a question about India's Taj Mahal, I refer the query to Neeraj Addagad. British parliament? That's Doug Shore's department. The Acropolis? Alexandra Tsakanikas takes that one. And after Shun-Yet Jan interprets Confucian thoughts for us, I respond in Mandarin, "Hen hao" ("very good"). Shen-Yet beams.

When I teach religion, my students are a natural resource. My current crop of youngsters belong to nine different religious faiths. I could offer a very dry lecture on the Russian Orthodox religion, but when you have Sasha Terentiev in the front row, why not give her the spotlight?

Students today are more tolerant and understanding of newcomers that when I was a child. Perhaps it's because most of our students are minorities and have faced discrimination themselves. When two Sikh Indians arrived in our district wearing turbans, I feared they would be picked on. But who's going to taunt them? The kid with the thick Italian accent? The Orthodox Jew who wears a yarmulke? The punk rocker with the earring? No one has said an unkind word to them.

These students are successful because they are hard-working, considerate, and good-natured. Some, like Shun-Yet Jan, serve as an inspiration to others. I recall the day when exuberant Shun-Yet burst into my room and exclaimed, "Four years ago I couldn't speak English, and today I was accepted into the Honors Program!"

Shun-Yet and the other foreign-born students have also provided some of our lighter moments — even when they didn't realize it. Recently, I announced to the class, "Next week we are going to begin studying the American Revolution."

Doug Shore's unmistakable British accent moaned from the back of the room. "This is my least favorite time of the year."

A few days later, I was addressing the class when I noticed Doug jostling with another boy.

"All right, guys, what's going on?" I demanded.

"Mr. Schachter," the boy complained, "Doug won't stop humming, 'God Save the Queen.'" Doug threw up his hands in resignation. It was not a good week for our British delegate.

Sometimes, when I look out at children with dark skin and light skin, with blonde hair and dark hair, and I hear their accents and drawls, I envision us taking the ultimate class trip: around the world. We could visit our students' relatives, sample the local foods, and pick up a few foreign phrases. This experience would enhance my students' knowledge of the world around them, and who knows – by the end of the trip, I may even be able to pronounce their names!

30

In Praise Of The Class Mother

Educational Oasis, January/February, 1990

Way, way back in time, before mainstreaming, bilingual education, and resource rooms, there was the class mother.

For years, she has been overlooked, overburdened and sometimes overweight. Nevertheless, history books have ignored her. In such monumental works as *The School and Society* by John Dewey, *How Children Learn* by John Holt, and *The Learning Society* by Robert M. Hutchins, there has been no mention of this vital ingredient of our education program. Every good little schoolchild knows that Abraham Lincoln walked six miles in the snow every day to school, but what has always been omitted from the story was the person who followed in his tracks an hour later with his lost lunch box and gym shorts. That's right, his mother.

Now, if Mrs. Lincoln wasn't the first class mother, then it was probably Mrs. Alexander Graham Bell (she had a phone) or Mrs. Betty Crocker (she could make cupcakes). Regardless of who was the first, the important thing to remember is that these women have toiled for decades in relative anonymity for the betterment of our schools.

The job, admittedly, was easier in the old days. Yesterday's class mother helped out with parties, reminded parents of school activities, and fetched the doctor when a child got too close to the lion's cage at the zoo. Today's class mother does all of that plus head committees on child abuse, missing children, drug and alcohol awareness, fingerprinting, Neighborhood Watch programs, latch-key kids, and how to handle a death in the family. And, despite smaller classes, class mothers frequently make more phone calls than their predecessors did because of the growing number of divorced households.

When I was a child, you could easily identify the class mother. She was less intimidating-looking than the teacher but was still a figure of authority in her own right. She went about her business in a way that never interfered with the teacher. She was the good tooth fairy, Mary Poppins, and Mother Teresa all rolled up into one. If the school nurse was ever absent, I figured she'd make a good substitute.

These women always wore "class mother" outfits – clean, neat and efficient. They were all housewives, all happily married (or at least gave the appearance of being happily married), and their children were usually among the nicest in the grade. As far as I can recall, the class bully's mother was never a class mother.

But, that was all 20 years ago. Now that I'm a teacher, I am in a position to make several observations on the subject: For one thing, these class mothers sure seem a lot younger than when I was a student. In fact, they frequently look about six years older than their children. Today's class mother might even swap clothes occasionally with her daughter. And, more often than not, an increasing number of mothers work outside the home. (This could lead to conflicts. A second grade teacher recently planned a trip to the museum. There were only two places for chaperones, but four mothers wanted to go. One smartly attired woman stalked up to the teacher and declared, "I took a year off from a successful law practice to go on these damn trips and I'm not going to miss this one." She didn't.)

Most class mothers aren't that obstreperous. The majority that I've dealt with are quiet accommodating, even a bit mischievous. On a recent overnight trip to Boston, our school principal was awakened at 1:30 a.m. by a pounding on the door. When he answered it bleary-eyed, he encountered four Groucho Marx look-a-likes who promptly squirted him with their loaded water pistols. The class mothers fled into the night, their mission accomplished.

Though they can be frivolous, and even silly at times, these class mothers are concerned about their child's performance in school and some will do almost anything to make sure their child doesn't fall behind. I remember when I taught in a new school building. On that first day, students entered the room looking nervous in their surroundings. Most clutched notebooks with pens peeking out from their rear pockets. I gave the class an encouraging smile until I spotted the individual in the third seat of the second row. It was a woman in her forties, notebook open, pen in hand. (I knew our district had a strict retention policy, but this seemed a bit too tough.) The kids who trembled when they looked at me absolutely shook when they spotted her. For some reason, I didn't question her appearance (after all, she had been on time and well prepared – a good role model for her peers), but I did catch up with her at the end of the period. "My daughter is ill and I didn't want her to fall behind," she said quickly as she filed out the door. "Can't talk. I'll be late for science."

That was my first introduction to Mrs. Temero, fill-in student and class mother.

Mrs. Temero was one of those dedicated class mothers who spend endless hours at school. In fact, some mothers seem to be at school more often than their children. I've had a few occasions when I've been tempted to call a kid at home and give him an update on how his mother was doing in school.

Mrs. Winthrop was one of those indefatigable mothers. I recall seeing her one day as she bustled around in the office. She was scooping up brochures and applications when she scurried past me. "You're doing great work, Mrs. Winthrop," I called out, and then added teasingly, "but didn't your last child graduate in 1978?"

She turned around and smiled. "Shhh, don't tell anyone," she whispered. "I just love being involved."

31

Addressing Others By First Name

Educational Oasis, March/April 1990

I made the transition from student to teacher fairly easily. Learning the material, maintaining discipline, and keeping the records organized had been a snap. But, I'm having a hard time with names.

It's not that I can't remember them, it's just that I don't know how to address people.

It's been especially difficult at school. I attended the North Shore schools in Glen Head and six years after graduation I returned to my alma mater to teach social studies. And the problem arose: What do I call my former teachers? For weeks I addressed them as I had when I was their student, until my former social studies teacher, Mr. Pappas, came up to me and said, "Saul, please call me George." The next day my former English teacher suggested, "Look, it's Marion." So I tried, but it was hard. I had known these teachers such a long time that it was difficult to change. It was like calling my grandmother "Jennie." In school, it was easy to call the chairman of the science department "Ira" (he arrived after I had graduated), but there was no way I could address the hall monitors (who were my friends' mothers) as Rosemary, Gertrude, and Ida.

But slowly things improved. After a few weeks I was on a first-name basis with my colleagues, but at social gatherings there were some awkward moments. I would greet my former English teacher and his wife with "Hello, Bob and Mrs. Blitz." Similarly, when I met my former math teacher it was with "How are you, Linda and Mr. Shanler?" Linda's husband encouraged me to call him "John," and I felt more comfortable. But then Linda got divorced and married Mr. Cohen, who didn't encourage me to call him anything. I just wave to Linda and her husband now.

Dealing with my students posed problems – especially since many of them were my Little League players when I was in high school. They now had to address me as "Mr. Schachter." This created a bigger problem than the one I faced in going from the formal, "Mr. Pappas" to the more personal "George." For years they had known me as "Saul" or, if they liked me, as "Good ol' Saul," or "My buddy, Saul." But, now that I was an authority figure who could control their destinies (I gave out the grades), they had to change their relationship to me.

I once had my younger sister, Louise, in class. She was perplexed. Being my sister, she surely couldn't address me as "Mr. Schachter," and if I were to have the respect of the class, I couldn't tolerate her calling me "Sauly" in front of 25 students. So, to avoid any embarrassment and to cut down on her giggles, she didn't call me anything. In any case, the students have conformed and address me as "Mr. Schachter," though an occasional "Hi, Saul!" can be heard from around the corner.

And finally, dealing with my students' parents has presented me with similar "How do I address them" problems. Initially I call them "Mr. and Mrs. ... " but when I see them for years on a social basis, the formalities are dropped. I am a bit dismayed when parents I don't know greet me with "Hello, Saul," at our initial meeting. Until I know them better, I try to keep things on a more professional level, refraining from calling them by their first names.

I'm confident that I'm making progress in adapting to this new stage in my life. To me, learning all the proper forms of addressing people is like comprehending the metric system. It's going to take a while to understand all these conversions, but I'll get the hang of it. And, if it's too difficult, I'll sell my house and move back in with Mom and Dad. Or is it Mom and Mel? Viv and Dad? Oh, life was simpler when I was a kid!

32

And Now, 2.2 Seconds With Saul

The Washington Post, March 14, 1990

I was watching "60 Minutes" when the telephone rang.

"Hello, Mr. Schachter, this is Whitney Gould from '60 Minutes.' Mike Wallace is going to be reading your letter tonight and we were wondering if we could send a news crew to your house to interview you for the 11 o'clock news."

My response was less-than-eloquent.

"Huh?"

Then it hit me. My letter, critical of the way CBS handled the Andy Rooney affair, was going to be read by Mike Wallace before 33 million Americans.

"Sure," I said. "Why not?"

After hanging up, I sprung into action. There was not enough time to vacuum the living room, but I scooped up all the newspapers and deposited them in the bedroom.

The sweat suit and four pairs of shoes were tossed behind the desk. My own attire, the flannel shirt and jeans would have go to.

I rummaged through the closet. The three-piece suit would be, admittedly, a bit much. I settled on a blue sport shirt, matching blue pants, dark socks and shoes.

I then called friends, relatives, and anyone else who happened to be in my area code. And, I paced around the room.

At 7:53, the restored Andy Rooney concluded his comments and Mike Wallace appeared on the screen. "In the fallout from the whole affair these past weeks, I've received more letters than I care to contemplate... When I talked about Andy's suspension from '60 Minutes,' my favorite letter said this:

"... My family listened to your brief comments about Andy Rooney last week and we couldn't believe what we heard. I felt so embarrassed for you..."

"... 'CBS forced him to say those things,' said my mother. 'He's an old man, he doesn't know what he's saying,' said my father trying to defend you...

" 'He was paid off,' said my sister... 'You blew it, Mr. Wallace.'"

And, the letter was signed by me.

"Well, to the entire Schachter family and to all the others who wrote me in a similar vein, my motive was to try to make peace, to explain without explaining. I wish I had done it better ..."

"...All is forgiven, Mike," I said soothingly to the television.

"But," concluded Wallace, "all's well that ends well."

That's when the phone rang. Nina Sautkulis. Uncle Gerry and Aunt Bernice. Jon Seiden. Former student Tibbie Romm. Mrs. Droogan. David Kliman. The David Kliman whom I have not seen in 15 years? Yep. Cousin Carole. Mom. And on and on for 40 minutes until the CBS cameraman and reporter arrived, and then I decided to take the phone off the hook.

We made small talk, a microphone was fastened under my shirt, and then it was lights, camera, action. I was asked a host of questions about Andy Rooney, Mike Wallace, and "60 Minutes."

I sat there before the bright lights, smiling, looking relaxed, but trying to avoid disastrous wedding videos where I've appeared hunched over, tongue-tied, saying "yeah" and "ya know."

In 15 minutes it was over.

I then waited nearly two hours for the 11 o'clock news. I answered more phone calls, took a shower (forgetting that I had already taken one a few hours before), and resumed my pacing.

When the news came on, Andy Rooney's return was the lead story. After a brief summary, anchor Brian Williams announced that "the letter read on the air at the end of the broadcast was written by Saul Schachter of Sea Cliff, New York."

And, then on the screen was Saul Schachter of Sea Cliff, New York.

"To suspend him for speaking his mind – or not speaking his mind, he denied saying it – I felt was wrong."

And that was it. I must have been on the screen for 2.2 seconds. If I sneezed I would have missed it. Later on, I heard it happened so fast that friends and relatives were rewinding their videotapes, because they hadn't heard what I had said. My blue shirt looked fine, but my appearance was so quick I could have been wearing a pajama top and no one would have noticed. I didn't care. My one-sentence debut on the "CBS 11 O'Clock News" had been a success.

I went to bed at 11:30, but didn't fall asleep until 12:30. And, then I awoke at 4 a.m., wide-awake, staring at the ceiling. I rolled over and was able to catch a few more hours of sleep.

The next day was wonderful at school. I signed autographs, showed the video to my students (and acknowledged their applause), and thanked the various well-wishers. My letter, a friend pointed out, was mentioned in Newsday.

But, then it was time to return to the real world. It was fun. I enjoyed my brief fling at fame, but in considering Andy Warhol's famous line about everyone being famous for 15 minutes, I couldn't help by think: Hey, Andy, I've 14 more minutes coming to me!

33

My History Heroes Come To Life

Educational Oasis, March 4, 1990

I've chatted with Robert Redford, and I've met Woody Allen, but for me there's nothing like meeting political figures. Sure, Redford has charm and Allen is funny, but introduce me to the Secretary of the Interior or the Deputy Chief Inspector for Public Words and I'm in heaven.

My political celebrities are like no other. Their world is fast and exciting, yet they live in practical anonymity from the general public. They never seem to be besieged by screaming fans. Autograph seekers don't seek them. Their groupies often number one or two. You will probably never see them lounging by the pool on *Lifestyles of the Rich and Famous*. And, their marital woes will never make the front page of the *National Enquirer.*

But I don't care, I follow their careers on television and read about them in the newspapers. And, if I can meet them in person, then I've achieved the ultimate high. Recently, I reached that ultimate high.

I had just finished eating my Friday night dinner when my former professor Mike D'Innocenzo called.

"Saul, I've got an extra ticket to the Lyndon Johnson Banquet at Hofstra University tonight. If you can get here by 8 p.m. you'll be admitted."

I looked at the clock: 7:05. "I'll be there," I yelled into the phone, and by 7:50 – I was.

The Lyndon Johnson Banquet! This dinner was one of the highlights of Hofstra's three-day conference examining the Presidency of Lyndon Johnson. Over 150 dignitaries were involved, and since I was a social studies teacher and politics buff, this was for me.

I took the elevator to the tenth floor of Hofstra's library to meet Mike. The door opened and the 1960's came to life. Over in the corner was James Farmer. Talking to a tall woman was Nicholas Katzenbach. Who was that fellow talking to Robert Weaver? Why, it was Wilbur Cohen. I strode around the room as if I were a regular at these affairs. I nodded at Floyd McKissock and acknowledged Henry Fowler. But it was tough keeping up this act. I mean, here were the men and women who were the movers and shakers of my youth.

I came down to Earth when I spotted Mike. He greeted me warmly and we chatted a bit before heading for the elevator that would take me down to the dining hall.

I stepped into the elevator and noticed the short fellow to my left. It was Harold Wilson. Harold Wilson – the former Prime Minister of England! He was here in *my* elevator. We rode down to the lobby in silence. The door opened and there stood Lynda Bird Johnson Robb and her husband, Charles Robb, the former governor of Virginia, and perhaps future Presidential candidate. I briefly fantasized that Lynda Bird might break out and cry, "Saul, baby, is that really you?" but she did no such thing. She merely said, "Hello," and I returned her greeting.

Shortly, we were in the dining hall. Mike D'Innocenzo, a 1984 congressional candidate, seemed to know everyone and he introduced me around. "Ralph," he said to Ralph Caso, the former Nassau County Executive, "this is Saul Schachter." We shook hands.

Mike introduced me to others who in turn introduced me to their friends. "Sargent Shriver, this is Saul Schachter." "William Bundy, this is Saul Schachter." I was ecstatic. But, after a while, my name began to take on new forms. "Barbara Jordan, this is

Sol Sheckler." "Harry McPherson, this is Sol Sockler." "Ramsey Clark, say hello to Paul Shacker."

"Nice to meet you, Paul," said Ramsey.

"It's a pleasure," I responded.

After twenty minutes, I was introduced to Ralph Caso again. I had come full circle.

When this ritual was completed, I joined the various dignitaries at table #28. I sat between a Hofstra dean and a Hofstra trustee. Across from me was Adam Yarmolinsky, a prominent Johnson Administration official. Conversation flowed smoothly, waitresses poured wine, toasts were offered, and I began my second dinner of the evening.

Hofstra officials welcomed the guests and Governor Robb spoke briefly. Hofstra President James Shuart, noting that it was not practical to introduce the 150 dignitaries present, advised us, "Just turn to your left and your right and recognize them." We did.

At one point during a break, I noticed that no one was talking to Harold Wilson. I couldn't believe it. Here was a man who know Churchill, DeGaulle, Brezhnev, and Adenauer, and no one had a thing to say to him! He reminded me of high school prom queens who are so gorgeous, they intimidate all the fellows who might want to ask them out. But, on this evening, Mr. Wilson didn't look too gorgeous. Actually, he seemed a bit forlorn. I figured that he's probably been to a thousand of these affairs and probably had no idea where he was. I excused myself from my table and approached him.

"Mr. Prime Minister," I said, extending my hand. "It's an honor to meet you, sir."

His eyes twinkled and he bowed his head slightly. "Thank you," he said, shaking my hand.

And that was it. Not one of the world's more scintillating conversations, but I couldn't pull up a chair and ask him what he'd been doing the past twenty years. He seemed to be a nice man and I felt better for having gone over and for saying hello. I returned to my seat.

I joined in the conversation, but at the same time I was mesmerized by the scene around me: foreign ministers from France, India, Belgium and the Netherlands; New Dealers from the Roosevelt era. At the next table, two men were discussing something in French. I was like a little boy in the candy store while these men and women were enjoying their class reunion.

At one point, I spotted Alexis Vogt's father, Robert, a dean at Hofstra and one of the organizers of the Conference. Alexis was one of my favorite students. I had her the year before when she was a quiet and shy student. Now, I watched her in a long dress, mingling easily with the people who helped shape our world before she was born. I beamed with pride as I realized how much she had matured, with only her braces and occasional giggles belying her age. I caught her eye and smiled, and she smiled back.

Later in the evening (who knew what time it was? I certainly never looked at my watch), CBS commentator Bill Moyers, the former Johnson Press Secretary, delivered an eloquent, moving speech about Lyndon Johnson. For over an hour, he regaled his listeners with stories of his late boss. When he finished, the crowd roared to its feet, giving him a standing ovation.

It was now after 11 (I finally did look at my watch), and although dessert had not yet been served, some people began filing out. For many of them, the day had been a very long one. I, however, was not about to go anywhere. I spoke to some people I had met 500 introductions ago, and we chatted over ice cream and pudding. Finally, when there was only a handful of people left, I headed for the exits with Alexis Vogt, her mother and grandmother.

As we walked out the door, I couldn't help but think about the future Richard Nixon Conference. I'd like to shoot the breeze with Dick and Pat and see what Spiro's been up to. And, who knows, maybe Harold Wilson will be there. I'd introduce him around, and if no one wanted to talk to him, well, he could sit at my table.

It's the least I can do for an old friend.

34

Living In The Community
In Which You Teach

Educational Oasis, September/October, 1990

Sometimes I see my students at the most unusual times....

I remember a cold November evening, after 11, when I heard a knock at the back door. Groggy from having been awakened from a deep sleep, I opened the door and there was Noah Schwartz, age 12. He was concentrating on the paper before him. "Mr. Schachter," he said, without looking up. "I don't get question number 6. Was it Ferdinand Magellan or Ponce de Leon?"

Now, I don't usually get midnight callers, especially my students, but it was nice to know that Noah felt comfortable enough to seek my help. Many of my colleagues, however, wouldn't dream of living near school. "Are you kidding?" said one teacher. "What about my privacy? Can you imagine what my house would look like the morning after Halloween? I'd have to get an unlisted number." She paused. "And in the summertime I really don't want them to see me in my bathing suit. No thanks, I'll live elsewhere."

Not me. I'd rather live here.

I guess having grown up in this community and having gone through the schools where I presently teach might make my decision to stay a little easier to understand. But I enjoy my students. Oh, there are days when 3 o'clock arrives and I wish the school buses would take them to another planet, but that's a rare occurrence. And, yes, taking in a movie and discovering what appears to be your entire homeroom giggling and whispering about you in the back can dampen what started out as a promising evening, but that's O.K. The positives outweigh the negatives.

For one thing, it's nice to bicycle to school. It's only twelve minutes away. Pedaling past my students in their pigtails and Mohawks on a bright brisk morning makes me feel like a modern-day Mr. Chips.

But, more importantly, by living in the community I can see my students excel in areas outside the classroom. Over the years I've attended dozens of their piano recitals, softball games, and local theater productions. Seeing them perform outside school helps me reach them inside school.

Some of my students are stunned to learn I have a life beyond North Shore. During my first year, I taught third and fourth grade. One afternoon the doorbell rang, and when I opened the door, two of my students, selling Girl Scout cookies, looked at me aghast. "You live in a house?" whispered the smaller one. I was tempted to reply "Well, I was getting tired of living in the classroom, surrounded by blackboards, chalk, and tiny tables, so I traded it in for this pad." But I didn't.

Over the years I've enjoyed watching former students grow up and take on responsibilities. Pick a store or shop in the community and you'll find a former student. There's Alie in the bake shop, Scott at the drugstore, Robert at the ice-cream parlor. And the ironies are delightful: The girl who couldn't add numbers is now working at the checkout counter at the supermarket. (So that's why my 14 items cost me only 36 cents.) The kid who was always in trouble is studying to be a cop. And now the students that I used to whirl past on my bicycle drive past me.

And then there's my life at Waldbaum's…

In some communities, the big meeting place is the town hall or the library. But in my town, it's the local supermarket. As the years roll by, I wonder why we schedule so many parent conferences when I seem to get more covered at Waldbaum's.

I was squeezing tomatoes recently in the produce section when I heard a woman's voice. "Jeremy failed the social studies test, didn't he?" I looked up and met the mournful face of Mrs. Rabinowitz. "Yes, he did," I said soberly.

As I made my way over to the zucchini, I gave progress reports to Mrs. Whitaker, Mrs. Dugan and Mrs. Cocchilado.

Most of the parents I encounter abide by the unwritten rule of not discussing their child's grades while I'm food shopping. For others, the temptation is too great. They begin with, "I hate to bother you…" But I don't mind. I've learned to give succinct responses. And if they catch me on the deli line or at the checkout counter, it's O.K. I'll give more detailed responses because I'm not going anywhere. Occasionally, I can work out a tradeoff. In the past month I've given Mrs. Dubinski, Mrs. Schroeder, and Mrs. Alexander an update on their children and they've helped me determine how to tell when a cantaloupe is ripe and the proper way to cook veal cutlets. We both emerge happy.

And in June I get sneak previews of what lies ahead. Near the frozen foods, a mother will approach me with her arm around a young child. "Mr. Schachter," she will say proudly, "this is Corina. You'll probably get her next year."

I look at the child and smile warmly. "I hope so," I say, "It'll be fun," – just as long as she doesn't appear at my door at midnight!

35

Feeling At Home
In The Soviet Union

Newsday, October 28, 1990

The first few days of my vacation, I ran the Moscow Marathon, drank tea with Nikita Khrushchev's daughter and mastered the Moscow Metro system. Each night I went home to my family. But, it wasn't my wife and kids who waited with dinner (I'm single). It was, rather, a Soviet family who practically adopted me during my visit last summer under the auspices of *American-Soviet Homestays Inc.*, an Iowa-based tour company.

Not knowing what to expect, I had brought three books to read during my visit to families in two cities. But there really wasn't time to get beyond the introductions. I was too busy attending weddings, giving dancing lessons and being interviewed on the radio. Or you could catch me squeezing tomatoes with the locals at the open markets, hopping on and off local buses and giving directions to confused tourists.

And, just when I was developing an affinity for sitting around with my extended families slurping borscht, it was time to leave for home.

For 16 days in August, I was part of a group of Americans who were placed with families in Moscow and in Frunze, a city in the south central part of the Soviet Union, a couple of hundred miles from Mongolia in the republic of Kiergizi.

The families we stayed with were on holiday during our

visit and served as our tour guides. In Moscow, I lived with Valentina Svoren, a 51-year old divorced science writer and her about-to-be-divorced daughter, Natasha, 23, a biologist (After meeting dozens of their friends and relatives, I had a feeling I was the only person in the Soviet Union who wasn't divorced. Two or three generations living under one roof, it seems, strained marital relationships).

Natasha's English was good, and Valentina, who had only studied for four months, wasn't bad. Their flat was larger than I had expected, and I had my own room. Though their lives were not easy, Valentina and Natasha worked tirelessly to make me feel comfortable. Every morning Valentina made me porridge and raisins with a Cuban orange on the side. I'd wash it down with Bulgarian tomato juice. The other meals were plentiful and hearty.

One night I raved about Valentina's apple cake; it appeared two more times before the week was up.

Valentina helped me get into the Moscow Marathon when I thought I wouldn't be admitted, and Natasha stayed with me at the starting gate until the race began. She had an appointment and had to leave, but a few miles into the race, there she was on the side, cheering me on.

In the evenings, it was off to visit Uncle Sergei and Aunt Tania or cousin Mikhail or Tolya or Ilya or Jana. Relatives, friends, friends of friends — I met them all. And there was always food emerging from the kitchen: cabbage soup, crepes, tomatoes, chicken, fish, watermelon, stuffed peppers, cutlets, plums, apples, and sweets. Their generosity was limitless. One night, the flashbulb on my camera failed to work. A cousin handed me his flash, and when I wanted to return it, he waved his hand at me. "No," he said. "It's yours. A gift from me." Another relative offered me his watch. I think if I had looked longingly at the color television set, I could have come home with that, too.

I was also able to get out on my own. I walked all over Moscow, checking out record shops, bookstores, listening to sidewalk poetry readings, hearing pro-Gorbachev speakers, hearing anti-Gorbachev speakers, marveling at the Hare Krishnas dancing in the streets.

I had been in the Soviet Union in 1978 and, at that time, couldn't find anyone who was willing to speak to me. Now, 12 years later, I couldn't find anyone wouldn't speak to me. Many of the conversations were very sad: Soviet Jews, suffering great persecution, being forced to flee to Israel. Others who never had any intention of leaving were now emigrating because all their friends had left.

The younger Moscovites wanted to practice their English with me and asked me questions about Michael Jackson and Sylvester Stallone. Middle-aged women wanted to know about Phil Donahue. Phil Donahue? At first I couldn't figure that out. Then I remembered. Donahue had done a series of shows in the Soviet Union and they were televised in Moscow.

Every other day I checked the lines at McDonald's in Pushkin Square---they went on and on. The wait for a quarter-pounder was at least three hours. I also learned that most of the people on line were Russian tourists from outside Moscow who wanted, literally, a taste of Americana. Every day I took pictures of the lines from a different angle---but I never had a lens wide enough to capture the magnitude of the crowd. Occasionally, I'd wander over to the Arbat---the artists' pedestrian walkway—to see the line at Baskin-Robbins (Usual wait: 45 minutes). There were, of course, the lines for bread and other necessities, but there were also very long lines for shops that sold only cigarettes---some of which never opened at all.

After line-watching, I'd head over to relax in a small park. One day I met a 16-year old girl who chewed gum, found school boring, her parents boring and most of her classmates boring, but who liked boys and American movies and music.

"Who's your favorite singer?" I asked.

"Ella Fitzgerald," she replied.

We talked for a while more, and when we parted she smiled and called after me, "Wasn't I entertaining?"

One day, an uncle of my host family, an editor at a science magazine, invited me to tea with his colleague, the daughter of Nikita Khrushchev, a charming woman in her 50's who led an independent life traveling the world. I was warned not to discuss her father or pose for a picture with her, but we did get to discuss current events, although on a somewhat superficial level.

At the end of each day, I'd take the Metro or the bus back to my family's flat. In the late evenings, exhausted from all the activities, I'd retire to my room. I could hear Valentina next door, listening to tapes and practicing her English.

It was a sad day when we parted.

From Moscow, it was on to Frunze, a four-hour flight. When we landed, our hosts were waiting for us. We felt like children up for adoption. "Are you my mother?" an elderly American called out playfully to a woman in her mid-20s. Another member of our group scanned the awaiting patrons, wondering aloud, "Hmmm… Whom would I like to go home with?"

Three-fourths of my new family had turned out to greet me: Alexander, a reporter for Tass; daughter Maya, 21, a theater critic and aspiring actress (she played Cinderella at age 6), and son Vladimir, 20, her stamp-collecting brother. Marina, the mother, was home.

Only Maya spoke English well.

Flat #2 was larger than the Moscow one; the hospitality and food were on par. Marina's pierogis rivaled Valentina's apple cake.

Alexander, Vladimir and I swam at the local sports club. Maya and I spent an afternoon at the local town hall attending weddings (Five days a week, weddings are held there; Saturdays are the big days with 60 couples taking their vows. It cost $2.75 to register and about $9 for the service, the music, and the photographs. The brides all wear white gowns, the groom and best man suits, but the parents and the other guests dress casually. "It's too hot for the others to get dressed up," Maya explained. After 10 minutes, the service is over and the next couple marches through.)

Later, Maya and I visited her favorite theater, where actors and their wives (usually other actresses) work and live. Their salaries of 100 rubles a month ($16, a third of the average salary) are so paltry that couples and their children often sleep in their dressing rooms. Most of these marriages, Maya told me, will end in divorce. "Their careers often come first," she said.

The next day I treated Maya and her friend, Marat, to a three-course meal. The tab came to $2.10. The conversation was more dear: We talked of politics and emigration and American unemployment. In the evening, it was back to the flat, where I was teaching Maya how to disco dance. The lessons must have went over well, because the next night her friend Marina appeared at the door, saying that she, too, would like to learn. Maya and I took to the floor every night in the family living room.

Occasionally, we watched Soviet television. I saw a professional-looking Soviet production of Sherlock Holmes, a film about old American musicals, the evening news (good coverage of the Iraqi invasion), and a "Tribute to John Lennon" concert somewhere in central USSR. It was amusing to hear Beatles songs with Russian accents.

On the last day, I passed up my swimming session to make my debut on Soviet radio. Vladimir, though his connections at Tass, had arranged for this interview, and I adroitly answered questions about my impressions of Frunze (friendly city), what I would tell my friends back home about Frunze (nice people) and whether I would return someday (I hoped to).

The last evening, we all went over to a friend of Alexander's for a party There was good food, dancing, and talk. One woman I met edited the personals column in the weekly Frunze paper. These ads cost 30 rubles ($6), a hefty sum for the average comrade who makes 300 rubles a month. She told me about the woman whose anonymous personal ad landed her a date with her ex-husband—and they both had a great time; about three women who married their correspondents in jail; and personals placed by a man in Canada and one from China. I couldn't let this opportunity pass. I, too, placed an ad. The woman promised to forward the responses.

As the evening wore on, the atmosphere grew melancholy. A couple, friends of my host family for more than 30 years, said their goodbyes. They were leaving for Israel the next week. Our host, 50ish, a Boris Yeltsin look-alike who had regaled us with bawdy stories and songs earlier in the evening, told me how sad his life was. His father, he said, was murdered by Stalin. He rarely sees his two children, who live with his ex-wife. And, if he ever married again, he said, the woman would probably leave him after a month.

After a week in Frunze, it was time to begin our trip to New York. We flew into Moscow and had to travel across the city to another airport for our flight to the States. From our bus window, we surveyed the city we had left only seven days before. It almost felt like being home again. Before reaching our destination, we were to make a quick stop at the hotel to drop off two colleagues from our group who were extending their stay. As we approached the hotel we could see a large crowd outside. What was going on? A revolution? Was Gorbachev overthrown? Pulling up to the curb, we could make out the faces. It was our Moscow hosts. Somehow, some way (they didn't know each other), they had found out we were coming in for a one-minute stop. I quickly scanned the crowd—and there was Natasha. I bolted out of the bus and we embraced. She talked fast, I talked fast, and we hardly heard what the other was saying. And, then, too soon, I was being ushered back onto the bus. As I said goodbye to Natasha, she pressed a package into my hand: It was Valentina's apple cake.

36

Marathon Man

Newsday, October 28, 1990

I was extremely excited when I arrived in the Soviet Union to run the Moscow Marathon until I discovered that nobody had ever heard of it.

It was a Friday night, and the marathon was scheduled for the next day. My "host mother" (I was staying with a Soviet family) didn't know what I was talking about. Neither did her 23-year old daughter. Phone calls to their friends and relativesl similar reactions: Marathon? What marathon?

"Call the police!" I shouted, sure that the information I had read in an American publication about the date of the race was accurate.

"It begins at 2:15 near Lenin Stadium," one police officer said. A small item in Pravda mentioned a marathon starting at 4 p.m. Three more phone calls confirmed that it was actually starting at 4:15 p.m.

But first I had to register. My host mother, Valentina, took me down to the fairgrounds the next morning at 11. The place was abuzz with excitement. Banners proclaiming the "Moscow International Peace Marathon" hung overhead. This was the first co-sponsored Soviet-American sporting event. Prize money of $25,000 would be awarded to the winner.

Valentina and I strode into one office, but disappointment set in when one sullen official said, "Sorry, it's too late to register." No, you should have come last night, said another. From booth to booth, we went. Heads shook disconsolately, hands waved us off. It didn't look good.

But, Valentina wouldn't take nyet for an answer.

We finally found someone willing to register me. It was 11:45. "You have until noon to sign up," the official told us. Then the official told us we would have to go to Gorky Park to pay the entrance fee of $45. There seemed no way I could make it by noon. "My friend here just flew in from New York (that was correct), he's a fellow scientist (well...not quite), and he's very tired from the trip (surprisingly, I felt wonderful)." She looked at her with hopeful, mournful eyes. "Well, all right," said the official, and she initialed the papers and handed me my number (476). I was in.

At just past 4, the runners started lining up. At 4:12—three minutes early—we were off. I soon found myself running with Ivan, from Latvia, who jogged carrying the Latvian flag. We ran along the Moscow River, passing Red Square, a housing district, a 250-year-old cathedral, and then the Kremlin with its beautiful gold spires.

The crowds along the route were enthusiastic. But, after a few miles, I was getting thirsty. A cluster of volunteers stood at the side of the road, dispensing something to the runners. I ran over into the crowd, hand outstretched, and received a wet sponge. Hmm. This was different. Up ahead, containers of cool water were being distributed.

At seven miles, we passed the British Embassy. Then it was over to the Exhibition Hall and Gallery and October Square. At nine miles, we ran began an ascent up a hill for 2 ½ miles. An official periodically called out our times, but since the announcements were made in Russian, I couldn't tell exactly how well I was doing.

At 11 miles, it was up Leninski Prospeckt (my host family lived there). Farther up the street we passed the home of Mikhail and Raisa Gorbachev.

I soon ran into Sharon Levy from Denver, Colo., one of the 200 Americans in the field of 10,000. Sharon was carrying a little camera, and we spent the next few miles taking pictures of each other, sometimes retracing our steps to get a better background shot.

At 17 miles, I was really fatigued. We ran through Gorky Park, where an opera singer was performing. The music was not particularly uplifting. I wondered if she knew the theme from "Rocky."

We then crossed the Krimsky Bridge, the Stone Bridge, and ran back past the British Embassy. We had run more than 21 miles. Less than two miles down the road was the Kremlin again. I was fading. All the people I'd run with were way ahead. My thighs began to ache. My legs felt heavy. The distances between water stops seemed to grow longer.

At the 22-mile mark, I committed the unpardonable sin— I walked. For about half a block. Walking, however, seemed to be as a difficult at this stage as running. I began to jog again. Under the Crimean Bridge, under a railroad bridge, and then I saw the final stop: Lenin Stadium. The path became narrower, the crowds lining the road became louder, and somehow I was gaining strength. I passed one runner, then two, then three. I passed Ivan the Latvian, still carrying his flag. I heard someone call out, "Go, Saul, go!" and turned to see Denver's Sharon Levy cheering me on. I entered the stadium, and the lights were on. I headed into the final lap. I looked into the middle of the field and there, oddly, was a Soviet baseball game in progress.

Up ahead, I saw the clock: "4:17.22." My previous best time was "4:15.01," set in Washington the year before. Boy, if I hadn't posed for many photographs I might have beaten that time. My head was dizzy by now. But somehow I was able to sprint across the line. I looked up at the clock: "4:17.56." I was handed a certificate, but I was distracted by tugs at my shirt and my shorts from some of the Soviet runners.

At first I couldn't figure out what they wanted. Then it hit me. They wanted my smelly shirt, my smelly shorts, and my smelly sneakers. I graciously declined.

37

A Dance Class For Singles Has An Added Twist

Atlanta Jewish Times, 1991

Eager to meet new women, I signed up for a "Dancing for Singles" adult education class at a nearby school.

I arrived so early the first night that the school wasn't open yet. The custodian let me in where I waited in the hot, stuffy gym. In a few minutes, Larry, an accountant, arrived. At 35, he was enthusiastic about the class and the opportunities it would afford to meet new women. Other men, all in their late 20s or early 30s, strolled in. We made small talk and stood near the door to await each participant.

The first woman to arrive was cheerful, confident-looking, and was about 65 years of age. The second one was pushing 70. Our faces dropped. The next woman was a few years later. It seemed each woman who arrived got progressively grayer and slower. Only one woman in the class was under 50.

At 6:30 p.m. our instructor, a Liberace look-a-like, arrived with phonograph in tow. "All right ladies and gentlemen," he announced, "let's line up opposite a partner." I turned around and faced Edna, a heavy-set woman with a sad, but hopeful face. Larry, the accountant, was paired with Helen, a little dynamo whose gray hair was tied up in a bun.

I looked up and down the line. It appeared all the men were dancing with their grandmothers.

I tried to make light of the situation. When we began doing

the waltz, I whispered to Larry, "Maybe we can double-date some-time." During the opening bars of the rumba, I cooed, "Edna told me I could pick her up at 7 at Federation Apartments."

Evidently, Larry was not amused by the situation for he failed to show up the second week. Larry was not alone. Five other men bowed out.

I returned and found the ratio of women to men was now at least 3 to 1. In fact, there were only Rico, Jan, Juan, Ernie, Bill and myself to dance with 18 elderly women. And Bill didn't want to be paired up. "I'll just watch," he said.

When the evening started, I danced with Edna. But with the women far outnumbering the men, I soon found myself in great demand.

After one song ended, I dashed over to Helen. Then I joined Jean, did the rumba over to Anna, and shimmied back to Edna. I felt like one of those rent-a-dates who has been to 28 proms.

While I felt proud to be doing my civic duty, I wasn't progressing very well with my dance steps. Each woman danced differently: heavy Edna was hard to budge, Jean wanted to lead and Anna, who was hard of hearing, was always a few steps behind.

Helen, however, was fairly graceful and a good sport to boot. I found myself dancing most of the time with Helen.

Conversations were awkward initially. I told each woman that I was a teacher, but they revealed little of themselves. Were they widowed? Did they have children? I found myself talking about meeting actress Helen Hayes, critiquing a Clark Gable movie and recalling famous people who died that month. At the rate I was going, I was surprised I didn't mention how life was much better during the Depression.

By the fifth week, some of the women had begun to drop out, but I hung in there. I was disappointed when class began and Helen failed to materialize. I was reunited with Edna, but minutes later, Helen – *my* Helen! – appeared, and we were back again, the Fred and Ginger of the adult education class.

By the end of the 10th and final week, I was getting pretty good at the rumba, the cha-cha, the waltz, and the Lindy Hop. Initially signing up for the course as a way to meet nice, young, single women didn't turn out exactly as I had planned. But it was fun. I might even return!

38

My Word Processor Collapses (And Do So I)

Computor Edge, January 24, 1992

For three years, my Amstrad PCW9512 word processor produced beautiful, neat, crisp manuscripts. Then I decided to paint my bedroom.

I unplugged my word processor, moved it to the living room, painted my gold bedroom white, and moved back my word processor.

I plugged in my word processor, slipped in a disk, and the menu flashed on the screen. I had started an article and there were a few corrections to make. I pressed the <E> key for "Edit," but a "W" came out. I pressed <Can> for "Cancel," but the spelling key came sliding down the screen. <Exit>, <Enter> and <Delete> all had similar creative effects, though not the ones I wanted. I sat back in my chair and cried. Why didn't I leave my bedroom gold? Gold is a nice color.

I turned off the machine. I turned on the machine. I tried the "Edit" key again. Out came the "W." I touched the "Edit" key lightly. Same effect. I stabbed the "Edit" key. Same effect. I tried the other keys, but none worked properly. In fact, my word processor was working as if it was leaning to the left: It was following commands one key over.

I pulled out the manual and found my problem on page 358: "Typing produces all the wrong characters." It suggested I unplug the monitor and plug it in again. That maneuver failed. Then it offered the following advice: Consult your dealer.

My dealer told me he doesn't sell Amstrads anymore, they're on the verge of bankruptcy, but thank you for calling.

Amstrad, a British company, has an office in Texas. I called the office, heard a recorded message urging me to stay on the line, and then I was disconnected. Three more calls resulted in the same response. I tracked down a computer company in Illinois. "We have a branch office in Hicksville (15 miles from my house)," a voice said. I called the Hicksville office, described my problem, and was relieved when a voice told me he could fix it. I bundled up my word processor as if it were a sick child, found the office 45 minutes later, and after another 30 minutes left the office with the repairman still scratching his head. "I can fix the newer models, but not this one," he said.

After returning home, I pulled out the yellow pages and was amazed and slightly overwhelmed by the 2,651 names of computer experts, computer consultants, and computer repairmen in Nassau County. I dialed a few numbers. No luck. Never heard of my model. Try so-and-so. So-and-so didn't know.

My cousin, Gail, who had paid a small fortune for her computer's repair, suggested a place in Port Washington. Friendly people, but they repair Zeniths, no Amstrads. I called a student's father – our local computer expert – but he couldn't help. My mother sent over the phone number of the guy who fixed her camera. "He sells computers now." I called him. She was right. He sells computers, but he doesn't fix them.

I hung up the phone. I couldn't believe this. Three years of my life were on four disks and I may never see them again. Letters to friends, articles for newspapers and magazines, lessons for my Social Studies classes, tax records. What did I do before my word processor? Boy, life was simpler back in the late '80s. I looked around the room and my eyes fell on my beloved VCR. Now, don't you go on the fritz, too, I pleaded.

I didn't sleep much that week. I lay awake at night thinking of what could be the matter. I was certain the problem lay in the keyboard. If I could only open the keyboard… maybe there's a wire loose. But the back was sealed shut. No screws, no clips.

On Day 7, I contacted the company in Illinois again. They could probably fix the machine. There's an initial fee of $40, said the woman on the other end. There's labor costs, there's costs for parts, there's shipping costs... I was writing all this down, but I was running out of paper. Also, my quick deductions indicated that the repairs would probably cost about half what I paid for the machine. Forget the repairs I said to myself. "How much would it cost for a new keyboard?"

"That would be $140, plus $6 shipping," she said.

Well, that was cheaper than what the overall costs would be. "I'll call you back in an hour," I promised.

I sat back in my chair and reflected on the situation. I really had no choice. I stared at the blank screen of my word processor. I jiggled a button, pushed a few keys, and was ready to call back the woman in Illinois when I flicked on my machine for one last, no doubt futile, try.

I slipped in the disk, the menu appeared on the screen, and I pushed the "Edit" button for an article I had been working on about Alaska. And, lo and behold, there it was! I pushed the "Delete" key and a word disappeared. I restored the word. I pressed <A> and the letter "A" appeared on the screen. My Amstrad was back! I gently turned off the machine, turned it back on, prayed quietly to the gods of the major religions, and opened my eyes. There was Alaska, ready to go!

I called Illinois, thanked them, but told them that I wouldn't be needing them. "I figured it out," I told them confidently. I called my mother, my student's father, and my cousin Gail who, with pride in her voice exclaimed, "I am so happy for you."

My thoughts turned toward the future: if I ever paint my room again, one thing's for certain: the Amstrad is not going anywhere.

I'll paint around it.

39

Why Do I Visit Synagogues Abroad When I Don't Go To Services At Home?

Inside, Spring 1992

Whenever I travel, I make it a point to visit the neighborhood synagogue. On my various journeys, I've attended services in Poland, Czechoslovakia and East Germany, to name but a few. And I've had a Passover seder in Mexico, celebrated a wedding in the Soviet Union and witnessed a bar mitzvah in Alaska.

All of which might not seem so strange, were it not for the fact that I never go to synagogue at home. I'm not exactly sure why. I consider myself a good Jew. But while I am certainly proud of my heritage, I have never been enamored of the services themselves. Still, because of my feeling for Israel, growing anti-Semitism around the world, and my own ethnic pride, I want to make sure that Jewish communities are not silenced and that they continue to flourish. Even in the United States, in towns where the number of Jews is miniscule, I seek out the local shul.

This past summer, I spent time in both Missoula, Montana, and Fairbanks, Alaska. In Missoula, I was reading the local newspaper one day when I noticed advertisements for various churches in town. But no synagogues were listed. Wondering if a Jewish population existed at all, I contacted the editor of the religion page who put me in touch with someone named Scott Greene. Was he a rabbi? A cantor?

Scott Greene turned out to be neither. He was a dentist. And not only was he head of the 40-family Jewish community in Missoula, he was also a native of Glen Cove, New York – only 10 blocks from my house in Sea Cliff.

There was no synagogue in Missoula, Greene told me. Instead, services and Hebrew school classes were held in the basement of a friend's house. Greene hoped to find a rabbi for the High Holy Days in the fall, but otherwise it was a "self-service" congregation. "We do it all," said Greene proudly.

Although there were no summer services in Missoula, Fairbanks offered weekly Friday night worship. Intrigued by an ad in their local paper for evening services followed by a potluck supper, I called the number listed. I explained to Joe Notkin, the synagogue's president, that I was from out of town and interested in visiting their congregation.

"This week will be a bit different," Joe said. "Instead of pot-luck dinner, there's going to be a double bar mitzvah – two brothers born 11 months apart."

That sounded good, but I had no ride. "Don't worry," Joe said. "Rachel will pick you up.

At 6:30 the next evening, a car pulled up. An Asian woman rolled down the window and asked, "Saul?"

"Rachel?" I answered, somewhat surprised.

"No, Rachel is sick. I'm Tan, Joe's wife. I'm taking you to the bar mitzvah."

I got into the car and sat back as Tan headed toward the chapel at the nearby Air Force base. On Friday night and Saturday morning, she explained, their chapel was transformed into a synagogue. After services on Saturday, however, the Stars of David came down, the crosses went up and the chapel became a church.

As we drove along, I also learned Tan's life story. She and Joe had met about 10 years before in Thailand. She was divorced with two children; he was teaching English. They fell in love, got married and moved to Chicago. An architect by trade, Joe was of-fered a job in Fairbanks at three times his old salary. Off they went.

Tan paused as we approached the base. After clearing se-curity, we pulled into the parking lot where I met Joe. A friendly guy, he instantly made me feel welcome and introduced me to the others. There were about 100 families in the congregation, more than half of whom were the result of intermarriage. Indeed, in Joe's family, Tan remained a Buddhist, but her children were being raised as Jews. Only two months earlier, their daughter had been bat mitzvahed.

We entered the chapel, and I sat down to enjoy the services. Leading the bar mitzvah was a young female rabbinical student from Philadelphia who was interning in Fairbanks for the sum-mer. She was ably assisted by her husband, who was born into an Italian-Catholic family but had converted to Judaism at the age of 18. The two bar mitzvah brothers were up on the makeshift bimah (stage) and read portions from the Torah as their father strummed a guitar in the background. At one point, the rabbinical student sang along with a group of youngsters, who must have represented about a dozen races. Definitely an interesting mix up there.

Following the celebration, Joe made the weekly announce-ments and alerted the congregation to the fact that a board meeting would be held in the basement of a nearby Wendy's restaurant. Afterwards, I congratulated the participants and thanked them for their hospitality. I was driven back to my hotel by David and Lil-lian Goldfarb, a couple in their 40s, originally from Chicago (half of Fairbanks seems to be made up of transplanted Chicagoans). On any given day, David works from 8 to 4, comes home for a brief nap, eats dinner and, during the summer months stays outdoors with his wife until midnight or 1 a.m. gardening, hiking or explor-ing. Thinking that his evenings were similar to my afternoons, I left Fairbanks feeling very close to its Jewish residents.

But my first experience in synagogue-hopping remains my most enduring memory. I was in Moscow in 1979, during the Brezhnev years. Tired of museums and art galleries, I sneaked away from my tour group and found a synagogue. Looking and feeling conspicuously out of place, I was approached by a few congregants who muttered, "Watch what you say, the KGB is around." I nodded and entered the synagogue, a once beautiful edifice now in obvious disrepair. The service was simple, yet I was quite thrilled to hear Hebrew chanted in the middle of a Communist country.

After the service, I was besieged by many older people, who stuffed addresses and phone numbers of their New York relatives into my hands, urging me to contact them when I returned home. I did so and also wrote back to the Moscovites. I never received a response.

But eventually, I did hear from Marina, a young woman I had met briefly on that trip. She and her Russian-speaking mother had somehow gotten out of the Soviet Union but were stuck in Vienna. Marina desperately wanted to come to the States, but the only way she could enter the country was if she had a relative here or a "romantic interest." Marina did have a relative in Brooklyn – who had never met her and didn't want to – so having known her less than an hour, I became her "romantic interest."

I contacted the Hebrew Immigration Assistance Society (HIAS) in New York, filled out several forms, put up a little money to help her when she arrived, and waited. In the meantime, Marina and I corresponded. We exchanged life histories and I did my best to keep her spirits up. "You give me hope," she wrote in one letter.

Six months later, Marina and her mother landed in New York. Wanting to make her first day in America special, I took her to Jones Beach, McDonald's and a disco. She seemed entirely blasé about it all. As it turned out, the evening at the disco was less than wonderful. Marina was denied entry to the club because the manager was checking identification and she had left her passport back in her room. Although she was 24, Marina looked about 17.

"Identification?" she screamed. "What is this, Russia?" And she stormed out.

Despite that mishap, Marina adapted well to her new country, and we have remained friends. HIAS found a place for her to live in the Russian section of Far Rockaway until she got a job at a bank and could afford her own apartment. She subsequently married a fellow Russian Jewish émigré and settled in New Jersey. We hope to see each other again soon.

In the meantime, I'm planning to continue my travels. Who knows what faraway synagogues I'll discover or what interesting people I'll meet? The experience is sure to be memorable.

40

South Africa As It Dismantles Apartheid

The Denver Post, August 23, 1992

When I announced to my friends that I would be taking an eight-day trip to South Africa, the reaction was less than enthusiastic.

"It's too violent there," a friend from New York City said. "Sixteen hours on a plane?" said a friend who commutes from Connecticut to work on Long Island.

"It's such a repressive country," said a friend who had traveled to China, the Soviet Union and Romania.

But, acknowledging the difficulties, I went ahead anyway. And, I'm glad I did.

I visited South Africa because I have been fortunate enough to have seen most of the world, but I had yet to visit this country. I like adventure. And, because now, with the dismantling of apartheid, it is an exciting—albeit uncertain—time to be there.

I stayed with families in suburban communities, took public transportation and talked and talked to people at bus and train stations, pubs, shops, bookstores, and beaches. All were willing— even eager—to talk about apartheid, and I came away from our discussions with sympathy for all sides in the dispute. Nearly all the whites to whom I spoke favored ending apartheid, but preferred slow, transitional approach.

"You can't give the vote to people who only have a first-grade education," was the common refrain. "And, they aren't ready yet to run a country."

"Give them education, teach them to contribute to society, and all of South Africa will prosper," said the whites—and blacks. And yet, despite the hopeful rhetoric, couldn't help but feel at times that I was back in 1940s America.

Whites often referred to "our blacks" as if they were chattel. Black maids—and most white families seem to have one—were frequently addressed in a condescending manner. Whites would speak disparagingly of the blacks crammed into vans that whizzed by each morning in search of work. One white secretary, a very nice person otherwise, was very upset that "some coloreds (people of mixed origin) make more money than I do," as if that were a crime.

Most whites complained that more than 40 percent of their salaries go to taxes, many to programs that are assisting blacks. And, "the blacks don't pay taxes," which might sound like a reasonable complaint were it not for the fact that for years the blacks have made a pittance for a salary and have been denied proper schooling and opportunities.

In an attempt to soften their rhetoric, the whites would point out that there are hard-working blacks, they sing beautiful songs and in their honor every year, the country holds a "Coon Competition," whose specifics made me squirm.

Yet, despite their carping, most whites, in my small informal polling, and judging from what I read in the newspapers, favor the reforms taking place. In a special referendum called while I was there, 70 percent of whites supported the reform policies of F.W de Klerk's administration.

Still, most whites are worried about the future and young families are moving abroad—many of them to Toronto. "There are many opportunities there," said one young doctor. And, those who are left behind and alarmed by the sharp surge in crime have barricaded themselves behind high walls and elaborate security systems.

Among the blacks—and I wish I could have met more of them—was a sweetness that was endearing and a little sad. I expected bitter and frustrated individuals, but met none.

Unemployed blacks would politely ask me on the street if I needed my house painted or if they could do odd jobs around my property. When I was lost in Johannesburg, one man who worked across the street at a bank (making a tenth of the salary of the white women beside him doing the same job) told me he insisted on personally escorting me the ten blocks to my destination.

Even during the highlight of my trip—a van tour of the desperate communities in Soweto, South Africa's largest black township—I was greeted warmly. I half-expected our van of comfortable whites to be pelted with rocks, but all I encountered were smiling, waving children and stoic adults.

Still, I was not blind to the fact that the crime rate among blacks has skyrocketed and that just before I arrived, a white teacher recently assigned to a previously all-black rural school had been murdered by an angry mob of local blacks.

So, what's South Africa like for the single traveler? Well, for one thing, it's difficult to get lonely. I met a woman on the flight over, and the next day she gave me a full-day tour of Cape Town. (We saw each other once more and spoke on the phone before I moved on to Johannesburg).

Terese, a Liverpool native, and I had drinks down at the Cape Town waterfront. Magid, the former mayor of Johannesburg (and one of my New York students' cousins), spent parts of two days with me, discussing politics, introducing me to important figures and taking me to out-of-the-way places. At one fish and chips place, I met Dena, a cashier—an American editor on leave for a year so she could work at odd jobs around Africa—and the next night we had dinner at a Mexican restaurant discussing life in South Africa.

And there was Blanche Rust, a woman I met while using her phone. She worked for a bank in a small office. We chatted a bit, and then I left to tour the Johannesburg Star newspaper office. While touring the Star's facilities, I said to myself, "I wonder if Blanche would have lunch with me?" I returned to her office, asked her to lunch, she said she'd love to, and 90 minutes of delightful conversation followed.

So, these were carefree days. The weather was beautiful. It was February, and the temperatures hovered around 80 degrees with little or no humidity. Cape Town's palm trees and beaches made me realize why it's considered one of the world's most beautiful cities.

There was no language barrier. Throughout South Africa, the people spoke English (along with Afrikaans), newspapers were interesting and informative, the top 40 tunes and patter on the radio were fun to listen to, and the prices were cheap (a bus ride cost 40 cents; a lunch I put together of two pieces of chicken from a take-out place, apple juice and a bananas set me back $1.30).

And, yet, I was always aware that I was still a distance from Paradise. The first glimpse of that came at the train stations. The reforms have officially ended segregation—but everyone still "knows his place." There are first-class and third-class trains (but no second class). In the days of apartheid, whites would travel in comfortable first-class cars and blacks would be confined to the less-expensive, overcrowded, hard seats of third class.

Now, officially, anyone can travel on any train. However, when I considered traveling third class, I was courteously but firmly directed by whites to first class. There were a few blacks in first class, but I never saw a white emerge from third class.
When Terese, the Liverpool lass, and I sipped drinks and listened to music down at the waterfront there was nary a black in the place, except for the waiters.

"Blacks are free to come," one white man assured me, but his companion whispered, "But, they know they're not welcomed here."

On my last day, I was due to depart Johannesburg on the 9 p.m. flight. Having seen all I had wanted to see, and curious about Pretoria, the capital—a mere 58 miles away—I took a bus to the airport in the morning, checked my bag in a 25-cent locker, and took another bus to Pretoria, a 45-minute ride (there's no direct bus route from Johannesburg to Pretoria). There, I spent the day walking around the city, an easy place to traverse.

At 5 p.m. I boarded the bus to take me to the airport. It

started to rain—only the second time I encountered rain, and both times, when I had finished my sightseeing and was settled comfortably and safely aboard a bus. I thought about the places I had seen: Cape Town, Johannesburg (a pretty city, despite its critics who say people live there only because of job opportunities), Pretoria and Soweto.

In Cape Town, I took a cable car up Table Mountain, whizzed by a nudist camp, and happened upon a Malay wedding in the park (one of 74 being celebrated there that day). I went down to the Cape of Good Hope and saw where the Atlantic Ocean converged with the Indian Ocean. Nearly, I followed in the footsteps of explorer Bartholomeu Dias and Vasco da Gama. Sadly, I never saw the acclaimed Kruger National Park on the east coast, nor took the Garden Route from Cape Town to the city of Durban. I never saw a museum.

But, I'll be back. I would love to see Kruger and Durban. I would love to get together again with Edy, Terese, Blanche, and all the other nice people I met. And I would love to return to a South Africa that has successfully ended apartheid and where all groups could live together peacefully.

Soweto Accessible On Tours From Johannesburg

The township outside Johannesburg, so often in the world's headlines, is not just a newsmaker. It's home---to 2 million black South Africans.

Violent and tragic, Soweto crystallizes the plight and hopes of South Africa's black population.

It's possible for travelers to visit this huge cluster of black communities on tours available out of Johannesburg. The best are run by Soweto Tours, organized by the Soweto Town Council. I joined such a group of foreigners, including three other Americans, three Germans and an Australian.

Our guide, a black Sowetan, told us about life in a calm, matter-of-fact way:

●Nine languages are spoken among the residents.
●Unemployment is around 50 percent.

•Many people still have to use outhouses.

•Until 1976, the residents could not legally purchase alcoholic beverages.

• There have been improvements (a new university is being built nearby), but most people still live in abject poverty.

We passed Winnie Mandela's former home (painted in black, green, and gold—the colors of the African National Congress), and I even had a chance to knock on the gate of ANC leader Nelson Mandela's fine new house (he wasn't home).

It's possible to take a local bus from Johannesburg to Soweto, but locals—both black and white—said it would be dangerous to do so.

Visitors who arrive in Soweto by van with a local guide are perceived as Sowetans' contacts with the outside world. Those who come by bus have no such cachet.

41

My Slipping Popularity

Newsday, November 2, 1992

I think my popularity is slipping. I don't know why but the evidence seems overwhelming — just check out my birthday cards. When I was growing up, my neighbors' annual wishes written at the foot of their Hallmarks would conclude with "Love, Bill and Mary" or "Love, Betty and Joe." That was nice. They cared about me. I cared about them. But, in recent years, their enthusiasm seems to be waning. I now receive cards signed "Fondly, Bill and Mary," or "Fondly, Betty and Joe." What's with this "Fondly?"

My former classmates seem to feel the same way. For over 15 years, old school chum Diane Bedeer and I have been exchanging birthday greetings, concluding our wishes with "Love, Saul," and "Love, Diane." But, two years ago, I received her missive with the following closer scrolled on the bottom: "Sincerely, Diane."

"Sincerely?" What about all those times I helped her with her Latin homework? And, who was it who taught her to ice skate? Who encouraged her to run for class vice president? (Granted, she lost by over 140 votes, but that surely wasn't my fault.) Well, maybe Diane's closer was an aberration. But, no. The next March 28, a Garfield birthday card arrived and there at the bottom of the greeting was the start, "Sincerely, Diane."

I immediately contacted the police. Was I on their 10-most-wanted list? Have I racked up too many parking tickets? Have complaints come in from my neighbors when I've mowed the lawn too early in the morning? No, no they assured me, my record was clean.

Hmmm… it's a mystery. I pulled out my old high school yearbook to see if I had overrated my popularity. On page 96: "All my everlasting love, Harriet." Sweet girl. But I couldn't help but wonder: Who the heck is Harriet? And, Harriet, honey, your love may be everlasting but I surely haven't seen any of it. Here's another one: "Love ya oodles, Guess Who." I'm still trying to guess.

Now, I know we sometimes go overboard with our demonstrations of affection. We kiss and hug people we can hardly tolerate. We praise a child's excruciating piano recital, we awake from a deep slumber just before the lights come on to rave about someone's vacation slides. But, if our loved ones haven't changed, if they are still as wonderful as they've always been, well, I say, we should show it!

Without fail, to my closest and dearest friends and relatives, I still sign "Love, Saul." My parents, those old reliables, have always come through: "Much love, Mom and Dad." Now, *that's* better!

But, what's going to happen when this anti-love epidemic hits them? Will they too, succumb to "Fondly, Mom and Dad" or "Sincerely, Mom and Dad"? I have this recurring nightmare, that on my next birthday, I'll open my parents' card and there it will be: "Your friends, Mom and Dad."

I shudder at the thought.

42

The Siberian Communication Gap

The Washington Post, November 22, 1992

My troubles with Alex began with the laundry.

I had just arrived in Siberia on the final leg of a 16-day homestay trip to Russia. I filled a big bag with dirty laundry, leaving a change of clothes on a chair in my room.

Sauntering into the kitchen of Alex's flat, I held up a container of detergent and said I would do my laundry later that evening.

Alex nodded. "Yes," he said.

I set out to see something of Irkutsk, and when I returned I saw laundry hanging on the line outside the third-floor balcony. My laundry. My clean laundry. I raced up the steps and into the flat. There, next to my bed where I had left it, was the bag of dirty laundry. Outside on the line, my last set of clean clothes was dripping.

Bag in hand, I returned to the kitchen where Alex and his wife, Valentina, were sipping tea. I calmly related what had happened, and Alex started shouting. In Russian. Was he yelling at me? Was he yelling at Valentina? I never got a translation. Alex swiped the bag from my hand, and a few minutes later, Valentina, rubber-gloved was on her knees in the bathroom washing my clothes.

I spent much of the first night in the bathroom with an upset stomach. And I was still weak when I sat down for a late breakfast the next day.

"Just some tea and bread, please," I said to Valentina, who didn't speak English but seemed to understand.

Alex announced that he was going to visit his mother at his summer home. Would I care to join him? "Well," I began, "I'm not feeling very well.."

Alex waved off my protestations. "It's just a little walk across the way," he said, reassuringly. I agreed to go.

For the first 15 minutes, we walked along a pretty path in the woods. Then the path disappeared and suddenly we were traipsing through swamps and bogs, trying to balance ourselves on rocks across streams. An hour had passed, it was warm and humid, and I was getting thirsty. "We're almost there," Alex called back to me.

The hike itself wasn't so bad, but the mosquitoes were unrelenting. (Alex, who had stripped his shirt off minutes into the hike, didn't seem to notice). Onward, and not quite upward, we went. By the time we arrived at the summer house after 2 ½ hours of hiking, I was spent. I slumped in a small chair drinking hot water for an hour while Alex climbed the side of the house to check on his birds.

When we returned, by bus, to the flat, I showered and felt much better. I told Alex I'd be going out that evening, but there was a problem. I'd be out late and didn't want to disturb him when I returned. Could I have a key?

"It's ok, I will be awake."

"I might be back after 1 a.m.," I said.

"No problem, I understand."

At 1:15 a.m., I stood outside the apartment building. The front door was locked, which meant I couldn't reach Alex's third-floor apartment, which was also locked. The apartment building, six stories high, was completely dark.

In the still of the evening I finally realized that every time Alex said "yes" or "I understand," I was in trouble.

I circled the apartment building. No sign of life. I considered the options, of which there were not many. I couldn't sleep outside. I could, perhaps wake up Alex's neighbors so they could contact him.

What could an angry mob do to me? Send me to Siberia?

I began by throwing pebbles at the first-floor window. A light went on, a couple of heads appeared in the window, and the lights went out. I knew someone was watching me, so I started jumping up and down frantically, yelling, "Americanski! Americanski!" (That's about the extent of my Russian.) Finally the window opened reluctantly. A middle-aged woman and two kids peered out. "Alex," I said, motioning upward. "Alex."

The elderly woman, looking – not surprisingly – a bit suspicious, asked me "Family name?"

I couldn't think of it. Fortunately, I had written down Alex's phone number. I gently approached the window with it. The old woman backed off slightly, but I smiled reassuringly. "Alex," I said, as I pointed to the number. The woman disappeared.

A few minutes later, Alex was at the front door. Wordlessly, he led me up to the flat, shaking his head. I apologized, but it seemed to do no good. I figured I would be grounded for a week.

The next day was uneventful, until Alex mentioned that he wanted to take me on a 12-hour hike the following day. Three others from our tour group had agreed to go. I thanked him profusely, but mentioned that I still wasn't feeling well enough to go hiking.

"I understand," Alex said.

That evening I was out until 2 a.m. and returned without a hitch (Alex had given me a key).

At 7 a.m., there was a knock at the door. It was Alex. Beside him were two backpacks loaded with food and equipment. "Let's go!" he said, looking a little like Theodore Roosevelt before attacking San Juan Hill. I smiled wanly, thanked him, and told him I was still too weak to hike. When it dawned on him that I intended to roll over and go back to sleep, he stormed out in a huff.

I tried to spend the day sightseeing, but I never did find downtown Irkutsk.

On my last day, I had a few hours to kill before our tour

group's picnic was scheduled. I was determined to find downtown.

I calmly, clearly and slowly explained to Alex my intentions. "What tram do I take?" I asked.

He thought for a moment and responded, "No. 1." Good.

"And what time do I have to return so we can catch the boat to the island?"

"12:30 p.m."

Very nice.

Camera in tow, I set out, walked to the main road, waited a few minutes and caught the No. 1 tram. I paid two cents for my ticket and sat down. About seven blocks later, the tram stopped to pick up more passengers, then turned around. I couldn't believe it! In a few stops, I'd be back at my original embarkation point. I jumped off the tram.

I never did find downtown, but wandered about for a few hours and returned to the apartment at 12:20 p.m.

When I opened the door, I saw Alex coming down the steps. "Where were you?" he demanded. I pointed out that I was returning 10 minutes early. He was furious. "I said to return at 11:30. Come on, we're late!"

We caught the boat, the picnic was a success and the next morning we Americans bid farewell to our Russian hosts. Alex shook my hand firmly and said, "Well, how did you like your visit with us?" Before I could respond, he said, "And, no jokes."

For the first time, I laughed. I apologized for the confusion, apologized for not knowing Russian, raved about Valentina's cooking, and thanked him for his hospitality.

He bowed his head and nodded. "Yes," he said. "I understand."

43

Reading Large-Print Books And Feeling Guilty About It

Newsday, November 15, 1993

Like millions of other Americans, I am reading — and enjoying — John Grisham's mystery, *"The Client."*

But I'm feeling a bit guilty about the whole thing. You see, I'm reading the large-print edition that I took out from my local library. I had been No. 12 on the waiting list for the normal-sized book and couldn't wait much longer when I spotted the large-print edition sitting on the shelf next to other large-print books. I quickly signed it out.

Reading a large-print edition is really quite an experience. For one thing, each edition appears to be at least 9,000 pages long. That could be a bit intimidating until one realized that there are only about 20 words on each page. Reading a book like this gives a person the opportunity to wallow in false bravado: "I've been reading, *'The Client,'*" I'll say to the stranger on the train next to me. "Just read 1,000 pages in two hours." If he looks unimpressed by that feat, or recognizes that the author is not the most challenging writer, I'll add, "but, of course that was a bit easier than the 800 pages of Tolstoy's 'War and Peace' I read during breakfast."

Still I feel uneasy. Why? Well, the print is so large that I feel like a kid who's been left back five times in the fourth grade. And I feel guilty. I keep thinking of those little old ladies and little old men, who can't enjoy this copy because I'm reading it (even though the librarian assured me there was no waiting list for the large-print edition). Even when I left the library, I wanted to cover the book in a brown-paper wrapper lest anyone sees me, a 37-year old fellow with 20/20 vision (with my glasses), absconding with a copy of a large-print book.

And, finally, I feel like I'm cheating. Everyone else in my neighborhood is waiting patiently for this book and I, in a sense, jumped to the head of the line by taking out the large-print edition. It reminds me of the time I attended the Dublin Horse Show. When the competition ended, there were thousands of people waiting for buses that could hold perhaps 40 people each. I was near the back of the queue and estimated that it would be a couple of hours before I could board a bus. I didn't want to wait. I couldn't wait. I'm from New York – The Impatience Capital of the World. So what did I do? I walked a few blocks behind and picked up the nearly empty bus before it arrived at the Dublin Horse Show stop.

What's in my future? Will I start to drive on the shoulder to avoid traffic jams? Will I order Hindu meals on airplanes so I'll get served first? I hope not. I don't handle guilt well.

44

That First Day Back
At School Is Truly Unique

Newsday, August 20, 1994

The new clothes are hanging by the door. The shoes are polished. The lunchbox is stuffed with peanut butter and jelly sandwiches.

It's my first day of school.

Actually it's my 33rd First Day of School (as a student and teacher). And, although I'm probably more nervous today than I was when I first entered Glen Head Elementary School back in 1961, I'm glad to be back. There is a great feeling of renewal, a fresh start. I like school. I look forward to meeting my new students, catching up with colleagues on their summer adventures, and, after a couple of days, I'm ready to start a new vacation.

That being impossible, I return to class to face my new seventh graders. Every year I have an advantage over the students. They are coming in from three elementary schools, they don't know two-thirds of their classmates, they don't know the rules or routine of the building, and I do. If I tell them to be on time for class, they are on time for class. If I tell them to take out a pen, they take out a pen. I have power and their unquestioning respect. All of which lasts for about two weeks.

But, oh, those two weeks are glorious. On opening day, I sit the students in alphabetical order and learn their names in four days (three days if they don't change their shirts).

Most of them won't admit it, but they're glad to be back, too. That first day they rarely speak. By day two, they're showing you pictures of their friends from camp, their baby brothers, and their gerbils. Your students from last year, the new eighth graders, most of whom have grown a foot since June, pop in to say "Hi," and you take pride in their newfound poise and confidence.

But, for some students, the first day of school provides a rude awakening. My friend, Betty, teaches kindergarten and she told me about the little boy who came to class the first time the kindergarten session was extended from a half-day to a full day. The little boy arrived at 9, enthusiastically completed his responsibilities, dutifully followed the rules, worked well with the other youngsters, and at 12 noon, thinking school was finished, put on his jacket, said goodbye to the teacher, and started out the door. When Betty stopped him and explained that kindergarten was now a full day, he put his hands on his hips and, clearly disgusted, said, "Who the hell signed me up for this?"

My students, too, had a problem with the schedule on the first day of school a few years ago. When the school bell rang at 2:50 p.m., ending the day, students gathered up their belongings and departed. I did some paperwork in the faculty room and then returned to my classroom around 3:30. There, in the first three rows were about a dozen of my new students. It seems in elementary school, they had to get the teacher's permission to leave at the end of the day. They didn't realize that in junior high, you can leave when the last class ends. I smiled and gave them permission. They returned the smile, sauntered out, thanking me for my kindness.

I sat back in my chair and thought to myself: There is nothing like the first day of school.

45

Airport Angst

The Washington Post, November 20, 1994

Crossing the jungles of Africa or the plains of Mongolia has always been easy for me. Eating exotic foods, making myself understood when I don't speak the language, negotiating my way through unfamiliar territory — all aspects of travel that are exhilarating. It's trying to get home from the airport that's tough.

Last year — over the objections of friends and relatives — I went to Cuba. "It's too dangerous," said one concerned friend. "What will you eat?" said another, familiar with the food shortages. But I went ahead, had a terrific time, flew back from Havana to Florida — and sat at Miami Airport. For 10 hours. There had been a snowstorm in New York and both Kennedy and LaGuardia airports were shut down. Finally, after midnight, we flew into LaGuardia, where I discovered — at 2:30am — that the buses had stopped running, limousines were grounded and cabs were spotted as frequently as J.D. Salinger. But finally I corralled one, headed out at a snail's pace, reached my Long Island home by 4 a.m., showered, slept two hours and at 7:15 a.m. staggered off to my job.

Leaving for trips, I used to let my family drive me to the airport. But there was always a big scene: Mom hugging me tight, Dad surreptitiously stuffing a few extra bills into my pocket, my sisters fighting back tears.

Now, things are easier. I take the Long Island Railroad to Jamaica, where I catch a bus to the airport. Returning home, I reverse the order. Very simple, inexpensive, no big deal — usually...

This year I went to Vietnam. Again, some of my friends and family didn't think it was a good idea. "You'll get malaria," said one. "What happens if you get into trouble?" Indeed, Vietnam was a country new to the world of tourism — no one knew what to expect. But I went ahead and had a terrific time.

On a Monday morning, I flew from Bangkok to Taipei, to San Francisco to New York — a trip taking nearly 27 hours. After arriving in San Francisco, I noticed a United Airlines flight leaving an hour earlier than the one I was scheduled on. I switched flights and got home early.

I walked into my house at 8:30 p.m. and called my parents. No answer. That's nice, I thought. They're out for the evening. Then it hit me: *Where* are they out for the evening?

I called their neighbor, and sure enough, they had gone to the airport. Oh, great. My parents haven't picked me up at the airport since the Carter administration. I'm thinking: The plane will come in, there will be no Saul, and Mom will be upset. So, here I am at home, sitting by the phone, worrying about my parents — after traveling nearly 30,000 miles, avoiding malaria and hepatitis and taking 27 hours to get home. Finally, they called.

Traveling would be so nice if I could just avoid airports.

46

I Have A Crush On The U.S. Postal Service

Newsday, December 5, 1994

Shhh… don't tell anybody but I love the U.S. Postal Service.

I'm also a big fan of the telephone company and multiplex movie theatres.

And, I'm not afraid – well, not too afraid – to defend these much maligned institutions.

I'm amazed at the overall success of the Postal Service. As someone who regularly misplaces his keys, his wallet — and still can't locate his winter jacket — I'm astonished that my letters, mere dozens among the 550 million that the service handles a year — always reach their destination. (And, I'm delighted when the mail — especially like the one from a 6-year old former neighbor addressed to "Saul, Sea Cliff" — reaches me.)

I send a lot of letters overseas and for a mere 50 cents (or 45 if I use an aerogramme), I can reach a friend in Europe or Asia in a couple of weeks. For 29 cents, I can send news to friends and relatives as far away as Hawaii. In more ways than one, the Postal Service delivers.

Which reminds me of the telephone company. I recently called a friend in Alaska. It was just after 11pm , we spoke for three minutes and the bill came to just 39 cents. A similar three-minute call to a friend in Peru came to $2.51. Not bad.

And American operators are the best in the world. I remember trying unsuccessfully to get the local operator when I was traveling in Ireland. A friend informed me that sometimes Irish operators don't come on the line. "It depends on their mood," he said. That's not the case with American telephone operators. They are nice and have patience. I've considered dating a few, and I will… if I ever get to Seattle. Or Helena. Or Boise.

Movie sophisticates lament the arrival of multiplex theatres, but not me. When I was growing up, towns had one movie theatre showing one film (if the town had a movie theatre at all). If there was a film I wanted to see, I often had to travel 10 or 15 miles to see it. Today, my area has a multiplex theatre that shows six films, and sometimes seven. And, I'm delighted. I can walk to see my favorite flick. Critics complain that some of these new theatres contain only 10 or 12 rows. Well, how many rows does a person need? As long as there's room for me, I'm content.

So, there you have it. During this year, let's resolve to be a little nicer to the Postal Service, the phone company and multiplex theatres. And, while I've got your attention, how about a few kind words for disco? The greatest music to dance to. It'll come back, you'll see.

Shhh … just don't tell anyone I told you so.

47

Becoming Friendly
With A Chinese Woman

Sawasdee Inflight Magazine (Thai Airways), March 1995

I met Cathy Zhong in 1981 when I spent the summer studying Chinese in Shanghai. I was 25, she was 18. There were 200
foreign students, mostly from the United States, West Germany,
and Canada. There were almost as many Chinese students on campus, who because they were denied summer jobs (Chinese students
were not permitted to work), spent the days studying, studying and
studying. They were urged to talk to us so they could practice their
English, but not to get too friendly. The foreign students liked the
contact — we wanted to practice our Chinese — but it got mo-
notonous when we found ourselves discussing the same mundane
subjects over and over again. That is, until I met Cathy.

Cathy (she prefers her Anglicized name to her given name
of Mingyi) was nearly 5' 10" tall, slim, and one of the most beautiful girls I'd ever seen. If there was ever a beauty contest in China, I was convinced she'd be the first "Miss People's Republic
of China." We hit it off from the start. Cathy loved to talk about
everything. We went to the zoo, saw a Charlie Chaplin Film Festival (where we sat in the best seats in the house for 40 cents), and
Cathy entertained me in her crowded (eight in a room) dormitory.
This last act shocked her friends. From the horror on their faces, I
thought Cathy was on the verge of being executed, with me next
on the guillotine.

Anyway, I was gone by the summer's end, but Cathy and I wrote to each other over the next four years. In 1985, I returned to teach English in the northern part of China and saw Cathy in Shanghai, where after graduating first in her class, she worked as a teacher. She liked her job, but was restless. She wanted to come to America to study. I considered sponsoring her, but before I signed the necessary documents, I made sure I read all the fine print (A friend of mine had sponsored a Polish student, who upon arriving in America required $2,300 in dental work, all of which came from my friend's pockets. I did not want to be in the same position). By sponsoring Cathy, I was in effect becoming her American guardian. She was accepted to Hofstra University which is ten miles from my home in Sea Cliff. Hofstra informed me that insurance (available at $30) would cover Cathy in the event that she required medical attention. I was grateful for that. I agreed to be her sponsor. I was responsible for her tuition, housing and food. Cathy had enough money to cover her air fare.

It took over a year of paperwork, phone calls, scary times (the Chinese government keep tightening the restrictions on students leaving), and long letters between Cathy and myself before any progress was made. Cathy was worried about the crime in New York, would she be able to adapt to a new environment, and was she making the right decision to leave her home for at least two years. I did my best to assure her that all would be fine. And, on a chilly fall evening in September, 1986, Cathy Zhong arrived from China.

Any doubts that Cathy had that she would not succeed here were dashed almost immediately after she arrived. Cathy came on a Saturday night and on Monday, showing no ill effects from jet lag, took the English entrance exam. She scored 97 percent. Within the first week of school, she found three jobs on campus. She later tutored five students from China, Cyprus, Japan and Iran in English. After living with me for two weeks (and securing rides from my friends), she moved in with a family near campus who housed and fed her in exchange for babysitting. Later, she lived with a recently widowed woman who merely wanted companionship. She stayed there for two years.

Soon after arriving, Cathy developed a strong affinity for chicken and American movies. She bought contact lenses. She passed her driver's test. She was not impressed with Chinatown, but loved the New York City Ballet. She strolled down the seedy side of New York's 42nd Street, gazing at a marquee of a "XXX" film and said "Only $1.99. Why, that's cheap."

And she has become very, very popular. Cathy said to me that no one in China ever told her she was pretty. Here, she's been told. A friend of mine gave Cathy a bicycle so she could ride to school, but she made so many friends there (especially male) that her transportation problems were soon over. For a while, more mail was coming to my house addressed to Cathy than to me. When her house was burgled, the investigating policeman, according to Cathy, "talked one minute about the crime and sixty minutes about me." She received (and still receives) invitations to dinners for Thanksgiving, Christmas, Chanukah, Easter and Passover. The Lions Club invited her to address its members and the president was so taken with her that he hired her to speak on a weekly basis at the local elementary schools. For four years, he took her out to lunch at least once a week. An elderly gentleman who frequented the restaurant where Cathy worked told me seriously that he hopes to adopt her (which would be difficult considering Cathy's parents are still living). And, finally, during that first spring, Cathy felt compelled to call twenty-two prospective suitors and tell them that she was sorry, but she must curtail her social activities, she really had no time for them and that she must study, and thank you and good luck.

That first year was particularly memorable. At the campus restaurant, she served George H. Bush. After I paid for her first semester's tuition for three classes, Cathy applied for and (surprise!) received a scholarship for the next two semesters. (Two years later Cathy presented me with a check for that first semester's tuition). In addition, Cathy landed a job teaching the Chinese exercise, 'tai chi,' twice a week at Hofstra. It was really impressive to see Cathy's name and biography in the Hofstra Faculty Guide. Cathy even began picking up some ethnic phrases. One night she called me and moaned, "Oy, I hate this damn linguistics book."

In 1989, Cathy got a job at LaGuardia Community College High School teaching English as a second language. She did some modeling and received an offer for a part in a Telly Savalas movie (She auditioned with hundreds of other Asian women, read one line, and was hired). She recently left teaching and now sells insurance for Mutual of Omaha (It seems every fellow she dates buys $10,000 worth of insurance). Agents receive a free one-week trip (Italy in 1992, Hawaii in 1993) if they sell a certain amount of insurance. Cathy sold enough insurance in 1992 to qualify for that trip to Italy, despite the fact that she only worked at Mutual of Omaha for two months (She received the trip to Hawaii in 1992 for nine months' work).

And now she's branched out working as a consultant. She goes to China a few months a year on business, making deals, and checking in on her aging parents.

Cathy has been in the United States for eight years. Any doubts that she would adapt to living in this country have been quashed long ago. She has an apartment in Manhattan, subscribes to *Cosmopolitan, Forbes, Fortune* and *Business Week,* and gives me stock tips and financial advice (some of which I even understand). I figure next week she's going to buy the Trump Tower.

I'm delighted that Cathy is doing so well. She has brightened a lot of people's lives, including mine. She meets everyone (Last winter, she met Richard Nixon and Rev. Billy Graham in a restaurant. Obviously stuck by her beauty, the former President said, "Are you an actress?" "No," replied the communist-turned-capitalist, "I'm a broker."

Although Cathy and I don't see each other that often, we get along beautifully. We have a standing date to celebrate each other's birthdays. That means a dinner which includes, of course, chicken, followed by an American movie.

I'm so glad she's here.

48

Looking For Mr. Roommate

Sawasdee, January 1996

When I began traveling with tours nearly 20 years ago, 99 percent of my companions were terrific and the rest were my roommates.

I don't know why that happened. Individuals who seemed to be wonderful people when first introduced frequently turned into monsters. The mild-mannered guy at dinner had an explosive temper. The charming assistant principal, my roommate in Africa, harassed so many women that he was sent home to Ohio after one week.

This, I concluded, could not continue. So from that moment on, I interviewed all prospective roommates. I inquired of others what they knew about them. And, since I've become more diligent, I've had some terrific experiences. In fact, a few have been my roommates on subsequent trips. This year, a friend from Germany had agreed to accompany me on a trip to Vietnam with *Trans China Tours*. We had discussed it for over a year and everything was proceeding smoothly until he informed me that he couldn't get the time off from work. He had just started a new job and couldn't leave.

The single supplement charge was over US $500 and I didn't want to travel by myself, so I started making phone calls. I contacted friends who liked to travel and had the time and had the money. But, those friends who wanted to go to Vietnam, ("Great!" "Sounds terrific!"), didn't have the US $3,000 for a 10-day trip. And those friends who had the time and money were less than enthusiastic about traveling to Vietnam ("Vietnam? You've got to be kidding"). My situation looked bleak. Until I got a Christmas card from John Johnson.

John Johnson was a 75-year-old retiree living in Florida. We were on the same trip together to the former Soviet Union in 1990. I hardly knew him, but he had faithfully sent a Christmas card each year. This year's card filled me in on all of John's activities from the past year, but I could sense that John, a widower, was feeling a bit lethargic. "Haven't been anywhere since China in 1991," he wrote. "Can't find anywhere exotic enough."

The bells in my head rang loud and clear: I telephoned him. I described the trip. "Sounds good," he said. "Can I call you back in two days?" "Fine," I replied.

John called back in two hours. "Let's do it!" he said triumphantly.

In the subsequent weeks, we swapped newspaper articles on Vietnam. I got my shots; John got his. With the recent lifting of the US trade embargo, I expected the Vietnamese to welcome us warmly. It was to be an exciting trip. Traveling to an exotic country, sampling the local foods, meeting the people. I had one concern: Would I recognize John at the airport?

It was a reasonable question. I couldn't quite remember what he looked like. John flew out from Florida; I left from New York. We were to meet in San Francisco where we were to board the same United Airlines plane for the flight to Bangkok. There we would spend the night, before leaving the next morning for Hanoi.

It didn't quite work out that way. When I arrived at Kennedy Airport, I was told by the ticket agent that my flight reservations were cancelled. "Oh, great!" I groaned. After what seemed like an interminable delay, she continued: "The flights were overbooked so we're sending you to Tokyo and then on to Bangkok." I described my dilemma to the agent. "Don't worry, your friend will find you."

Thirteen hours after leaving New York, I arrived in Tokyo. I didn't see John, but I did spot Joe Rosta, a childhood friend I had last seen around 1969. He was going to Bangkok on business. After exchanging pleasantries, I set out to look for John. I spotted a kindly-looking grey-haired man sitting by himself in the terminal. I ambled over, smiled, and said, "Hello, John!" The man returned the smile and said, "Sorry, I'm not John." Embarrassed, I slunk back to the sanctuary of Joe Rosta. Four hours later, I lined up for my boarding pass to Bangkok. The man in front of me carried a bag with the tag, *Trans China Tours*. John!

On the seven-hour flight to Bangkok, we re-introduced ourselves. John had worked in many jobs including a plant manager, and manufacturing engineer. John and his wife had once quit their jobs and sailed around the Caribbean for a year. Later, he and his family lived in Puerto Rico for two years. As we were touching down in Thailand, John was describing to me his plans for a summer trip to Eastern Europe. He was definitely not a couch potato.

From that moment on, we got on excellently. John never complained, never sat still. He was interested in everything mechanical. He also really knew his flowers, animals and architecture and, since I'm quite ignorant of these things, I learned a lot. On my end, I loved mingling with the locals, finding out about their lives, and I'd pull John into our conversations — so we complemented each other well.

Vietnam was a pleasant surprise. We didn't know what to expect when we left the States, but we need not have worried. The food in Vietnam was plentiful and good, although the people were another concern. How would the Vietnamese treat us? — especially with the war still vivid in the minds of most Vietnamese.

Again, no problems. They were wonderful. As we walked down the streets, old folks would smile and the children would run over and enthusiastically try out their 20 words of English. I felt that if we'd extended our stay, we could have been elected mayors of Vietnam.

Most of the tourists were French (occasionally, we'd run into a handful of Americans), and they, too, were treated with kindness. Only the Chinese seem to be met with disdain ("They occupied our country for a thousand years," a guide told us. "You and the French were here less than 20.")

Each city was varied and interesting: Hanoi, with its moderate temperatures (68 degrees in February) was very pretty, with wide boulevards and well-kept parks; Danang was bustling, Hue had its famed China Beach; Ho An had some wonderful architecture; and finally hot, exciting Ho Chi Minh City, with its old markets coexisting alongside the many new hotels and shops.

During the last two days, we went off on our own. John took a boat down the Mekong Delta, and I enjoyed poking my head around the side streets of Ho Chi Minh City. At night, we'd reunite for dinner, swapping tales of our adventures.

And, finally, it was time to leave. John was spending an extra day in Bangkok, but I had to return to my students in New York. We bid farewell to each other at the hotel and promised to keep in touch. "I'll send pictures," he called out as I ducked into the cab for the ride to the airport.

As my plane flew over the United States and prepared to land in New York, I let out a sigh of relief. Everything had turned out perfectly: Vietnam was beautiful, the people were warm and gracious and John had been terrific.

And as I reclined in my chair, a magazine in my hand, I thought ahead to the future: I wonder if John needs a roommate in Eastern Europe....

49

A Yankee Pedaler's Progress Thru Iowa

New York Daily News, May 26, 1996

> *"It was the best of times. It was the worst of times."*
> -Charles Dickens

It's quite obvious. Dickens rode RAGBRAI. Who else could so succinctly and accurately describe the annual seven-day bicycle ride across Iowa?

Now in its 24th year, RAGBRAI — the (Des Moines) Register Annual Great Bicycle Ride Across Iowa — satisfies Dickens' contradictory criteria and it attracts more than 10,000 riders from all 50 states and nearly 20 countries.

Bikers descend on Iowa in late July and battle the heat, rain, strong winds and occasional tedium to ride from the west end of the state to the east. They curse, complain, mope and swear they'll return the next year. And many do.

As a New Yorker, I had read about Iowa's fabled bicycle ride for three years. Skimming over the parts describing the fickle weather, I preferred reading about the international community of riders, the delicious food and the friendly hospitality. I signed up. Herewith is my account:

We leave early on Sunday from Sioux Center, a religious town of almost 5,000 people, mostly of Dutch descent. They've provided 5,000 free continental breakfasts!

The terrain is fairly flat and the temperature is in the mid-70s. But as we'll see each day, it's a long haul: seven to eight hours on a bike riding past cornfield after cornfield.

Other riders aren't very talkative and I could use a radio. But, then, I discover "The Pancake Man," who sets up his stand every morning 20 miles into the RAGBRAI route. And, so, I established a routine: I'd rise at 5:45 a.m., pedal for almost two hours until I came upon The Pancake Man, who'd feed me and thousands of other bikers pancakes, sausages and orange juice – all for $4. A nice break.

In Algona, Harold Reit, a retired baker, earns a spot in the Guinness Book of World Records by making the world's longest cake — 2,100 feet stretching six blocks through the town (I have two slices). At Gopher College, we are made "honorary graduates" and, in the evening, there is a rugby game and a "graduation dinner" for VIPs — riders who have finished all 24 RAGBRAIs. The two street dances? I slept through them.

The next day, we pedal through Corwith, which calls itself the "Town with a Heart" (red hearts have been painted on the pavement to mark our route). Along the road, the rumor spreads that one biker has proposed marriage to another. Ah, romance.

I ride with an elderly man whose shirt proclaims: "Don't give me no jive. I'm 75." But the shirt is an old one. "I'm really 80," he grins.

Goodell has a Hawaiian theme: a luau with a cardboard palm tree and greeters wearing grass skirts. In Westgate, a worker from the Interstate Power Co., up high in his truck's basket to check the lights downtown, obligingly carries dozens of bikers' cameras with him and takes photos of the throng below.

In Oelwein, a woman is counting riders. I'm No. 5615 at 12:30 p.m. "Where are you from?" kids yell out to the riders. At each response there is a polite applause. When it's my turn and I shout, "New York!" a loud cheer erupts. Very nice. I might move here!

In Masonville, a woman and her sons are raffling off a goat, $1 per chance. I buy one.

Midweek, the weather changes. It's getting hotter, the hills are steeper and a strong wind is blowing. Many have dropped out and I am tired. What started as a leisurely endeavor has developed into an obsession to finish. But I still want to have fun. Roaring through Cedar Rapids, I pass some girls who hold up signs reading, "10," "10," "9.99," "9." I yell back to the last one, "I'll try to do better!"

And then it's Saturday, the final day. I get up at 4 a.m. for the 67-mile ride to Burlington. It's drizzling and in the distance, lightning flashes. Can't see a thing on the gravel road. The light rain gets heavier. Feeling tremendous guilt, I pass The Pancake Man, but I have to make my 1:15 p.m. flight to New York. I pause at a stand where a group is giving away food and gratefully accept two muffins and an orange for later. The rain gets even heavier, but it only strengthens my resolve. At 9 a.m. I stop to eat my orange and chat with the locals. A man gives me a Gatorade.

As we near Burlington, the end is in sight. We race through the center of town, crowds lining the street. Kids lean over to slap our hands. There's one more obstacle: a killer hill. I feel I'm going to pull a hamstring. I eat my last muffin and roar down Snake Alley, reputed to be the world's most crooked street.

I roll into Burlington at 10:15, and soon after we reach the Mississippi River for the traditional "bike dip." It's quite a scene — a mass of humanity. Senior citizens are taking Polaroids of us for $2. (The money goes to support their organizations). I'm interviewed by two local TV stations. "Would I do it again?" I laugh and reply, "Ask me in six months."

Finally, I change my clothes, catch my flight, and with memories of The Pancake Man, Snake Alley and my prospective goat in my head, I fasten my seat belt and drift off to sleep.

$O

Growing Up In Glen Head

Newsday, December 15, 1996

In 1953, when my newlywed parents announced they were moving from Brooklyn to a new development in Glen Head, the reaction among friends and relatives was unanimous:

"Where's Glen Head?"

Even today, to many lifelong residents of Long Island, Glen Head is still no more than a dot on the map. But perhaps that's what makes Glen Head so special. It enjoys its anonymity.

Glen Head, originally settled by the Matinecock, was probably first spotted by a Dutch sea captain named Adrian Block in 1613. Because easterly Long Island offered other harbors with closer proximity to the ocean, Glen Head — and Hempstead Harbor in general — had no whalers or captain's houses on its shoreline.

I grew up on Glen Cove Drive (where my parents still reside), among other children of young parents. There were games of touch football in the street, and behind the American Legion Hall, hide-and-seek contests, and then refreshments afterwards in the kitchens of the Osmans, the Kennedys, the Morganellis, and the Klimans. Birthdays were a neighborhood event. In the summer, we'd bike down to Tappan Beach to swim until darkness set in, and in the winters we'd bundle up to go ice-skating on Scudders Pond. It was a scene Norman Rockwell would have envied. Our community was one large extended family. It wasn't unusual for me to have breakfast with my parents, lunch with the Osmans, and dinner with the Morganellis (Now at 40, I've tried to continue this practice, but the Osmans and Morganellis aren't too thrilled with the idea).

As an adult, I returned to teach at the North Shore Middle School, my alma mater. Now I teach my classmates' children. We've come full circle.

And Glen Head's charms remain the same.

Children still play in the street, though I notice more hockey games than football. The old makeshift football field behind the American Legion is gone, but in its place are four new Little League baseball diamonds. A soccer program attracts over 700 children each year. This past summer, local residents, led by Mike Lennon, Bill Zukas and Jim Collins, created the "NSPAL Roller Hockey League" down at Tappen Beach. For children — and their parents — Tappen hosts free evening concerts during the long, lazy summer months.

"Glen Head's a unique town," says Carl Wnuk, who has owned the Glen Head Hardware Store since 1946. "It's a place surrounded by other villages that have few or no stores. The people from Brookville, Greenvale, Roslyn Harbor and even some from Sea Cliff, come here to shop."

"Glen Head is a friendly place," agrees Neil Caggiano, who has owned the local flower shop for more than 30 years. I enjoy going up the block to the deli every day — and along the way shaking hands with my friends and customers. Everyone waves to each other in Glen Head."

A bedroom community of commuters who work an hour away in Manhattan, and blue-collar workers and local professionals, Glen Head is a good place to raise a family. The Memorial Day Parade still attracts a large crowd, as does the Little League parade. People still remove their hats when the National Anthem is played. Nick the Barber still cuts hair in his shop near the train station (he's been there since 1955). Post office and bank employees know you by your first name. Restaurants abound, including Pappagallo's, The Iron Horse, The Station House, Gabriel's, Cornucopia and The North Shore Café.

"The people in Glen Head are very involved in the community," adds Caggiano. When eighth-grader Jason Napolitano was stricken with leukemia in 1992, the community rallied around him and his family with a series of fundraisers that helped defray his medical costs. (Today, Jason's cancer is in remission and he is an active 12th-grader at the high school). "We helped Jason through Rotary, and we raised over $70,000 for the 'Gift of Life' program to bring over 82 kids from Russia for emergency medical treatment. It's a caring community," says Caggiano.

That attitude seems to have permeated the school system, too. North Shore youngsters are active volunteers. "Some school districts require their students to participate in community service," says Public Relations Director Marge Malone. "But North Shore's program is strictly voluntary and we still get 80 percent of the student body who do so." The district sponsors a Community Chorus, a Community Symphony and a Summer Band open to all adults in the community.

The schools are one of the reasons that home buyers are attracted to Glen Head. Another is the relatively low taxes, made possible because a LILCO power plant in Glenwood Landing contributes a share.

Although I moved next door to Sea Cliff in 1983, Glen Head is the place I always return to. The Klimans, Morganellis, Kennedys and Osmans still reside at their original addresses. There is something special about Glen Head people. Ann Osman still calls me the night of the Academy Awards to compare Oscar selections. Jane Costello, who moved away in 1960, never forgets to send a birthday card. And in the supermarket, I occasionally run into a longtime resident who says, "I hear nice things about you from your students. I'll tell your mother."

It's that kind of place. To some, it may be a spot on the map, but to this teacher, Glen Head spells "h-o-m-e."

$1

Cruise To Antarctica, The Very Last Holdout

The New York Post, February 24, 1998

I hate the winter, get bored easily with nature, and get seasick just looking at ships.

So what did I do last Christmas? I took a cruise to Antarctica.

Why would anyone go to such a place? Well, for me and for 20 of my shipmates, it was our last continent. Few people have been there (indeed, in 1996 only 4,500 tourists visited Antarctica). And, in many ways it's the last holdout: No Gap or McDonald's have been built. Just gorgeous ice floes and sea lions and penguins. Thousands of them.

As a teacher and a traveler, I had always wanted to see Antarctica, but time constraints made it difficult to book such a trip. (Tours are only offered in winter – Antarctica's summer. In July and August — Antarctica's winter — temperatures can go down to -80° F). I settled on Marine Expeditions, a Toronto-based organization, that offers relatively inexpensive voyages.

Our group of 80 (representing five continents) met in Santiago, Chile, where we spent the day after Christmas strolling around this pretty city in shorts and t-shirts as temperatures hovered around 95°.

Then we flew to Ushuaia, Argentina, the southernmost city in the world.

On the third day, we boarded the Akademik Ioffe, a Russian scientific research ship that four years ago was converted to a cruise vessel. There were 51 crew members, including 44 Russians for the eight-day trip. We would spend two days crossing the mercurial Drake Passage to get to Antarctica, four days at the continent and two days getting back.

I quickly settled into the routine: At 8 a.m, a buffet breakfast; at 9, a lecture; at 12:30 p.m., lunch (soup, salad, and quiche). In the afternoon, another lecture followed by a snack. Dinner (choice of meat, fish or vegetarian) at 8 p.m. Meals were informal, the food plentiful and good (Cruise-lovers looking for midnight meals will be disappointed. They don't exist). The evening's entertainment was a movie (either Hollywood or National Geographic).

I made myself right at home, taking self-guided tours of the ship. There was a small gift shop, a well-stocked library where I spent a great deal of time, and a "workout room" which, sadly, consisted of one barbell and a broken treadmill. (I got my exercise walking up and down the ship's steps 20 times each morning.)

At mealtime, I talked with my traveling companions. There was Mary Lou and Paul, a deaf couple who have three adopted deaf children. There was Derek, 83, and Ann, 70, a delightful pair from Kenya. There was the energetic Van Striker family from Idaho: Mom, Dad, two teenage daughters and Grandma. Not a whiner in the bunch. By the second day, we were all best friends.

After dinner, I usually skipped the movie because I had more pressing issues: defending my title against all of the ship's elderly ladies as the undefeated Scrabble champion. Some of them were tough — and stubborn.

Following Scrabble, I'd head off to the sauna (right across from my room), a shower, and sleep.

On Day 5, we arrived at Antarctica.

My roommate, Carl, a 43 year old teacher, and I prepared for our landing. I wore a hat, boots, gloves, snow pants and a wool turtleneck over a t-shirt. Carl, being from Southern California and unaccustomed to cold weather, wanted to do it right, which meant layering. He pulled an long underwear, a shirt, a sweater, another shirt, another sweater, a windbreaker, two hats, two pairs of gloves. I think he was wearing nine layers of clothes.

"I'm ready," he intoned, walking off like Lurch, from *The Addams Family*.

In fact, he was more than ready. With temperatures never dipping below 35 degrees, the perspiring Carl was down to two layers of clothes by the third day.

Unable to land directly, we took Zodiacs (small motor-boats) for the five-minute trip to the continent. What a glorious sight! Magnificent mountains! Shimmering ice floes! Amazing animals!

For four days — once in the morning, and once in the afternoon — we'd walk and hike among the wildlife for a couple of hours, taking pictures and returning to the ship at our leisure.

And something wondrous happened: I became a nature lover. I took notes at the lectures and read books on Antarctica in the ship's library. When we landed on the continent and saw the penguins and the sea lions and the birds — and not a single human being — I was hooked.

I became enchanted with the penguins — especially the chinstrap penguins — and I watched for hours as they fed their young beneath them. We were told not to get closer than 15 feet from them. They obviously hadn't read the handbook and literally engulfed me. We enjoyed each other's company.

And, then, too soon, it was time to return to the Zodiac. We would have one more landing in the afternoon before our two-day trip back to Ushuaia.

Unlike the previous tour group who had to scrub six of the eight landings because of turbulent seas, we had had a relatively calm trip.

And, then just before our final landing, our luck ran out.

We hit choppy water that sent waves crashing against the ship. But we had all been prepared for such an occurrence; since the first day, we had been taking Dramamine to ward off seasickness. While it prevented nausea, it also kept us in perpetual state of sleepiness. Indeed, it wasn't uncommon to walk around the ship and see bodies strewn all over, slumped in chairs, dozing on tables.

We slept and slept. Each night, I'd get eight hours of sleep, have breakfast, read a bit, and go back to bed. Sometimes I had two naps in a day.

Well, on that stormy afternoon of the last landing, the boat was careening to the left, careening to the right. It was nearly an hour before our scheduled 4 p.m. departure for our last landing on Antarctica. Some of the passengers heroically made their way to the bridge. (Being the brave fellow that I am, I was taking a siesta.)

Anyway, at 3:15, the announcement came over the P.A. system, "Due to rough waters, we have canceled the last landing."

I went back to sleep.

Two days later, on January 5, we returned to Ushuaia. That evening, we boarded the plane for the flight to Santiago, and then I went on to New York. Arriving early the next morning at Kennedy Airport, I zipped off to school.

I was looking forward to seeing my students, but as I sat there reflecting on the previous two weeks, I had to admit: I missed my penguins.

52

Holiday Helpers
Mind The Store

Newsday, April 12, 1998

Charlotte Abelson works every Easter, Christmas Eve and Christmas. But she's not looking for any sympathy.

She prefers working the holidays.

Abelson arranges for Jewish volunteers to fill in at the front desk at the North Shore Community Hospital at Glen Cove so that the Christian desk volunteers can have the day off to celebrate the holidays with their families.

"I had been the president of the North Country Reform Temple and I was looking for something that we could get involved in to help the community," says Abelson, an ebullient 68-year old decorator from Glen Cove. "I spoke to people at the hospital who said they would love to have replacements during the holidays. So, we did it."

The first year was 1977. "We really didn't know what we were doing," she says, laughing. "We were afraid someone was going to die at the hospital on our watch."

But no one did and the volunteers grew more comfortable filling in. They greet visitors, answer phones, deliver flowers, keep track of admissions and discharges, and help patients get television service.

Anything else? "Well, one year we had a drunk Santa Claus roll into the lobby of the hospital," Abelson recalls. "He was singing madly and wanted to go upstairs to all the floors to sing … he said he was bringing good cheer. But, the good cheer was really in his belly. Finally, we had to call Security."

And just like the hospital volunteers that they substitute for, the volunteers have learned a couple of new things over the 21 years. "When computers came, everyone was afraid to sit at the desk," says Abelson.

Over the years, Abelson has been overwhelmed by the response from the Temple members. "When I started this, I used to hand out three-hour shifts," she says. "But now we have so many people calling, some of our shifts are only one hour."

Last Christmas, 32 people helped out; this Easter 16 people volunteered.

"We have some people who have left the temple and still continue to volunteer." She pauses and smiles. "I can't believe it's been 21 years."

§3

Telling Kids Not To Do Something Backfires

Newsday, November 2, 1998

As a teacher of adolescents, I have been following the debate over teen smoking with great interest.

Despite all the evidence that smoking can and does lead to emphysema, lung cancer and early death, young people have been lighting up in record numbers. The United States has spent millions to teach kids not to smoke, but to little avail. Experts cite stress, peer pressure, and cigarette advertising (e.g. Joe Camel) as prime reasons, but I think they're all missing the boat.

I believe, without any scientific evidence, but after observing youngsters during 19 years of teaching, that the main reason they're smoking is: They're told not to.

What happens when kids see a "Keep Off the Grass" sign? They step on the grass. Tell kids not to smoke and they'll line up at the vending machine. They're kids! (A colleague once said that if there was a campaign to do away with orange juice, kids would guzzle it by the gallon.)

Now, smoking is a serious problem. And, to be honest, short of a jail term or expulsion from school, I don't know what the solution is. But telling kids not to smoke is not the answer.

A number of years ago I was teaching in our high school. It was the school's 25th anniversary. A big celebration was planned. Local historians, long-time residents and former students were invited back for the part. The entire community was excited about the upcoming gala – except for the students.

They had no enthusiasm for it. When an organizer of the party, asked at the meeting how we could get the kids to come, my wise old department chairman said, "Have the principal come out against it." (Now, there was a man who knew young people!).

In my school in recent years, we've had a problem with hats. Some teachers (and obviously, some students' parents) don't mind if students wear hats in school. Others — like myself — feel it shows poor manners and contributes to a slovenly appearance and poor performance when it comes to work.

In my class, my policy is that if you're caught wearing a hat, I will confiscate it and return it after the next major holiday (Groundhog Day and Flag Day don't count). Anyway, it's been a fairly effective policy except that with some students, their bodies are Human Pez Machines: I remove one hat and another immediately replaces it. It's an ongoing battle.

Last year, a colleague in the math department was clearly exasperated over the hat issue. Every day there was another student wearing a hat in defiance of the rules. She finally threw in the towel. She announced that the upcoming Friday would be "Hat Day." Wear any hat you want. Big, small, loud, quiet. She didn't care. She talked it up every day leading up to the big event. And, when Friday arrived she walked into the class and was stunned by the sight she saw: No one was wearing a hat.

There is a lesson there.

54

The Yeast He Could Do

Newsday, January 5, 1999

During our school vacations, I am usually off exploring exotic places such as South Africa, Vietnam and Cuba. But last February was different: I stayed home. More specifically, I stayed in the kitchen.

I don't know what happened to me. Usually, a one-pot and three-ingredient guy, I went on a rampage: On Monday I made stir-fried pork; Tuesday was Dijon turkey meatballs; Wednesday was turkey meatloaf; Thursday was vegetable lasagna, and finally, Friday, it was bread from scratch. (I was completely transformed. At one time in my life I wanted to be the 20th century version of Marco Polo. By the end of the holiday, I was becoming Julia Child!)

It was an amazing week.

I would start my adventure in Farmers' Bazaar in Glen Cove, where I met the most helpful women. Forget singles' bars and dances, the place to meet women —— albeit usually elderly women — is the supermarket. Helga helped me with the pork selections. Eleanor assisted with the spices. When I was leaning over to pick up low-fat butter for my bread-baking debut, Elizabeth shook her head. "For cooking, buy the regular butter. Low-fat doesn't work."

I had found a white bread recipe, with a sidebar of wonderful helpful hints. I borrowed an instant-read thermometer from my sister, Marjie, and set it to work. I read through the directions. In water that was 108 degrees Fahrenheit, I dissolved the yeast. I measured all the ingredients accurately. I used unbleached flour, and I was going to omit the salt until I came across this order: "Never leave out the salt. Not only does salt add flavor, it controls the actions of the yeast." Since I didn't want to mess up the action of the yeast, I put in the salt.

I used a mixer for the flour. I kneaded the dough. I folded it toward me, pushing it down and away with the heels of my hands. I was supposed to "give it a corner turn," but I didn't know what that meant, so I gave it a twirl.

I placed the dough in a large, greased bowl, turned it over, covered it with plastic wrap and, then – I hit a snag. The directions said, "Set it aside to rise in a warm spot about 80 degrees." Hmmm. It was 37 degrees outside and 69 degrees inside. There was only one thing to do. I called my neighbor, Mrs. Moran, the "Irish Soda Bread Queen" herself. Mrs. Moran is a sweet woman who left Ireland in 1942 but maintains the most lovely Irish brogue. "Aye, Saul, 'tis a problem," she said. "Here's what I would do. Turn your thermostat up to 80 degrees." I followed her advice. As my house slowly became a steam bath (I was soon down to a t-shirt and shorts), I looked in on my bread and, sure enough, it worked.

I returned to my manual. "For a soft, tender crust," the author wrote, "gently brush the top with milk before baking or butter the crust after it comes out of the oven." I used the milk.

After it was baked, I removed the bread immediately from the pan and cooled it on a rack to prevent the crust from becoming soggy. "Don't slice it for about 20 minutes, regardless of how tempted you are by the aroma." Boy, was I tempted, but I behaved myself. Finally, at 6:40 p.m., nearly five hours after I began, I cut off a piece of my bread and placed it in my mouth. It was delicious. I cut off another piece. Five pieces later, feeling a bit doughy myself, I decided that was enough.

As I put away the pots and pans, I thought ahead to my next vacation. Originally I had planned to go to Central America, but now I have bigger and better plans. I've outgrown white bread. It's on to bagels and bialys. Maybe even a pumpernickel raisin bread. All I can say is: Clear those aisles at Farmers' Bazaar. Ladies, I'm coming back!

§§

Looking For
Long-Lost Luggage

The Sunday Oregonian, June 27, 1999

Most of us, at one time or another, set out on our own personal odysseys. Ludwig van Beethoven, despite deafness, composed nine symphonies. Sir Edmund Hillary, defying the odds, conquered Mount Everest. Wilma Rudolph overcame the debilitating effects of childhood polio and won an Olympic gold medal in track and field.

On the morning of July 3, 1998, under a sweltering sun, I set out alone from Atlanta to fulfill a 20-year dream: to find my lost luggage.

It was a Samsonite XCV3, hard and rugged, and had been with me through the good times (camp) and the bad times (camp). And, on my first voyage overseas to Africa, after I disembarked in exotic Senegal, I waited patiently for it. But, it never appeared. Calls to the airlines were fruitless, and I was forced to soldier on alone.

I purchased other luggage, but I never forgot my Samsonite XCV3. And then last year I heard about the Unclaimed Baggage

Center in Scottsboro, Alabama (population 15,576), the final rest-
ing place for all the lost and unclaimed airline luggage.

It was the news I'd been waiting for.

The Unclaimed Baggage Center (also known as the UBC)
sent me directions and a brochure. And off I went.

It would prove to be a difficult undertaking. For only the
second time in my life, I was driving a rented car. The trip, according to my associate at the UBC, would take 2 ½ to 3 hours from
Atlanta. Timing was important to me. I had to return by 3 p.m. if I
hoped to make my 4:05 flight on Kiwi Airlines to Orlando, Florida.
I withdrew a log book and made some calculations: Leave Alamo
Rental at 7 a.m. Arrive at UBC at 10 a.m. Search for two hours
and secure Samsonite. Leave Scottsboro: noon. Return safely to
Atlanta: 3 p.m.

It didn't quite work out that way.

For one thing, the directions were a bit off. The Alamo attendant laughed at the ones the UBC sent me and issued a new
version beginning with, "From the highway, turn off at Exit 168."
I drove for more than an hour, but because of the heat and lack
of sleep I missed Exit 168 (I was at Exit 150, and the numbers
were dropping precipitously when I realized my mistake). I turned
around and 30 minutes later reached Exit 168. It was after 11 a.m.
and according to my directions — "Go 30 miles on 168, make a
right on 159, and then a left on 35 to Scottsboro," I still had a ways
to go. I calculated that by the time I arrived in Scottsboro it would
be time to turn around. I revved up the car to 70 mph (15 mph over
what this environmentalist/safety-conscious driver usually traveled, but, hey, I had a plane to catch!) and roared on.

By 11:30, I reached Route 35 and a sign pointing to Scottsboro. *Scottsboro!*

But, it proved to be a tease.

There was no Scottsboro – at least not for a while yet.
"Scottsboro: 19 miles" read the sign. 19 miles! I couldn't drive
70 mph on these country roads. Perhaps 55 – if I didn't cross
paths with a cow. I drove on. At 11:50, feeling as if I were making little progress, I pulled into a service station and explained

my dilemma to two retired gentlemen talking by the pumps. "The Unclaimed Baggage Center? Well, you're only two miles from it," one drawled. "But if I were you and wanted to make that flight, I'd turn around right now."

As my head drooped, he continued, "And, I'd forget those dang directions. I worked at Delta and here's what I'd do. I'd scoot over to 72, head east, and then take 75 South all the way to Atlanta, but you better get a move on."

But a move on to where? Do I abandon my dream of re-uniting with my Samsonite XCV3 so that I could pal around with Mickey and Disney World, or do I show some fortitude, some courage and hope God (or someone else in the office) leads me to the Promised Land and reconciliation with my luggage?

I stayed the course.

And, by noon, I arrived at the Unclaimed Baggage Center in Scottsboro.

It was an immense place, covering 25,000 square feet. There were shirts and pants and hats and computers and cameras. But my Samsonite? It was long gone – if it ever arrived in the first place. And, its contents? Clearly, 22-year-old underwear and socks were not the key factor here. I wasn't nearly as nostalgic for them as my trusty companion, my Samsonite XCV3.

But the deals were incredible: $50 for a suit; $200 for a computer; $7 for a shirt. I wanted to stay, oh, I wanted to stay, at this, the greatest of all garage sales. But, I couldn't. I had that flight to catch to Orlando.

So, at 12:30 p.m., I slipped behind the wheel of my car and sped off in search of Route 72. I found it and soon was head-ing off toward Chattanooga, Tennessee. Tennessee? My third state in seven hours? (I began to wonder if there was an Unclaimed Unclaimed Baggage Claim Center – UUBCC – for lost northern-ers …) And, although I was heading east, I discovered I was also heading north. I'd never make it back to Georgia in time.

I stayed on Route 72 awhile, switched to 24 (a shortcut to Route 75) at the suggestion of another gas station attendant (should I have a reunion of all these direction givers next fall?) and found

Route 75 as a thunderstorm erupted.

I sped up to 72 mph. It was 1:30 p.m. when I saw the sign: Atlanta – 100 miles. At 2 p.m. it was down to 68. At 3, realizing I didn't have a clue as to how to find the airport, I pulled into another gas station for directions ("Follow 75 to 85 South and follow the signs to Montgomery. When you get to the airport, go north"). At 3:10 p.m., I returned my car to Alamo, caught its shuttle bus, and at 3:40 p.m., made it to the front of the line at the Kiwi check in counter where I asked for my boarding pass for my 4:05 flight to Orlando.

The attendant looked at me pleasantly and said, "Those 4:05 flights were permanently canceled on Aug. 1. We'll put you on the 8 p.m. plane."

She slapped an identification label on my luggage, "This is so you don't lose your bag. Have a safe flight now, you hear?"

56

Have Cheerios, Will Travel

Newsday, August 24, 1999

When I travel each summer to exotic places, I'm fairly easy to please.

I don't need four-star hotels, I don't require room service and I don't expect a limousine to greet me at the airport.

All I need to make me happy is a daily morning bowl of Cheerios. Or granola. Swimming in skimmed milk. With a banana sliced on top, a handful of raisins, orange juice and a bagel – or the nearest thing to it.

Don't get me wrong. I'm not one of those Ugly Americans who whine for two weeks about being too far from McDonald's. I've lived with a Siberian family, ridden a camel in Egypt and climbed Masada in Israel. And I've made sure I've eaten the local delicacies: I've had reindeer in Finland, a calf's head in Mexico and octopus in Japan. All very nice (once).

But, when it comes to breakfast, well that's where I become "Tony the Tiger." I must have my cold cereal. And fruit. And orange juice. Something robust. Something healthful.

When I first started traveling, I would pack my clothes, my camera, my guidebooks and — my breakfast. Not knowing if the country I was visiting had a supermarket with an extensive cereal aisle, I took my own: small boxes of Cheerios. But, alas, each box seems to contain about six Cheerios. Not good.

So, on subsequent trips, I began stowing away Pathmark's Jumbo No-Frills Granola. But that practice didn't last long because the box seemed to weigh a ton (actually 32 ounces), took up half my suitcase and friends wondered, after looking at my slides, why I always seemed to be wearing the same shirt. So, the jumbo boxes had to go.

I changed my strategy. After we had landed and unpacked in a foreign country, my traveling companions would go out to the beach or a museum. I would go in search of a supermarket. And I usually found one. I would stock up on cereal and bananas and orange juice and we all returned to the hotel that evening content. It was a good arrangement for 20 years.

Then, with a mixture of excitement and dread, I went to Mongolia. No Pathmark or Waldbaum's there. After landing the night before and being deposited in a drab hotel, our American group boarded a bus at 9 a.m. for our first field trip. The cool morning and occasional strong winds gave way to a warming sun. Twenty-five miles away on bumpy roads (only 3 percent of Mongolia's roads are paved) awaited our hosts for the day, a three-generation Mongolian yurt-dwelling family. The younger ones took some Americans horseback riding. Grandma milked the goats and another family member cooked another goat. While my companions were off hiking, I spent a few hours inside one of the yurts with others in the family.

The yurt is a round felt tent that has been the standard dwelling of Mongolians for 2,000 years. When my hostess excused herself to fetch refreshments, I looked around. For a moment, it seemed as if I had been transported to ancient times, if I ignored the motorbike parked outside and the nearby portable generator that powered the owner's television set and other modern appliances.

After a few minutes, my hostess returned with airag — a yogurt like drink made of fermented mare's milk and served in a brass bowl. Custom dictated that a drink of airag may not be refused, so I took a sip — it was pretty terrible — and passed it along to the others. Next came goat broth (very salty), goat cheese (not so good), and a slice of the goat itself (tough and unappealing). I did not ask for seconds.

By 3 p.m., it was time to go. I thanked everyone, and as I prepared to leave, I scanned the walls: framed pictures of the family and relatives, a photo of Lenin and, beneath it, on the floor, what was that box? I looked closer. No, it couldn't be. But, yes, it was. A box of Cheerios! An *old* box of Cheerios! How did ...? I didn't ask.

As I boarded the bus, I watched the yurt dwellers resume their daily routine that has changed little in the past 600 years — except perhaps for that one unique purchase…

57

The Schachter/Green Sister Express

Family Circle, September 1, 1999

Way before email existed and quite a few years after the Pony Express ceased operation, the Schachter-Green line began. Back then it was not a very extensive network. In fact, it operated only between two homes – my Aunt Bernice's in Falls Church, Virginia, and my mother Vivian's in Glen Head, New York. But it was a line that shortened the miles between two families as it carried their frequent correspondence.

I remember, even when I was a young boy, how often my aunt's letters would arrive at our house and how quickly Mom sent off a response. The two sisters were both young mothers, active in school functions and always chasing after their children. Early on, their letters were written on lined paper that never seemed quite large enough for all the news. When they got to the bottom of the page they would continue writing in the margins, around the corners and on the back of the envelope.

Overstuffed letters would arrive at our house with enough postage to pay for our college educations. Mom always enjoyed a good coffee klatch with her friends, but since Aunt Bernice couldn't be present for these events, sending letters was the next-best thing. Their correspondence was not the stuff of Gertrude Stein and Alice B. Toklas, but rather a summary of the week's events: what the kids and husbands were doing, who had the mumps, how the neighbors were faring and other tidbits.

As life got more hectic, Mom and Aunt Bernice started sending postcards, too. I guess they were always on each other's minds. Sometimes three cards would arrive in one mailing, all written on the same day with headings such as "7:45 a.m.," "12:30 p.m.," and "6:10 p.m."

Before going shopping, the two sisters often consulted one another through the mail, comparing size, cost and color. Occasionally, I'd go to the mailbox and retrieve a postcard that contained no salutation, no signature, no inscription of any sort except "Macy's - $14.95."

Eventually, Mom and Aunt Bernice started to include clippings from the newspaper with their letters. They exchanged local news stories, recipes, book excerpts and humor columns by Erma Bombeck. And they made sure to include the entire family. Aunt Bernice often enclosed articles for me on jogging, teaching and travel, and clippings for Dad on photography and Saabs (he had three of the cars in 15 years). If Dad was in the midst of wallpapering the kitchen, she would come through two days later with a clipping on wallpaper.

Since those days, their children have all moved away from home, but the Schachter-Green wire service has branched out and keeps humming along. Recently, I accepted my aunt's invitation to go to Virginia for a visit. Two days later, I received an envelope with no letter but a clipped advertisement of an airline's discounted fare between New York and Washington, D.C.

Mom has not been remiss in her communications with me either, even though she lives only two miles away. My mailbox is constantly brimming with recipes, household hints and articles — some illuminating, some baffling. "Catholics' Lag in Marrying Reported" announced one headline. I am not Catholic and I couldn't figure out why Mom had sent this to me. I called her. It turns out that on the same page as the article was an ad for hanging picture frames — an activity I was involved with at the moment.

So despite the occasional confusing communication, Mom

and Aunt Bernice keep us on their mailing list. There was talk in the family of buying computers for the sisters, but an error-free missive would be akin to receiving a form letter — it would seem impersonal and without charm. Mom and Aunt Bernice would never agree to it.

And come to think of it, neither would we.

58

Why Teaching Seventh Grade Is Better Than A Weekend Off

The Christian Science Monitor, September 20, 1999

My friends who work Monday through Friday look forward to their weekends.

I do, too, but sometimes I prefer Monday through Friday.

I am a teacher. I've taught everywhere from third grade to 12th — but much to the disbelief of my friends who teach elementary and senior high school — I like the seventh grade the best. The girls are sweet and innocent (the rolling-of-the-eyes and moodiness seem to arrive in eighth grade), and if they like you, they will do anything for you. Some even hope to bring you into the family. "Mr. Schachter, why don't you marry my Aunt Harriet, she's still married, but it doesn't look so good, so…"

The boys, on the other hand, struggle a bit. They seem to be half the size of the girls, cry twice as much, and have trouble remembering their locker combinations after long weekends.

But, they, too, can be charming and endearing. When one youngster finished a report on civil rights, he made a reference to the Ku Klux Klan. When this statement was met by baffled looks, he said impatiently, "You know, the CCC."

Today's youngsters are more tolerant than students of my generation were at their age. When I attended this school nearly 30 years ago (and I still bike there), the student body was 99.9 percent white. A kid coming from another country might have had a tough time surviving. But, as I look out at the faces of the students before me — the Indian kidding with the Korean, the Pole explaining an answer to the Iranian — I beam. This is one area in which the "good ol' days" were not better.

And, as they grow older, they remember. Last Christmas, Meredith gave me a new bell for my bicycle. Jamie, now a senior, calls me the night before school starts each year to wish me well. I feel fortunate to have attended many bar mitzvahs, bat mitzvahs, confirmations, weddings, second weddings and class reunions.

But it's been most fun having them "at the beginning" – in seventh grade. I'll never forget the time I gave a class on the American Revolution the day after the dancer and actor Gene Kelly died. It was two days before a scheduled test, and I reviewed the important facts about the revolution. Then I showed a four-minute video tape of Gene Kelly's memorable dance routine from, "Singin' in the Rain." One girl, whom I'll call "Alice," was absent. When she returned to class the next day to find out what she missed, I told her, "We had a review session for the American Revolution test, *and* I showed a brief clip of Gene Kelly in "Singin' in the Rain." Alice threw up her hands and clearly exasperated, cried, "Oh, no! Don't tell me *she's* going to be on the test, too!"

Sometimes, Monday through Friday is more fun than the weekends.

59

First Meal:
A Dash Of Planning, Practice

Newsday, October 12, 1999

When I moved into my new house, it was with a mixture of trepidation and exultation. I was afraid of the inevitable repairs that would be required, and my lack of manual dexterity only heightened my anxiety. However, I was looking forward to cooking. When I was a child, I had always enjoyed puttering around my mother's kitchen, but because it was her kitchen, I wasn't able to use it as much as I would have liked. Now, however, there were no such obstacles. Armed with six cookbooks, the experience from three adult-education cooking classes, and unbridled enthusiasm, I set out to equip my kitchen. I purchased a new refrigerator and stove, installed a new sink, and selected new pots and pans.

The first meal I concocted was a turkey casserole, steamed broccoli and white rice. I followed the recipe faithfully and sat down to a delicious meal. Following dinner, I cleaned up. It was a wonderful dinner except for one thing: I didn't finish washing the last dish until 11:30 p.m. It took me more than two hours to prepare the meal (not including buying the necessary ingredients),

20 minutes to eat it and nearly two hours to clean up. This was the first time I had ever watched "The Tonight Show" immediately after dinner.

Undaunted, I went ahead with my plan to be a self-sufficient cook. When I lived with my parents, I had alternated my breakfast menus: cold cereal, hot cereal and pancakes, and I resolutely decided to eat these same meals in my new home. Problem was, it took time to cook the latter two meals, and dirty pots and pans soon littered my sink. And I insisted on cleaning those utensils at the completion of each meal. By day two, I was getting up 30 minutes early to complete my breakfast chores and prepare lunch for later in the day.

With dinner, where I once felt satisfaction at a self-prepared meal, I soon felt only exhaustion. I discovered I was rushing through meals so I could get to the dishes. At one point, I was having dinner at 4:30 p.m., so I could be done by 9.

Finally, I realized, it was time to get organized. I studied the possibilities: it was too late to sell back the house. I couldn't quit my job.

I settled on the following plan: From Monday through Friday, breakfast would consist of cold cereal, toast, fruit and orange juice. Pancakes and hot cereal would have to wait until the weekends, when I had more time. I would prepare a chicken or beef meal (served with simple vegetables) twice and have leftovers later in the week. I would treat myself to a meal out once a week.

And it worked. Since then I have eaten three meals a day and have figured out time-saving devices in the process. When I'm preparing dinner, I stock containers with fruit, vegetables and assorted leftovers for my lunch the next day. I do all the dishes after dinner, instead of after each meal. I try to use no more than two pots (and preferably one) at dinner. And to avoid conflicts with my digestive system, I make sure I sit at the dinner table at least 25 minutes, even if I have finished eating.

With that newfound confidence and organization, I soon made dinner for my family and a few friends. I prepared a simple stuffed chicken breasts recipe, good conversation abounded, and everyone seemed to enjoy themselves.

    While the guests retired to the living room, I quickly washed the dishes and as I scrubbed the last pan, I looked up at the clock with satisfaction. Progress was being made. There were still almost four hours to go before "The Tonight Show" came on.

60

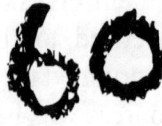

To See How Iranians
Live, Try A (Solo) Tour

The Christian Science Monitor, October, 26, 1999

As an adventurous traveler, I had fearlessly gone to South
Africa, Vietnam and Cuba without much worry. But when it came
to Iran, I approached things differently. With no diplomatic relations between the United States and Iran, and a presumed lack of
enthusiasm in Iran for Westerners and Americans in particular, I
decided it would be best to sign up for a tour rather than go alone.

So it came as a surprise after staggering off the plane in
Tehran at 1 a.m. and inquiring of my guide, "Where's the tour
group?" that he replied somberly, "*You're* the tour group."

I wondered if I should just get back on the plane. But I decided to stick it out — and I'm glad I did.

For one thing, there was my guide, Hassan, the curator of
the Archaeological Museum, was professional and very knowledgeable. And the sights we toured were beautiful. Just outside
of Shiraz, our first stop, we visited the incredible Persepolis and
climbed among Iran's most wondrous monuments built by Darius
the Great (550 – 486 BC). Nearby, we stood before the four Ach-
aemenid kings' tombs carved out of the cliffs. Our tour of Isfa-

han included a visit to the very long Naqsh-e-Jahan Square (Imam Khomeini Square) before we headed back to bustling Tehran, the capital. I wore shorts (the tour company — and Hassan – said it was fine), but women must be covered from head to toe.

Along the way, Hassan may have decided I was a very strange American tourist. He couldn't understand why I didn't want to see every last mosque, bazaar, and carpet shop. I did want to see those places, but I also wanted to see how Iranians lived. So we made a deal: I would sightsee with him in the morning, and after lunch I would explore on my own.

During my solo time, I went to the movies to sit with Iranians. (I couldn't find a theater with films in English or with English subtitles. The Animation Film Festival was the next-best thing). I went to malls and bookstores. I read English-language newspapers to see how the government saw the world. Then, I asked people if they believed what was written about in the newspaper. They spoke in English and were sometimes critical, but always looked around before commenting. I visited synagogues and talked to the congregants about how their lives were progressing. I always felt safe traipsing around. Iranians are very, very nice people.

I also took a lot of pictures — surprisingly freely — of unusual signs, women wearing chadors (the shroud-like garments that cover all but the face), the separate entrances for men and women and the "Down With USA" signs at the old American Embassy. All of which I couldn't have experienced had I been in a group.

I walked through cities with no destination in mind, poking my head into shops, smiling at people, hoping I'd receive a smile in return. I found that Iranians tend to be reserved in public, but I learned that behind closed doors the rules change: some drink and even use drugs. It seemed that from my informal poll of about 30 people that life under the shah was no picnic. The economy was better, but freedoms were stifled. After the revolution, there has been more freedom, but the economy is a mess. Neither government seemed to inspire much enthusiasm.

The trip went smoothly — until the last day. As I was

boarding the plane I snapped a picture of an intriguing looking sign: "Duty-Free Caviar." After I hit the shutter, I felt a hand on my arm, and a man who appeared to be a security official led me to an office. (I discovered later that generally you are not allowed to take pictures in foreign airports). Another serious-looking official wanted my film. I thought about not giving it to him (a crazy thought, as I had only taken five pictures) but reluctantly rewound it. They collected my passport and went into a back room. I looked at the clock: fifteen minutes before my flight was to leave. A few minutes later, they returned, handed me my passport, and off I ran to the plane.

When I landed in London, the first thing I saw was the same "Duty-Free Caviar" sign — right next to the one that read "No Photography." This time I kept the camera in the suitcase and thought instead of the past week: a lot of kabobs, pleasant weather (temperatures in the 50s and 60s in February) and nice people and sights. A super way to spend a week — it was particularly fun because I did it (almost) alone.

61

If Schools Could
Pick Their Students...

Newsweek, November 22, 1999

Critics of public schools have it all backward: we shouldn't let students pick their schools. We should let schools pick the students.

Let me cite a story — fairly typical among my teacher colleagues — to illustrate my reasoning.

A few years ago, a student I'll call "Jeremy" came to our middle school. He was disruptive and abusive to his peers, and he quickly became known throughout the school as a troublemaker.

The following year, in seventh grade, Jeremy was in my class. On the second day, the tall, lanky 12-year old let loose with a fusillade of profanity at the poor little girl to his right. I immediately threw him out of the room. The next morning I found a scathing letter on my desk from Jeremy's mother. In it she claimed I'd expelled her son because he "didn't have a pencil for class." Obviously, there was a communication problem here. A meeting was set up, the record was straightened out and the year went on more or less uneventfully.

In eighth grade, I heard that Jeremy continued to lie and be disrespectful. A couple of weeks after he graduated from our school, Jeremy's dad called me at home while I was having lunch. "We want to send Jeremy to a private high school. Could you write a recommendation?" I almost choked on my cucumber.

A recommendation? After all the grief he'd put me and my colleagues through? "He liked you," the father said quietly. And, in a way, I believed him. Jeremy did eventually settle down a bit in my class. His father probably asked me to write a recommendation because I was the only teacher he had a chance of persuading.

I grudgingly agreed, and a few hours later Jeremy and his parents were on my doorstep. They were on their way to Jeremy's interview.

"Oh, Mr. Schachter!" the mother cooed. "Thank you so much for writing this letter for Jeremy." This was from the woman who the year before had wanted my head for daring to discipline her child.

Smiling wanly, I promised, "I'll do what I can." Jeremy's dad handed me the school's questionnaire, and off they went.

I curled up in my big chair and looked over the categories from which I was asked to mark Jeremy from "outstanding" to "poor." "Performance as a student": I circled fair. "Scholastic ability" — fair. And then I paused. Uh oh. "Behavior," "Respect for others," and "Emotional stability." I looked up and down the form, but, alas, there was no "You've got to be kidding" box.

I read on. "Has any punitive action ever been taken against this student?" (I wanted to write, "On a daily basis? Hourly?") "Does the student have any exceptional abilities?" ("Yes, the ability to infuriate anyone he comes in contact with.")

The next day I called his prospective school and talked to the principal. I explained that I couldn't, in all honesty, write a favorable recommendation for this boy. "I understand," he said. "I just interviewed him and his parents." Jeremy, he said, showed no interest in the school or its program. His parents, on the other hand, spoke glowingly of his former school. When the principal pointed out the F's and D's on his report card, they pooh-poohed the marks. "He's a late starter," they said. After 45 minutes, the principal said, he had seen and heard enough. Jeremy was rejected.

I wish we could run our public schools like this. Schools, to me, are sacred and should be treated like places of worship. And teachers should be treated in a similar fashion. I once spent a summer teaching English in China. Every time I entered the classroom, students stood at attention. One child would bring me a cup of tea.

I don't expect standing ovations or a hot beverage each morning from my students, but it would be nice if teachers were treated with courtesy and respect instead of as doormats.

Students should be prepared for learning every day: they should be well-rested, fed and dressed properly. They should leave at home the baseball caps, the gum and the t-shirts with obscene messages. And at the end of the year, their teachers will evaluate them. Those who are hardworking and conscientious will be invited to return. The students who are disruptive will be sent to alternative schools.

Will this idea cure all of our nation's educational ills? No, it will not. There are many other problems. I think we have to do something about the inequities of school funding. I feel overcrowding should be eliminated and crumbling schools replaced.

These are problems that must be tackled. But first we must make sure that education is taken seriously. Letting schools pick their students would be the first step toward that end.

62

A Thank You
For Thank You Notes

Newsday, December 6, 1999

Even when he was wrestling with the world's problems, President George H. W. Bush found time to write thank you notes. Theodore Roosevelt did, too. And no less important a figure than Vivian Schachter, my mother, was — and remains — a big thank you note writer.

I remember, when I was a kid, Mom wrote thank-you notes to clerks, the mailman, the milkman, the sanitation workers and the school crossing guards. And, each June,nshe'd write my beleaguered teachers, thanking them for putting up with me all year.

Sadly, though, writing thank you notes has become a lost art. Dear Abby's and Ann Landers' columns are regularly filled with letters from distraught grandparents whose grandchildren have never acknowledged their gifts. And, at my school, I see a similar indifference.

We used to take our students — nearly 100 of them — on a three-day, two-night trips to Boston and Washington. When we teachers returned with our brood and staggered off the bus, dozens of parents would thank us and, invariably a day or two later, a thank you note would arrive in the mail. We appreciated that. But, in recent years, the busses have pulled in, the students have filed off, and parents would whisk them from the parking lot, with nary a thank you or even a goodbye.

So perhaps it's time we slowed down and start to think of others, to thank those who have been generous with their time and their deeds.

And we should teach our children to write thank you notes.

Indeed, says Judith Martin, who writes the syndicated "Miss Manners" column, the task should begin at birth, and the basic technique should vary only slightly through the years. "Miss Manners does not really expect the infant to thank the obstetrician for his efforts, though that would be nice," she notes dryly. "It is the parent who must be sure to associate the habit with parenthood from the beginning."

I agree and have attempted to continue the practice at school. I've tried to instill in my students the importance of writing thank you notes, although the results sometimes have not quite been what I expected. (After directing a class musical, I received a note signed by all my students which read, "Mr. Schachter, we want to thank you for your help and aggravation.")

Obviously, not all of them have to be somber missives. A few years ago, I sold an article to The New York Times. But, before it could be printed, a new editor came in, canceled the decision to print it, and sent me a "kill fee" check for $250. I wrote back, thanking the editor and urged him to "please reject more of my stories in the future!"

63

A Love/Grate Relationship

Newsday, February 1, 2000

Don't tell anybody, but I'm in love — with my food processor.

I must admit, however, it wasn't love at first sight. I had been resistant to buying one for the long time. First, there was the cost: nearly $150 for the machine. Second, I felt as if I would be betraying Grandma Schachter and all the other Schachters before me who chopped, minced, shredded, grated, sliced and pureed by hand. No easy way for those pioneers!

And, I was proud to continue this tradition — until last Thanksgiving. My cousin Gail was hosting for 12 relatives. My mother was making the stuffing, sister Marjie was bringing the creamed onions, and sister Louise the string beans. I volunteered to make carrot salad. A simple dish really: shredded carrots, diced celery, raisins, sugar, salt and mayonnaise.

On the Wednesday afternoon before Thanksgiving, I set out two packages of carrots and began grating them by hand. And grating them. And grating them. By 6 p.m. the sun was down, my right hand was getting raw and I still had five carrots to go. I finally finished, mixed them with the other ingredients and placed the completed product in the refrigerator.

The next day it was off to Gail's. Entering her apartment to a round of applause (the advance word on my carrot salad was very good), I lifted off the cover and proudly presented the dish to my dear relatives. As they peered in, "Ahhhhs" suddenly turned to

"Ohhhhs." My carrot salad looked as if it could comfortably feed three people. Everyone smiled benignly — and took very, very small portions.

Things had to change...

With the help of a very patient saleslady, I bought a food processor. Impressive-looking machine. It had a solid motor base, a work bowl, a cover with a large feed tube, a pusher assembly that slid over the feed tube, a sharp metal chopping blade, a serrated slicing disc, a shredding disc, a detachable stem that fit both discs and a plastic spatula.

All this to shred carrots?

At home, I set up the processor before me and lined up the various parts. In less than a minute I peeled the carrots, placed them into the machine, pushed the "on" button and ... voila! Nothing happened. I repeated the process. Nada. Removed the work bowl, returned the work bowl. Hit "On." Silence. Picked up the shredding disc — promptly cut my thumb. Off to the bathroom with bleeding finger. Found a Band-Aid, returned to the kitchen. Unscrewed everything, re-screwed everything. Hit "on." Nope. Unplugged the machine from the socket, plugged it into another socket, hit "on," and ... nothing happened.

Suddenly, I remembered a video that had come with the machine. I pushed the tape into the VCR. On the screen came a sweet looking lady named Beverly, but she wasn't particularly helpful either. Somehow — out of my view — she had aligned all the parts perfectly. When she dropped in her ribs of celery and tapped the "on" button, bingo! She had chopped celery.

I didn't know what to do. I gazed forlornly at my recalcitrant machine. I looked up at the screen at the bubbly Beverly now shredding cheeses and nuts and announcing, "And soon I'll be kneading 2 ½ pounds of dough in less than two minutes. And, you can, too!"

"Not me, Bev," I said wearily.

This couldn't continue. Something would have to change. I thought for a while and then did something that any self-respecting, self-reliant real man would do in such a desperate situation: I called my sister, Marjie.

"Heeeeeeeelp," I cried on the phone.

"Come on over," she said helpfully.

So, bundling up the food processor as if it were a sick child to be taken to the doctor, I drove to my sister's house. I set down the machine, she twisted the work bowl one way, adjusted the feeding tube and cover, popped the "on" button and vvvrrrrr, it worked! She dropped in the carrots and in less than a minute they were shredded.

Hooray! I had shredded carrots! I looked at her alignment and studied the way she had set up the machine. Thanking her, I bundled up my food processor and went home.

The next week, I prepared the machine for cucumber soup. Placed all the ingredients before me, set out the proper equipment, dropped in the cucumbers prayed to the gods of the three major religions, hit the "on" button and… it worked! And the soup was delicious.

From there it was on to chunky gazpacho! Crab cakes! Farmhouse hash! All fast. All very tasty.

Now six months later, I'm moving on. I've had my eye on this cute, sexy bread maker. If I bought it, do you think Grandma Schachter would understand?

64

In Any Language, Thumbs Up

Newsday, April 4, 2000

After spending six weeks teaching English in the northern Chinese city of Dalian, we 25 Americans, had developed a special fondness for our cooks. To show our appreciation, we decided to treat them to a "typical American meal."

Preparing a "typical American meal" there was no easy task. You couldn't run over to the local Waldbaum's and purchase what you needed. Instead, we had to scour the local markets. Fortunately, Dalian is a port city with a variety of Chinese and western foods, and we soon found that we had the ingredients for the evening's menu: salad, spaghetti and meatballs, garlic bread, apple crisp and beverages.

That accomplished, we returned to the kitchen to examine the facilities and divide up the chores. Bruce Mohs was responsible for the sauce, Jean Harper was in charge of the pasta, Steve Marineau took care of the apple crisp, and Carrie Sikorski handled the salad. I appointed myself supervisor and occasional interloper.

We soon discovered we were long on enthusiasm and short on utensils.

For example, Bruce had 12 jars of tomato paste, but they were sealed with wax. How to open them? He soon located a meat cleaver that did the trick.

Meanwhile, over at the pasta station, Jean was stirring the noodles in a large kettle with a coal shovel. She had developed a scooper by wiring a two-foot long bamboo handle to a large sauce pan.

While all this was going on, Bruce had acquired the services of an elderly Chinese man to regulate the heat on the coat stove by shoveling in coal and pumping the bellows from another room. A line of communication was established: If an American cook gave the thumbs up gesture, more heat was needed; thumbs down meant less heat was needed. This proved almost disastrous when Bruce, in a moment of gratitude for the man's efforts gave the thumbs up to the fellow, who promptly pumped the bellows and generated more unwanted heat. For this indiscretion, Bruce was banished to another room.

Meanwhile, Steven uneventfully baked the apple crisp, and Carrie quietly assembled the salad (alas, she couldn't find any lettuce).

During a lull, Jean put down her shovel and poured a bottle of China Red Wine into the sauce. "This," she declared triumphantly, "will really put the sauce into the sauce category!"

At 7 o'clock, dinner was ready to be served.

The honored guests — about 10 Chinese cooks — entered the dining room and sat behind their name tags on cloth-covered tables. Each table contained a basket of garlic bread and various beverages. A tape of classical music played softly in the background.

Brenda Marineau (Steve's wife), the youngest teacher at 25, began by offering a toast to peace and friendship between the American and Chinese peoples. A Chinese cook rose and responded with a speech that echoed Brenda's sentiments. Another cook stood and proposed a toast to Jean, probably our most attractive teacher. A third cook stood and proposed a toast to Jean. Before the next one could get to his feet to extol the virtues of Jean, we hurried through the first course.

The meal, needless to say, was a great success. Dinner was officially over at 9 p.m. (followed by one last toast to Chinese-American friendship and Jean Harper), and we thanked our guests for coming.

65

Poise, Style, Flashy Moves

Instructor, May/June 2000

After being a chaperone at school dances for 21 years, I've made an observation. Students today definitely have more poise that I or my contemporaries did back then.

I well remember my own seventh grade dances. About half the class showed up, and no one set foot on the dance floor for 30 minutes. Eventually, a handful of girls would summon up the courage to dance with one another. The boys either lurked in the bathroom or walked around with their hands thrust in their pockets, wondering when the whole painful experience would finally end. Usually, they made a token appearance at the very end of the dance and danced not with the girl of their dreams, who was out of reach, but with a "safe" girl – someone neither adored nor despised.

The seventh graders of this new millennium are different. Fairly soon after the music kicks off, nearly everyone is on the dance floor. And the dancing is terrific. For almost two hours, the energy and movement are nonstop. Oh, sure, there are guys who still circle the gym floor a hundred times before making a move, and an occasional girl who bursts into tears when she discovers that the boy of her dreams is a nightmare. But they're in the minority. Most of the students are there to have fun, and they do, dancing with numerous classmates — and even with their teachers.

Critics who complain that children don't know their history can't make that claim about music history. Today's youngsters are familiar with not only the musicians of the '00s (Celine Dion, Ricky Martin, Mariah Carey) but with the musicians of "ancient history" (the Beach Boys, the Beatles, Chuck Berry). They can Rock Around the Clock, Shake, Rattle and Roll, and Twist Again Like We Did Last Summer (how many people from the '60s — my era — can readily identify the music of the '30s and '40s?)

And they look smashing. Kids dress a lot better than they did 20 years ago — at least with the dress code at our school — and nowhere is that more apparent than at dances. The girls look like young Cinderellas in swirling dresses, balancing themselves precariously on high heels. The boys are impressive in neat suits and jackets. Some come with roses for their favorite girl. No bashfulness here.

My generation was indeed more sheltered — we didn't even know our teachers' first names, let alone how to dance with them. Not so today's kids, who are constantly exposed to a media without barriers regarding sex, language or values; who may contend with divorce or family problems. While much of their innocence is threatened, at the dance, at least, growing up is not so terrible. They are here to test out new roles, try on new costumes, and respond to music with enthusiasm. For me, a former wallflower, this change is a welcome one. Bring on the next dance!

66

Hello, I Must Be Going

Newsday, May 22, 2000

When it comes to parties, I keep thinking of that old Groucho Marx line: "Hello, I must be going."

That's because whenever I attend one, I'm usually the first to leave. It's not that I'm having a bad time. On the contrary, I usually love parties: good food, sparkling conversation, and interesting people — you can't beat it. But, I know when to go home.

At first, some of my friends took offense to my early leave-taking. "Aren't you having a good time?" they'd ask mournfully, offering more zucchini sticks and dip. "Everything was wonderful," I'd assure them. "I've just got to go."

I think it's a family trait. None of the Schachters can sit still for more than two or three hours at a time. We're active people: we skate, we walk, we bike, but we really don't sit. We couldn't survive living in Europe — leisurely two-hour lunches, sprawling three-hour dinners. Nope, in our homes, dinner is over and the dishes done in 45 minutes. We don't drink, we don't enjoy small talk, and no Schachter has ever stayed awake past 10 p.m.

Not only do I leave early, but unlike many others, I arrive on time. If the party is scheduled to start at 8 p.m., I'm there at 8 p.m. – usually alone with the host. This results in what seems like an eternity of idle chatter. I look around: Where is everyone?

I don't know how many times I've attended a wedding reception that's scheduled to being at say, 4pm and at 4pm, there I am sitting in my favorite blue suit, the sole guest, setting up tables and place settings with the waitresses and busboys. Where's everyone else? They were just at the ceremony an hour earlier, two miles away. Traffic isn't that bad. It can get frustrating.

One time I thought: why waste my time? I'll show up for a wedding reception fashionably late. My friend, Margaret, and her fiancée, Joe, were having their party on the Thomas Jefferson, a boat docked a 10-minute walk from my house.

At 3:30, I strolled — la-de-da — down to the boat. As I approached the dock, I could see the Thomas Jefferson. A majestic looking vessel, but, uh-huh, who did I see on the deck? It was — oh, no! — Margaret, Joe and all the other guests — all looking quite angry. "Where have you been?" asked Margaret, the not-so-happy bride. "We've been waiting to pull out for half an hour!"

I was stunned. I didn't know the boat was going to *leave* the dock! I mumbled some excuse and sheepishly joined the group. (And, since the boat would be bobbing about Hempstead Harbor for four hours, this was one wedding I couldn't leave).

So, since that experience, I'm never late for a party. But other habits don't change. When the hosts say goodbye to their last guests, I won't be among them — I'll be long gone.

67

Now Starring....
Murray Serether!

Active Times, May 2000

He's accosted Mel Gibson in "Conspiracy Theory," heckled John Travolta in "Primary Colors," and danced past Pierce Brosnan and Rene Russo in "The Thomas Crown Affair." But don't expect to see him up for an Oscar anytime soon. Indeed, you won't even find his name in the closing credits.

Murray Serether, of Glen Cove, New York, is an extra.

"You don't do this for the money," he says, laughing, of a job that pays $75 a day for 14-hour days. "But, it's been a great second career, even though a lot of my work never reaches the screen."

Serether's adventures began four years ago.

"My wife had passed away. I was retired, not doing anything," Serether says. "I saw an ad in The Jewish Week. They were looking for an 'older fellow' for a television commercial. I had always joked about doing television commercials. When I saw something on TV, I would say, 'Oh, I can do that. What's the big deal?' So I went for an interview, read the script, and they gave me two commercials right off the bat."

And, a new career was launched.

"My first commercial was for Imodium A-D," says Serether. "I was in the crowd at a basketball game, and this fellow was trying to get out to go to the bathroom. It took 14 hours to shoot. On TV, the commercial lasts about 30 seconds. If you look closely, you can catch me in the crowd."

Serether was then hired by a Japanese company that produces English lessons for Japanese living in the United States.

"I play a golfer named Mr. Rockefeller," Serether says. "I have a young wife and we play golf with another couple. I had about seven lines. It took four hours to shoot a 2 ½ minute commercial. They called me back for two more commercials. That was good — paid a little bit more."

Serether moved up to movies when he got a call from the casting director of "In and Out," the comedy starring Kevin Kline. "Got a tuxedo?" he was asked. He did, and one week later Serether was part of a crowd at the Academy Awards scene filmed at Lincoln Center.

"I was one of the movers and shakers in the movie industry," Serether says. "There were 1500 of us. A fun movie. Got to meet Kevin Kline, Tom Selleck."

As a youngster, Serether never felt the lure of the stage or the screen.

"I played in the high school band. Today, I go to movies, but I wouldn't call myself a movie buff," he says.

Although he's 72, the rugged-looking Serether lists the age range he can play as 55 to 60. "I'm fortunate that I have my hair, and I'm not turning gray yet," he says, smiling.

The look works well for such roles as a judge or attorney in the TV show, "Law and Order." In two years, Serether has appeared in eight episodes of the show.

"The agent would call me and say, 'Law and Order' needs an attorney. Wear a dark, navy blue suit. Carry an attaché case,'" Serether says.

He also appeared on television in "Dellaventura" with Danny Aiello ("a helluva nice guy"). Other performers he has schmoozed with include Mel Gibson ("friendly, but very, very short"), Tony Curtis ("we both came from the same part of the Bronx"), Emma Thompson ("a sweet lady"), and Michael Douglas ("not a friendly guy. His stand-in did all the work. Douglas came out, said his line and returned to his trailer").

Serether played a police officer in "Copland," with Sylvester Stallone; was in a bar mitzvah scene with 25 Woody Allen look-alikes in "Deconstructing Harry" and was part of any angry crowd that razzed "President" John Travolta in "Primary Colors" ("I was yelling, 'Get lost. Your mother takes numbers.' That sort of thing.")

His other film credits include "Meet Joe Black," with Anthony Hopkins and Brad Pitt; "China Coffee," with Al Pacino; and "Gloria" with Sharon Stone.

Serether is seeking to expand his resume.

"There is more money in commercials," he says. "That's my aim to get on a commercial. Something like Lou Jacobi as the Deli Man and the Cheese Man. I'd be good selling insurance on television or playing a doctor talking about HMOs.

"I'm looking for a TV commercial like Dunkin' Donuts' 'It's time to make the donuts.' The guy who did it just retired and he's traveling around the country now representing Dunkin' Donuts," Serether says. "That's my goal. Do one thing, have it run for 15 years, and get paid every time it runs!"

68

The Best Tastes Of Bermuda

Newsday, August 2000

In many restaurants in Bermuda, rather formal attire is required. Not so at Dennis' Hideaway in St. David's Parish. Indeed, if you arrive in a t-shirt and shorts, you might be overdressed.

Decidedly grubby — and proud of it — Dennis' Hideaway serves what may be Bermuda's best local food. For $32.50, you can order "the works," an array of dishes, including conch stew, mahi mahi (dolphin fish), herb-flavored shark hash, shrimp and conch fritters, and perhaps a bit of mussel pie. And, if you're lucky, bread and butter pudding might be tossed in for good measure.

Overseeing it all is Dennis Lamb, at one time a huge bear of a man but now somewhat physically reduced by the ravages of diabetes and circulation and heart problems. As he surveys his restaurant – a ramshackle pink frame structure with a scattering of picnic tables, most of them outdoor, and a few yapping dogs – Lamb says heartily, "I love cooking!"

He began at 13. "I was cooking at the government's biological station and then at 15 for the British army. I farmed, built bridges, but I always liked cooking. And people liked my cooking," he says. Lamb was encouraged to open his own restaurant ("Nobody in Bermuda does fish like you," he was told), and in 1968, Dennis' Snack Bar arrived on the scene. Word-of-mouth made his place a popular haven for the locals and the curious. And although it's far off the beaten track (St. David's is a 20-minute bus ride from St. George, which itself is a 45 minute ride from Hamilton, the capital), the famous and the not-so-famous have been drawn to this Bermuda treasure. "President Jimmy Carter found us," Lamb says. "John Wayne found us. People from all over the world. I've had them knock on my door at 2 in the morning and say, 'Mr. Lamb, we're hungry.'"

The secret to his success? "Just good herbs and spices."

Lamb was born in St. David's in 1925. "Until the 1920s there was no transportation in St. David's," he says. "Then a ferry service came in, and in 1937 St David's Bridge opened. Bus service started after that.

"Cooking was different then," he says wistfully. "We grew herbs, lived off the land and the ocean. We had tons of chickens, goats, rabbits, two or three cows." When he opened his restaurant in 1968, he had to sell everything. "Health inspector made us do it," he says.

But he maintained his garden. Indeed, cabbage for the coleslaw, beets, onions and peas that he serves come from his garden.

Lamb has been married twice. His first marriage (he was 19, she was 16) ended in divorce after nearly 30 years. Today he lives happily with his second wife, a mail-order bride from the Philippines he married in 1982 and her daughter, now 18. Since his illness, however, his first wife has checked in regularly on Lamb. "We all get along fine," he says, smiling.

Recently, Lamb turned over most of the cooking to his 38-year old son, Graham, known as Sea Dog (his six other children live elsewhere). On the day of my visit, I was the only guest, and Lamb and Sea Dog seemed happy to have company. (For the record, I had the delicious conch stew).

"People call for cooking advice," says Lamb. "I like the attention. And I've always like to sing for our guests. I haven't sung in a while since I got sick, but tonight..." his voice trails off. "Tonight I'm going to sing. At least, I'm going to try!"

69

A Teacher With
A Latitude Problem

Newsday, September 5, 2000

As a teacher, I've always tried to keep up with the latest technology — sometimes with unexpected results.

When video cameras appeared on the scene, I filmed my students reenacting *Washington's Crossing of the Delaware.* Pleased with the finished product, I invited an administrator in to observe the opening day presentation.

He came into the room, smiled at the young thespians and took a seat in the middle of the class. After a brief introduction, I slipped the tape into the VCR and voila! There was a very short George Washington urging his men on as they crossed the treacherous waters. It wasn't quite a scene out of "A Perfect Storm," but it was pretty effective. And then ... the lesson came crashing down when a student seated near the administrator threw up. (Did he get seasick?) As my students — a kind, thoughtful, helpful group — raced for the exits, it was left up to the administrator and me to try to comfort the obviously embarrassed student. As we put the room back in order, I turned to the administrator and said weakly, "Well, some kids react differently to my classes than others."

I didn't see him again in my room until four years later.

By then I was intrigued with computers. Not that I was particularly adept at it, mind you, but I was intrigued. I learned about the internet from our experts at school, and finally, on my own, I developed a geography lesson for my youngsters. It would be like a treasure hunt where students would perform a quest, surfing for the information I requested. The administrator — brave man that he was — returned to watch me teach another class. This lesson would count as my "yearly observation."

While I was happy to see the administrator back in my class, I was particularly worried about the kids he'd come to observe. They were extremely weak academically, most of them came from broken homes and a majority of them had emotional problems.

Undaunted, I plunged ahead. I was giving the students a lesson on how to measure lines of latitude and longitude. I used PowerPoint to present the material, slides flashing tantalizingly. I was a bit nervous, but everything was going smoothly. Then, the administrator in the back of the room raised his hand. "Mr. Schachter," he said gently. "I think you've got your latitudes mixed up with your longitudes."

"Huh?"

"What you've shown on the screen is backwards," the administrator said.

I stepped back and looked at the screen displaying my beautifully created PowerPoint slide. I scratched my head, but couldn't figure out what I did wrong. Suddenly, two students started explaining the correct way to measure latitude and longitude to me. One even came up to the front of the room. "No, no, Mr. Schachter," he said, taking the mouse from my hand and using the virtual marker to clarify the issue, "you do it this way." And he proceeded to show me.

I couldn't believe this scene. Here I was in the middle of an important lesson and I had fouled it up. Moreover, I expected these kids to make a snide remark like, "Hey, this guy doesn't know what he's doing" — and make me appear a fool.

But they didn't respond that way. They were helping out a guy who was in trouble. For the first time in years, I felt relaxed with an administrator in the room. The administrator put down his pen and watched.

When my students had finally explained to me what I was trying to teach them, I said "Ok, now I will give you this online activity and see how well you have learned how to measure latitude and longitude." But as soon as I said these words, it hit me again: Everything in the Web activity I had prepared was wrong. My questions were all based on my original incorrect assumptions. One student jumped to his feet and suggested ways his peers could straighten out my online activity. The administrator quietly got up and headed for the door.

"We won't count this one," he said smiling, as he left.

I sat back exhausted. "Whew!" I said, and looking over at my students — my dear students — I blew them a kiss.

70

To Invest Online,
Perchance To Dream

Newsday, November 29, 2000

When I was a kid, I had a friend who wanted to be president of the United States. Another friend wanted to play centerfield for the Yankees. A third wanted to star in a movie with Raquel Welch.

I had less lofty ambitions: I wanted to be a guest on "Wall Street Week with Louis Rukeyser."

I was totally intrigued by the show. First, there was my hero, Lou, whose hair was longer than my friends'. And then there were Lou's guests, those fellows (and occasionally, a woman) with aristocratic sounding names like Archibald Q. Bellingham, Reginald L. Huffington, and Arthur P. Wifflestoffer (to my pal Lou, they were Archie, Reggie and Artie). They all seemed to be millionaires or billionaires or zillionaires. And what I liked about them is that none of them seemed to work for their money. Lou's guests took their zillions and wrote a few checks (they called this "investing") and made more zillions! This was a show I wanted to be on!

But first I had to get through sixth grade.

It was September, 1968 and my teacher, Mrs McCarthy, a sweet, elderly lady, wanted to introduce her students to the stock market. She had us all contribute 50 cents each to buy a share of Reichhold Chemical (Mrs. McCarthy chipped in a quarter). The stock was selling for $11.25, and we are all pretty excited about the prospect of making money. My classmates talked about all the things they were going to buy with their stock market winnings: a Schwinn bicycle, new clothes, their own television sets. I, on the other hand, was dreaming of the first of my many appearances with Lou and Archie and Reggie...

We charted the stock's progress in the newspaper, and at graduation in June, 1969, Mrs. McCarthy announced that the stock was now selling for .... $11.25. We made nothing. Nada.

I was so disheartened that I stopped watching "Wall Street Week." Throughout my high school and college years I shunned *The Wall Street Journal*.

In 1981 I began teaching seventh grade social studies at North Shore Middle School, my alma mater. Like my colleagues, I put some money away each month in annuity. But they did more. They were involved in stocks and bonds and mutual funds. Some went into real estate. But I wasn't interested.

Then, on March 28, 1996 — in spite of all my efforts to avoid it — I turned 40. And, for me, it was a year of renewal. I resumed my old piano lessons that I had begun at 25 and ended at 25. I once again took ballroom dancing classes. I took computer classes. I baked a loaf of bread from scratch.

And I looked into the stock market.

I realized I was still curious. I read newspaper article. I occasionally leafed through *Business Week*. I learned from all kinds of sources.

And then I heard from a former student about buying stocks online. He encouraged me to contact Fidelity Bank. I did and spoke to "Frank," who told me to send in a check for $1,000 and set up an Ultra Services Account. The whole process was pretty easy. Fidelity sent me a password in the mail with which I was able to set up the online account. The fees, I discovered, were much less if I bought stocks on the internet as opposed to working with a broker. And I could bring up my account any time of the day on the internet and see what the value is at that moment.

It suddenly dawned on me: I had become my own Louis

Rukeyser! Who needed to be a guest on "Wall Street Week?" I started daydreaming about the possibilities of my own show: "Altamont Avenue Week with Saul Schachter." I'd invite Lou on the show! I'd have Mrs. McCarthy — who, God bless her, is probably 112 by now — as a guest! I'd double the number of escorts!

I sat back in my chair, closed my eyes and smiled. Life was sweet.

71

Why Would Anyone Want To Be A Teacher?

American Careers, Fall 2001

When I was in college, I was unsure whether I wanted to become a journalist or a teacher. After all, I had been an editor of our high school paper, wrote for our town's weekly and received an award for my work. But, I had also volunteered as a teacher's aide during my senior year and felt a pull towards education. However, after working as a summer intern at a major newspaper following my sophomore year, I made my decision: I would become a teacher!

My friends were baffled by my decision. Here I was working at a well-known paper, talking to famous people, and ... I wanted out?

This is what happened: I realized during my internship that the newspaper would was not such a glamorous one. The hours were awful. If a big story broke at 4:59 pm, you couldn't tell your bosses, "Sorry, I'm going home for dinner with my family." You had to stay. The pressure was incredible, there were lots of broken marriages, drug and alcohol problems, and not everyone got to cover the president. There were reporters covering school board meetings for 25 years – and they looked tired. The full-time newspaper world was not for me.

At the same time, I realized how much satisfaction I derived from working with children. Thus, a plan was hatched: I would pursue a teaching career and hope that I could write – but on a freelance basis.

So, I went ahead and earned my bachelor's degree in teaching. I secured a position at a private school and moved over to a public school until I received my masters. And, then, I was hired at my dream job — teaching social studies at my alma mater, North Shore High School in Glen Head, New York. After three years, I moved to 7th grade and have been there for the past 16 years. And, I love it!

I am very lucky: I am "self-employed;" that is I can teach whatever I want, in my own style, as long as I stay within the curriculum. And, I have the security of knowing I'll be receiving a paycheck every two weeks even if a lesson collapses!

As a teacher, I'm guided by one principle: Would I want to be a student in my own class? Toward that goal, I try to bring history alive, to have the students learn by doing. For example, when we study government, we turn the classroom into a model congress: students- as senators and congressmen- propose, write and vote on bills. I, as president, can sign them into law or veto them. Particularly controversial laws are examined by the Supreme Court (made up of nine students) who determine their constitutionality.

During our economics units the students run their own businesses, make money, lose money and some go into bankruptcy. During our law unit, students study famous cases and watch actual trials on tape for three weeks before we transform the class into a courtroom. Students portraying lawyers and witnesses — boys wearing suits and ties, girls in dresses — argue cases before a judge (yours truly in a long robe and gavel).

And happily, my students haven't changed as they've grown older. Last Christmas, Meredith Davids gave me a new bell for my bicycle. Jamie Penkower, now in college, calls me the night before school starts each year to wish me good luck. I feel fortunate to have attended many bar mitzvahs, bat mitzvahs, confirmations, weddings, second weddings and class reunions.

Teaching has been wonderful and the writing has not been neglected, either. Since 1980, I have sold 98 articles to *Newsweek, Family Circle, The New York Times, Newsday, The Washington Post,* and other publications. I truly have the best of both worlds.

72

A Housekeeper
Cleaned Up My Act

The New York Times, October 14, 2001

As a happy, contented, 44-year old bachelor who lives in a three-bedroom house, I recently did something I swore I'd never do... hire a housekeeper.

It was a tough decision. I had always been the type who had never felt comfortable having people work for me. For years I even was uncomfortable in restaurants because I didn't want someone serving me. At the end of the meal, my dates always had to restrain me from helping the busboys clean off the table.

Yes, I would hire a mechanic to fix my car because I'm not particularly handy. And, I have no problem bringing in an electrician to take care of the smoke that seems to be emanating from the wires in my kitchen. But hire a housekeeper? Pay someone to clean up after me? That was a tough one to swallow.

If I was ambivalent about this move, my family and friends were definitely not. That was because I could spend hours cleaning, scrubbing, dusting my home before guests arrived and the place still looked like a mess. I had to give in to the inevitable. It was time to make a bold move. It was time to hire Susana Ruiz.

She was a friend's housekeeper, a warm, always smiling woman. She emigrated from El Salvador to the United States 14 years ago and married Pancho, who was from Mexico. He is always smiling, too, and exudes just as much warmth. Having settled in a nearby town, they are now raising their two children there. After I made the initial inquiries, the couple stopped by to look over my house.

She did not speak English, but he did, so I communicated through him. When I explained that the house needed a complete overhaul, they nodded their heads vigorously. We agreed that she would work one day every two weeks for three hours. Because some things in my house needed immediate attention – the oven in the kitchen and the toilet, skink and tub in the bathroom — she said she would start with them. I gave her an extra key so she could let herself in while I was at work.

On the morning of her debut, I found myself thinking of Sam Levenson, the humorist. He once recalled that although his family wasn't rich, it was comfortable enough to hire a housekeeper, and that on the mornings when she was coming to work, his mother would rise early to clean up the house. She wanted to make the place look nice for the housekeeper. I found myself doing the same — scrubbing the oven door, fluffing the pillows and picking up the towels.

Then I stopped myself. After all, this is what I was hiring a housekeeper to do. I was becoming Sam Levenson's mother! I collected my briefcase, left the three hours' pay near the phone, placed a few goodies in the refrigerator and left for work.

When I came home that evening, the place was beautiful. The oven was spotless, and the bathroom sparkled. My bed was made, and the three dishes I had left in the sink were washed, dried and stored. Even a department store bag I had dropped on the living room floor was neatly folded and tucked away in the corner. I immediately called Mrs. Ruiz and relayed a message through her husband that she had done a wonderful job. I couldn't wait until her next visit to see what she would make shine.

I also soon found myself becoming a little tidier myself. For the first time since 1983, I started making my bed. Not only did I wash my dishes, but I dried them, too.

My friends and family were jubilant. More and more of

them wanted to come to my house, not to visit me but to meet the incredible Mrs. Ruiz. How did she do it? How did she transform the place? How did she transform me? These were amazing accomplishments.

Hiring a housekeeper was definitely the right move. I've become a new man. At restaurants I no longer feel obligated to help clean up after the meal. I don't wrestle with the valet parking attendants over my car keys. I let little old ladies help *me* across the street.

And, as I sit back in my big easy chair, a glass of wine in one hand, a can of Pledge in the other, I can't help but wonder: Can Mrs. Ruiz pull weeds?

73

Overreacting To 9/11

Newsday, December 3, 2001

Since September 11th, Americans have understandably been nervous about security. And nowhere is that more apparent than in the schools.

I teach in a district where most of our students are hard-working, well-behaved and a joy to be around. With caring teachers, our schools provide a comforting environment.

The World Trade Center attacks have changed everything. Since September 11th, our middle school has taken new security precautions. The entrance to the back parking lot is closed during the day after school begins so that all vehicles must enter or exit through the main entrance. All of the classroom doors that face our courtyard are locked. Visitors to the school must report to the office to sign in and receive a nametag.

But some parents are not satisfied. They want surveillance cameras, more guards, buzzer-entry systems, photo IDs, locked doors, keyless entries. And, ironically, in the same breath they say they want our children to feel secure and comfortable.

I understand their concern. In my daily personal life, I take security measures. I lock my car and house and leave a light on when I know I'm going to be home late. I avoid dark alleys. When I travel to Manhattan — a place I love — I leave my credit cards at home.

But I can't be locked up in my house. Indeed, since Steptember 11th, I've been to Manhattan more often than all of the previous year's trips combined (it's my own small act of defiance against the terrorists). A long time traveler, I am making plans for my spring and summer trips. I will be prudent (the hiking trips to Afghanistan and Pakistan are off), but just about every place else could be on the agenda.

And I really think it's far-fetched to believe that the terrorists are going to attack my little town. Whenever I give directions to visiting friends and relatives, they make it to my exit off the Long Island Expressway. But after that, they invariably get lost. Frantic phone calls follow and sometimes I have to hop into my car to rescue them. If my cousin Larry can't find me, I don't think Osama bin Laden and his crew will, either.

At school we want our children to be relaxed, and yet we're creating a fortress mentality. Students are no longer allowed to walk outside, past our fish pond and gardens, to reach their classrooms. For many, the only time they receive fresh air is at the 3 p.m. dismissal.

If I were in charge, I'd do the opposite: Unlock all the doors! Open the windows! Push the kids outside! Let them feed the fish! Sing with the birds! Make a pile of the leaves and … jump in!

Life is for the living. We should be vigilant, but we can't let the bad guys win.

74

Can A Jewish Man And Catholic Woman Find Love?

The Pittsburgh Post-Gazette, Thursday May 30, 2002

I always felt that I would marry a Jewish woman. I always wanted to marry a Jewish woman. But, after dating many, many Jewish women, I realized I always seemed to like their mothers better. And then I went out with Judy.

Judy (not her real name) was Catholic. I met Judy five summers ago during a 6-week program for teachers in Santa Barbara, but I hardly got to know her. A fellow New Yorker, she was an expert on Catholic theology, very sweet, and much respected by everyone.

A few times in the fall, we got together in New York City with another Santa Barbara alumnus. One day, I mentioned I enjoyed ice skating, and Judy said she liked it, too. We went ice-skating and had lunch and began seeing each other nearly every weekend.

Judy lived in the Bronx and taught at a "Second Chance" parochial school for tough kids. (She had a few sophomores who were eighteen years old). She had spurned offers of more lucrative — and less stressful — teaching positions. She made very little money and spent what she had on her friends and her adoring eight nieces and nephews. I called her the "Mother Teresa of the Bronx."

When we met, Judy and I were both 39 and had never married. I had lived a wonderful life. I had taught for almost 20 years in the middle school that I attended as a child and had had a successful "second career" as a freelance humor writer. I had traveled to over 70 countries.

Judy was the oldest of six children, all of whom had married. She said she loved me. And this was not a rash judgment on her part. She knew everything about me: the women I'd met while traveling overseas, the women I'd dated here.

After every weekend, she sent me a thank-you card which always arrived on Wednesday. If I asked, she said, she would marry me.

But I had concerns and felt awful about it.

First of all, she was Catholic, and although I'm not a regular at synagogue services, my faith is important to me. I would feel uneasy if my children were brought up Catholic. I would be uncomfortable having a Christmas tree in my living room. I realized that, with each passing day, I was feeling a stronger pull toward Judaism.

I also wished she shared my passions: movies, politics, '60s music. And I wished I shared her passions: theology, philosophy, ancient civilizations.

All that said, there were lots of pluses. Judy was very easy to be with. In the three years we'd been together, we knew everything about each other. She would have been very easy to live with, too. If I said, let's go rollerblading, she'd go rollerblading. If I wanted to go hiking in Nepal, she'd go hiking in Nepal. I, too, felt I was flexible. If she wanted to go to an art museum, I'd go. When her friend in Chicago became a nun, I accompanied her to the Mass and the activities that followed. It was really very nice and not a great burden, but Judy was very appreciative that I would do this for her.

She bought me sweet gifts: When the baseball season started, she got me a baseball book. On Chanukah, she baked a menorah made of brownies. She bought me bowls with the faces of the Flintstones, Bugs Bunny and my personal favorite, Tony the Tiger.

I had concluded that, after forty-three years of bachelorhood, I would not be an easy guy to live with. I had developed habits and foibles that would drive a future Mrs. Schachter crazy. I couldn't make coffee. I wouldn't spend a weekend redoing the kitchen. Not only didn't Judy not find these things offensive, she thought they were downright endearing! And she liked my humor (which, I knew, was not to everyone's taste).

Other positives: we were both low-key individuals. Neither of us was materialistic; neither of us smoked, drank, or swore. We could offer each other leftovers for dinner and be comfortable with it. We enjoyed reading the Sunday *New York Times* together. She said I was the only man she could trust.

But there was another problem. At 43, Judy's biological clock was ticking. I could be a father at 52, or 65 for that matter. (Although, when my child graduates from high school, I want to be able to remember the kid's name.) If we were 40, we could relax and date for years but we didn't have that luxury. Her ticking clock was not my responsibility, but I couldn't help but think about it.

I'd always felt that when I met the right woman, I would know it. With Judy, I went back and forth weighing the pros and the cons. This was not a way to decide on one's lifelong spouse. I've often wondered: Are there some people like myself, who perhaps, should never get married? My Jewish friends understood my hesitation about making a commitment. My non-Jewish friends all said the same thing after meeting Judy: "Grab her!"

On a Valentine's Day, I made my decision: I said goodbye.

That was more than 15 months ago. Since the breakup, I've often thought about my decision.

I liked Judy's family, and her dad would have been a terrific father-in-law. My family and friends were disappointed — they liked Judy a lot. Of course, so did I.

But while I was intrigued at first by our differences, as the relationship continued I had to admit that I yearned to be with someone who had similar interests and background as me. I looked at couples who have been married for 30, 40, 50 years and that often was the key to their successful relationship.

Still, I think of Judy and hope she is OK. I sent her a card when school resumed in September wishing her good luck, and last week I sent another one hoping she survived the school year intact. She hasn't replied. And I understand. I hurt her, and in situations like this a clean break is probably best.

75

Student Retention Is A Valuable Tool

Newsday, December 23, 2002

It was a decision implemented in 1996 in the Chicago schools. New York City schools adopted it and their new chancellor, Joel Klein, has embraced it. The decision: Ending social promotion of students and the retention — holding back — of those who do not pass required subjects. Now I hope it spreads to Long Island's schools.

As a 24-year classroom veteran, I truly love my students. But, when we turn out graduates who can't read or write or think, we're doing them a terrible disservice. They get out in the real world and fall apart. According to Lucille Cuttler, founder of Long Island's Project Literacy/Outreach, there are 20 million Americans who cannot read.

"And most of them received a diploma from high school," she says.

For the lazy, the combative, who do little or no work, I would favor retention. The reasons:

• A diploma should stand for something — that the student has successfully completed the work required.

•Retention should send a message to others in the classroom who might want to emulate their apathetic classmates: You, too, could be retained.

•And it would help keep standards and discipline in my classroom.

A few years ago I had probably my most difficult group of students. They were disruptive, belligerent, and wouldn't do any work. When I finally stood up in November and exasperatedly declared, "If you fail, there's a good chance you will be retained next year. The brash leader of the group stood up and said sarcastically, "Yeah, right. No one is going to keep us back." And he was correct. Critics who want to maintain the current system point out that students who are retained will suffer loss of self-esteem and that many will drop out of school altogether. I feel these are specious arguments. Self-esteem is gained through working hard and accomplishing a goal. You don't get any points for merely showing up. And, to those who worry about dropouts, it should be pointed out that many of them are skipping classes or school altogether. They already "dropped out."

New York has implemented state exams that students have to pass in order to receive their high school diplomas. But for many of our youngsters who have been promoted each year without mastering any skills, they will have little or no chance of passing them.

Unless they are retained – and helped – early. Retention is a valuable tool.

76

Don't Be Yellow: Smile, You Have The White Stuff

Newsday, March 7, 2005

I have worn glasses since I was in fourth grade and, despite my friend's pleas, never wanted to get contact lenses. I started losing my hair at 18, but never considered hair transplants.

But I have always hated my teeth — my yellow teeth (I was getting tired of sealing my lips during family photographs). So, recently I had "Brite Smile" treatments. (I rejected the "trays" you keep in your mouth for six nights while you sleep — sounded troublesome).

This was better.

Three 20-minute sessions (a fourth, if necessary) in one day. Mary, the dental hygienist, was ecstatic over my teeth: "So yellow!" she cried. "Much better than gray or black," she pointed out.

Mary took photos of my teeth, covered my face with dark glasses, put various contraptions in my mouth and began the three treatments. "Now, when we're done," she said, "you can only eat white or clear foods and drinks for the next 24 hours." She gave me a list afterwards.

I closed my eyes and thought of white foods: vanilla ice

cream, cottage cheese, sour cream, baked potato, chicken, cauliflower, milk. When I started running out of foods I thought of people: Vanna White. Perry White. Reggie White. Barry White. Buildings: White House, White Castle. And it was all so soothing.

After the third treatment, Mary examined my teeth and said, "It's almost there. How about one more treatment? I told her she could give me 10 more treatments if she needed to. She beamed and returned to work.

And so did I. Baseball teams: White Sox. Broadway: The Great White Way. Music: The Average White Band. But after almost 80 minutes, I started to struggle. Frank Lloyd White? The White Brothers? I don't think so.

Fortunately, Mary returned, withdrew all the stuff from my mouth and sighed, "They're beautiful!" She took pictures again and showed me the "before" and "after" shots. Quite impressive. My teeth were eight shades "whiter."

And all day I was smiling. A cop could have ticketed me for speeding and I would have smiled; my house's roof could have collapsed and I would have smiled.

For the next 24 hours I dutifully followed the food recommendations: Had yogurt and a banana (surprisingly acceptable) for lunch; that night had a dinner of chicken, cauliflower, and pasta with water. In the morning I dashed to the bathroom mirror to check on my teeth and breathed a sigh that they were still white (and still there). I proceeded to have breakfast of oatmeal, plain yogurt, banana and water. During those strict 24 hours, I felt like I was following a weaker version of Yom Kippur.

But it worked. My family and friends were impressed. My sister, Marjie, however, still thought there was room for improvement. "Those eyeglasses," she said disapprovingly, "went out in the 1980s. I'll go with you to get new ones."

I looked at her stern face — and flashed my new white teeth. She melted. "There's no rush," she conceded.

77

I Swear, Movie Vulgarity Is Just Too Damn Much

Newsday Aug. 15, 2005

When "Gone With The Wind" opened in 1939, a disgusted Clark Gable turned to spoiled-rotten Vivien Leigh and said, "Frankly, my dear, I don't give a damn."

Movie-goers were aghast. Did he just say, "damn"? Viewers complained. Church groups protested. But the offended word stayed and today it's part of movie folklore.

I miss those days. Have you noticed that no one says "damn" or even "hell" in the movies anymore? Oh, how I long for a "damn" or a "hell." It seems to have been eliminated from movie scripts.

"The Longest Yard," has, according to The Christian Science Monitor (which keeps track of these things), 130 four-letter words. The new "Bad New Bears" has 125, but the current champion has to be "The Devil's Revenge," with a (bleeping) 324 vulgarities. And, there is even a whole movie, "The Aristocrats," devoted to comedians telling the "filthiest, funniest joke in human history."

Why are so many films filled with vulgarities? To show

tough a character is? James Cagney, Edward G. Robinson and Humphrey Bogart never cursed, but they sure scared me. In fact, they scared the hell of out of me. Can you imagine Jimmy Cagney using a four-letter word? I can't even imagine him saying, "Damn."

Vulgarities add nothing to a movie. Indeed, they seem to be tossed in to get a rise out of the audience. They make a film slovenly, sloppy, distasteful.

As a movie buff, I see many films a year. And, although the best are as good as the best from 50 years ago, what most of the current ones lack is subtlety. I would love to see a crime picture without mindless violence, an adult drama without four-letter words, a sexy movie without explicit sex. Film language can be sexy without being offensive.

In 1944's "To Have and Have Not," when Lauren Bacall purred to Humphrey Bogart, "You know how to whistle, Steve, don't you? You put your lips together and blow," I got goosebumps. Still do! And from the irrepressible Mae West, "Too much of a good thing can be wonderful." Ah, Mae!

In recent years, three of the foremost practitioners of the "over-the-top, anything goes" filmmaking — David Lynch, Robert Altman and David Mamet — came out with "The Straight Story" (Lynch's), "Cookie's Fortune" (Altman's), and "The Spanish Prisoner" and "The Winslow Boy" (both Mamet's). They were well-written, intelligent, and, shockingly, they didn't have a four-letter word among them. After each film, I was so stunned the ushers almost had to help me out of the theater.

Now, I'm not calling for the complete elimination of strong words. If Clark Gable had instead said to Vivien Leigh, "Frankly, my dear, I don't give a hoot," it wouldn't have worked. But the original word was infinitely better than what directors today would have used in its place.

78

March Madness? Indeed, It Is.

Newsday, March 26, 2006

It's quite an event, "March Madness" is. It lasts nearly the entire month, with 64 college basketball teams vying for the nation's title.

They criss-cross the country, playing before packed arenas on national TV. CBS devotes hours to the tournament. The sports pages are packed with information and statistics.

Which leads me to wonder: When will these players attend class? Will they be studying physics on the bench during timeouts? Will they be arguing about the Protestant Reformation while practicing layups? I don't think so. Doesn't it bother anyone — their parents, their professors, university officials — that they are missing nearly a month of school?

Instead, they are playing in Dayton, Ohio; Greensboro, N.C.; Jacksonville, Fla.; Salt Lake City; San Diego; Philadelphia; Auburn Hills, Mich.; Atlanta; Oakland, Calif.; Washington, D.C; Minneapolis, and Indianapolis. And, this is just in March. Players at Georgetown University, for example, spent last October through February playing in Virginia, Oregon, Illinois, Georgia, Mississippi, New York, West Virginia, Indiana, Illinois, Wisconsin, Pennsylvania and Arizona. I wonder how much time is spent in libraries in those cities?

Don't get me wrong. I love sports. In high school, I played football, soccer, baseball, track, and basketball. I especially liked basketball, playing it into my early adult years. Although no one ever referred to me as "Air Schachter" (I couldn't shoot), I loved the passing, the defense, the hustling up and down the court. I appreciated the graceful play of others.

Today, I work out daily and avidly follow the New York professional teams. As a teacher, I encourage my students to play something — anything!

But, I don't support college teams. The whole environment appears unseemly to me. It would be nice if players practiced for a couple of hours after classes and had a weekly Friday night game. But that world disappeared long ago, if it ever existed.

Today's "amateur" college game forbids players from collecting endorsements, but it allows coaches to serve as hosts on television shows, incorporate their clinics and moonlight for companies such as Nike, which pays a handful of coaches between $120,000 and $200,000 yearly to distribute free shoes to their players. And, what happens to the players?

Many of the players weren't "college material" when they were admitted. And not only were they admitted, but many were given scholarships (blocking out deserving students who actually wanted an education). Only a tiny percentage make it to the pros. And the others? I shudder to think.

In the wonderful documentary, "Hoop Dreams," which followed the lives of two basketball players during their school years, there was a particular scene that drew great laughter from the movie audience. One of the high school players, a sad, inarticulate, lost young man, was asked what he wanted to major in at college. Head down, he mumbles, "Communications."

"March Madness?" Indeed, it is.

79

The Joy Of Junk Mail

Newsday, January 6, 2006

I don't like to brag, but I'm one of the most popular people I know. Just check out my mailbox and you'll see. It's overflowing with letters from banks, wildlife societies, hospitals-all inviting me to join their "family" (for a small contribution). Senior citizens want me, civil libertarians want me, farm workers want me. "Dear Mr. Schachter: You've been preapproved, selected, chosen, hand-picked." Two organizations say I may have won $20 million. And it's nice that they tell their friends about me. I once went on a trip to Israel. My acceptance letter was addressed to Sol Shockler. For a year, I received letters from eager organizations addressed to Sol Shockler.

Indeed, these folks are preferable to telemarketers who invariably interrupt my dinner or bother other members of my family. (My 76-year-old mother — whose father died in 1959 — was recently asked by a telemarketer, "Is your daddy there?" To which she replied wistfully, "Oh, I wish he were!")

No, I'll stick with junk mail. In an age when email has all but wiped out personal correspondence, I welcome these missives. But sometimes I think organizations get just a teensy bit confused.

During the Clinton administration, I received a letter from the National Rifle Association. I've long favored banning all handguns and have been a member of Handgun Control since its inception, so I must say I was quite honored to hear that the NRA wanted me to join. "Yours is a respected voice in the Sea Cliff, New York, area, Mr. Schachter. When you speak up, your elected officials listen." (Really? I've always had to vote for their opponents.) "We must stop Clinton." (I went to his inauguration.) The envelope contained a survey, and I dutifully filled it out.

"Do you think the government should have the power to limit the number ofguns you own?"

"Yes," I checked.

"Do you think the government should be allowed to store personal information on you just because you are a gun owner?"

"Yes."

"Do you think the government..."

"Yes! Yes! Yes!"

And so it went - and I mailed it in. (I wondered if I'd receive a Christmas card from Charlton Heston.)

My favorite letter came from an education company trying to sell me textbooks. I think the company picked up my name at a teachers' conference I attended. I remember writing down my name and position: Saul Schachter, social studies teacher. Evidently, someone felt it was a good idea to sort of merge those words because a few weeks later I received an invitation addressed to "Saul Stud." I kind of liked that. Saul Stud. I felt like trying it out on prospective dates: "The name is Stud. Saul Stud."

The letter began: "Dear Mr. Stud." I liked that, too. To my students I imagined me saying, "All right kids, show a little respect. From now on, it's no more 'Mr. Schachter' or 'Mr. S.' It's 'Mr. Stud.'"

That letter must have had the right effect. I bought 100 textbooks.

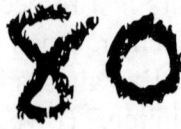

Turning Fifty

Newsday, July 7, 2006

As a society, we need to slow down. Department stores show their fall collections in April. Winter clothes clog the aisles in July. At the local pharmacies, St. Patrick's Day cards nudge the Valentine's Day cards off the shelves on Feb. 15. And half of my Sunday New York Times is delivered to my doorstep on Saturday.

Which leads me to wonder: Doesn't anyone want to stop and smell the roses? Obviously, we don't have time.

I turned 50 on March 28, but I was in no hurry to do so. I still ride my bike to work — the same one I pedaled when I was in high school. When I do drive, I never exceed the speed limit. I have three meals a day — eaten at a leisurely pace. I make sure I get eight hours of sleep and am told (by people other than my mother) that I could pass for someone 10 years younger. I was quite content to be 49.

But everyone else couldn't wait for me to hit 50. The AARP burst through first. It sent me an invitation to join my elderly brethren in September 2005 — when I was only 49 1/2! Birthday emails started arriving in late February welcoming me into my sixth decade.

A dear cousin sent me a Happy 50th Birthday card March

3. To be fair, she had me mixed up with Uncle Gerry, who turned 83 on that date. To make up for that lapse, she sent me two more Happy 50th birthday cards — reminders I didn't need. Despite the reminders from friends and geriatric organizations, I breezed into the final week oblivious to the changes occurring around me.

I was thrown off-balance when I awoke on March 28. My head was clogged, my eyes were itchy and my nose was runny. I knew that, as we age, our health declines, but I didn't realize that it happens *immediately.*

I recovered quickly, resumed my regular activities, feeling better about life, until the next day when the mail arrived: bills, a couple of belated birthday cards, and what's this? A brochure from Fay J. Lindner Residences — for assisted living. I couldn't believe it: AARP clobbers me six months early, Fay J. Lindner piles on the day after I turn 50. Stop the world, I want to hobble off.

In its pitch, Lindner wrote, "Elegant, private apartments, complete with tea kitchen, living and dining areas and full bathrooms, allow you to be on your own, but you'll feel secure knowing that you're never alone." And one of my future neighbors pictured on the cover looked about 97. Sigh.

Ah, life was so much simpler at 49. But, now, way ahead of schedule, I'm being pushed into senior citizenhood. Should I give in, move to Fay J. Lindner Residences and take up bingo? Sigh. Perhaps, I'll look up the 97-year-old.

Maybe she likes to bike ride.

81

Off The Beaten Itinerary

Newsday, August 13, 2006

As a teacher with many vacation days, I'm lucky to be able to travel extensively. But I hate talking about my trips when I get home.

It's not that I'm modest. When a friend asks how I liked visiting the Wat Po temple in Bangkok, Thailand, I smile but don't reply — because I can't remember if I ever saw the place.

"Wasn't Borobudur absolutely breathtaking?" a friend, Mary, asked me when I returned from Indonesia, while I scratched my head, ashamed that I had traveled 5000 miles from home and somehow missed the famous temple. Before I could answer, her husband, Barry chimed in: "The Borobudur is okay, but it doesn't compare with the Prambanan, does it, Saul?" Relieved that I had a choice, I made a fist and said adamantly, "No, it doesn't, Barry!"

Let's be upfront about this: I really am not interested in museums, churches, synagogues, mosques or ruins. And, pagodas? On two separate trips to China, having seen 23 pagodas (and probably some more than once), all I can say is "Pagoda, schmogoda."

For friends back home, I can put up a good façade, but it's wearing me down. Now I don't even send postcards for fear of the inquisition that will follow when I return. I gave my last slide show in 1982.

And, shopping? That endeavor ceased after my very first trip — to Africa — in 1976. I bought a large painting of an African village that my closest friends described as "ghastly" and a pretty native dress for my 4' 11" mother that was described by the store's proprietor as "one size fits all." It didn't.

I love to travel, but my interests are not the typical tourist's. I've taught English in China and Finland. I flew into Russia on a Friday evening and the next morning ran the Moscow Marathon. I worked as a volunteer at the Atlanta Summer Olympics and lived with families in South Africa. I took Swedish dancing lessons in Stockholm. These experiences I can remember. But they aren't what friends want to hear about.

My best defense? I spent a winter vacation in….Antarctica! It was wonderful. No museums! No art galleries! No exotic foods! When I returned, the inquisitors were ready. But so was I.

"Wasn't it bitter cold there?"

"No, in December, it's their summer. The temperature was in the high 30s, warmer than in New York. In July and August it gets down to 80-below."

"What type of wildlife did you see?"

"All kinds of birds: petrels, shearwaters, shags cormorants. Saw crabeaters…"

"Do crabeater seals eat a lot of crabs?"

"Actually, Barry, they don't eat crabs; they prefer krill, which are like shrimp. They filter them from the water using their cheek teeth."

A hushed silence falls over my audience. I've done it! My friends can't ask the usual picayune questions that usually trip me up. And I've gone on a trip and can actually remember what I saw!

I start to talk about why I prefer chinstrap to Adelie penguins and about the dramatic deterioration of the ozone layer over polar regions and how this could cause the world's oceans to rise with disastrous consequences.

I can't get myself to shut up. "And the albatrosses! Saw the wandering, royal, black-browed, the light-mantled sooty…"

I realize that maybe it's better for me to go to places that nobody else will ever visits.

I wonder if I can get a seat on the first flight to Mars...

82

Hating Autumn: I Want Spring!

Newsday, Nov. 25, 2006

Well, it's late November, it's 47 degrees, the wind is howling, and I'm still wearing my T-shirt and shorts.

I refuse to concede it's not summer anymore.

Call it autumn denial, call it autumn defiance. I don't know about you, but I'm not into this autumn business.

Colder weather, dark, dreary days, fallen leaves that require constant raking. Whose idea was all of this anyway?

And, what's with this turning back the clock so the sun disappears before 5 p.m.? Not in the Schachter house. The clock is staying right where it is. (Indeed, I'm thinking of moving it forward a few extra hours, so that the sun goes down around 8 p.m.).

And, there's another reason I don't like autumn: It leads right into winter, where things are only going to get worse: Colder weather, car batteries dying and the constant threat of snow and sleet and ice.

Nope, it's not for me.

It's not that I'm all that big a fan of summer (either the humidity or mosquitoes can wear you out), but I'll take it over autumn. First there's the food: So many wonderful vegetables and fruits: corn, zucchini, blueberries, strawberries and melons. There are free outdoor concerts. Trips abroad and domestically offer an exciting respite from the everyday stresses of life at work and at home. There is the promise of, quite literally, a beautiful day ahead (and a longer one, too).

Of course, there is such a thing as too much of a good thing: Years ago, I taught English for a summer in the middle of Finland, where the sun sets around 3 a.m. and rises around 5 a.m. Determined to "live like a Finn," I, too, went out hiking at 10:30 p.m., rowing at 1 a.m., frolicking with the girls in the lake at 2 a.m., until I realized — about three days into all this frivolity — that my body could not get by on two hours of sleep a night. Reluctantly, I began to turn in around 11 p.m.

Given a choice of all the seasons, I'd take spring hands down.

The sun emerges from its long winter slumber (as do my neighbors), the temperatures flirt around 70 degrees (good shorts-and-T-shirt weather), leaves decorate the trees (and stay there—not requiring any assistance on my part) and new flowers start to decorate the landscape. There is a sense of renewal, survival (we've beaten the fall and winter elements), of hope for the future. Unfortunately, in recent years, spring seems to have lasted only about two weeks.

So we're stuck with autumn. But I refuse to go down without a fight.

You, my friends, can be out there raking those mountains of leaves, shivering in your three layers of clothes, laboring under dark, threatening skies.

But not me. I'll be indoors in my T-shirt and shorts, munching on blueberries and strawberries (that I froze in August) forging ahead, happily contemplating that spring is coming.

83

Looking For A New Watch, With Thoughts Of Rosita

Newsday, February 17, 2007

When it comes to the electronic world, I refuse to join the 21st century.

Oh, sure, I have a DVD player, but I don't subscribe to cable, don't care for TiVo and have no use for a cell phone. And, I don't have a BlackBerry — or a Strawberry or a Boysenberry for that matter, either.

Regarding wrist-watches, I want a simple time-piece. Unlike my friend, Jared, whose watch has the capability to receive news, stock information, weather and sports scores, I want a watch that simply tells me the time.

Which mine did until the day I was leaving for a trip to England.

Without warning, it died. I went down to Radio Shack and told the clerk to sell me a watch, any cheap watch do. He picked out one from the shelf. It looked nice, it worked, the price was right — $7.99 — but he said, "It speaks Spanish." I wasn't sure what that meant, didn't really care, so I bought the watch and left.

Well, that night I was boarding the plane when suddenly

a strong female voice, without any warning, made an announce-ment: "Son las ocho de la noche!" Everyone jumped. I looked around wondering what was going on when it suddenly dawned on me that the voice was coming from my watch and was announcing the time in Spanish (it was 8 p.m.).

And, it proceeded to do this every hour.

In the beginning, it was kind of cute (I called it "Rosita," but she got on my nerves and everyone else's who received the "Rosita Jolt" (bewildered victims responded as if they were on "Candid Camera"). I enlisted the help of others, but we couldn't shut her off.

After arriving in England, I suffered from jet lag, but not Rosita. Every hour on the hour, she alerted the world to the time. (It got so bad, I found I was going into crowded places at 7:02 and 8:11 and 9:06, so others were not subjected to this).

But, finally, miraculously, Rosita went dormant. No more hourly announcements of the time. Life proceeded as before. And, then on a Friday night, I was at the movies when at 9 p.m., my long-comatose Spanish-speaking watch suddenly announced the time. The woman in front of me wheeled around to glare at me, so I wheeled around and glared at the woman behind me. She looked horrified, holding up her hands in protest.

This proved to be Rosita's last hurrah.

It's been three years since I had Rosita. I still don't have — and have no desire for — TiVO, a cell phone or an ATM card. But, I must admit, I miss my Spanish-speaking watch. It definitely had personality. Maybe it's time to go back to Radio Shack and buy a new one.

I wonder if they have a watch that speaks French.

84

Black, White And Read-
Well, By Someone!

Newsday, November 7, 2008

> *Were it left to me to decide whether we should have a gov-*
> *ernment without newspapers, or newspapers without a govern-*
> *ment, I should not hesitate a moment to prefer the latter.*
>
> - Thomas Jefferson

Every since I was a child I have loved newspapers. In elementary school, I brushed aside the teacher's attempt to get me to read *My Weekly Reader*. Give me *The New York Times* or *Newsday*, I said. I want the real thing! From 3rd grade to the 6th, I produced my own student newspaper. (Indeed, my obsession with newspapers interfered with my daily chores. My parents gave up asking me to take out the garbage because I'd always stop to read the newspaper beneath the bag and never make it out the door).

Today, whenever I travel around the U.S. or abroad, I always purchase the local paper to get a pulse on what is going on in town. What's doing in Des Moines? What's new in London? And, then after reading about them, I join walking tours, attend lectures — it makes me better understand a community.

"Newspapers," wrote Charles Lamb in the early 1800s, "always excite curiosity." I agree, but it seems few others seem to.

A recent report revealed 23 percent of Americans get their news from the David Letterman, Jay Leno or Jon Stewart. The

Center for the Study of the American Electorate reported that only 7 percent of the U.S.'s 18-24 year olds (a large percentage of the Leno/Letterman/Stewart audience) voted in the 2004 presidential primaries and that an estimated 30 million voters in the 18-30 age group did not vote in the national election. And, this indifference seems to extend to older adults as well. In my own survey of fourteen families on my block I discovered that only three others receive a daily newspaper.

It's a sad state of affairs.

We, the richest nation in the world, are producing a population of ignoramuses. According to the most recent Zogby poll, only 40% of Americans know that we have three branches of government and can name them. Fewer than half of all Americans know who Karl Marx was or which war the Battle of Bunker Hill was fought in. And, we don't read newspapers — and, we seem proud of it.

"I don't have time to read a paper," a friend (a teacher!) said to others at lunch recently before she launched into a review of all the television reality shows she saw the night before.

"There's nothing in it I am interested in," another added.

I was stunned. When my newspaper arrives, I'm like a kid let loose in a candy store. Should I begin by reading the amazing news about the deciphering of the genetic code or zip over to the story on the big change in Mexican politics? How about the report on early posters of flight at the National Air and Space Museum? The health benefits of eating tofu? The fellow who ran 3200 miles in fifty-seven days across America to raise money for charity? Wow! That's just in today's slim edition. The massive Sunday paper? That's Christmas, Thanksgiving, and the Fourth of July all rolled up into one! (And, I get the pre-printed sections from the Sunday paper on Saturday because, well, I can't wait!).

After the Declaration of Independence was signed in 1776, Benjamin Franklin announced, "A republic!" And then, turning to the other delegates, he warned, "If you can keep it."

Words we should heed as we elect our next President.

85

Getting My Students
To Bike Ride

NEA Magazine, Feb. 2008

At a party recently, I was escorted over to meet a young mother.

"Hello, I'm Saul..." I said, starting to introduce myself.

"I know who you are," the woman smiled. "You're the one who rides a bicycle!"

I had to pause. I'm the one who rides a bicycle? I never thought a bicyclist would be considered an oddity, but it's true. I draw quizzical looks from my 13-year old students when they encounter me for the first time on my Schwinn.

"Don't you have a car?" they wonder. And, I guess it's not a surprising question. The only bicyclists they have probably ever encountered are some of the poor South American immigrants that work in the area. Their teacher isn't poor, why is he on a bicycle?

It's a question that is probably only posed in the United States. In Europe, a continent with a high standard of living, many people ride bicycles. Early in the morning, men in their suits and women in dresses, pedal off to work. Perhaps the high cost of gasoline encourages them to opt for "pedal power," but I think not. They enjoy riding.

I do, too. I live only a mile from school. So, I ride my bike. I can arrive at my destination in twelve minutes, ten — if I make all the stop signs. I ride because I like to stay in shape and I enjoy the activity. After a hearty breakfast, I love getting out in the brisk mornings, pedaling through my neighborhood to school, my brief-case balanced on the handlebars. I wave to my friends preparing to leave for work and to the intrepid walkers, hoping to shed a few pounds, shuffling briskly through town.

But, when I pedal through my community — a community in which I was born and raised — with its well-manicured lawns and tall trees, I wonder: Where are my students? Why aren't they biking?

Oh, I see them.

But, they're waiting at the end of their driveways for their parents to drive them to school — and some live only five blocks away! (By the time their parents emerge from their house, they could have walked to school!)

And, once I'm at school, refreshed and eager to start the day, I look at my students and sadness overwhelms me: Many of them are so lethargic. I find each year they're growing increasingly overweight. For some of them, getting out of their chairs requires a major effort.

I'd love to say, "All right, kids, put away your history books (That would draw a loud cheer or two). We're going bike riding."

And, off we'd go! Through our own Sea Cliff and its magnificent Victorian homes! To Planting Fields to admire the flowers! To Roslyn to feed the ducks! And, for the great finale, we'd pedal off to Baskin Robbins for a scoop of ice cream! (If it had been a particularly grueling ride, we'd reward ourselves with *two* scoops!).

We'd laugh, we'd sweat, we'd enjoy each other's company. And, at the end of the day, no need to call Mom and Dad: We'd find our own way back!

86

School's Out For Summer, And So Am I

Newsday, June 28, 2008

I hate to admit this, but as a teacher I feel guilty about having my summers off. My free time in the summer has always made my friends a bit envious. I travel to exotic places, read books, swim, play tennis and bike ride, but I feel sort of miserable about the whole thing. I feel that I should be out there earning a living with everyone else. I put in a lot of hours during the school year (occasionally more than what the average worker puts in during the calendar year), but when the summer rolls around and people go trudging off to work, I feel guilty.

Now, I don't let on to others that I feel awful about my situation. My friend stopped by on his way home from work and from his car asked how my day had been. He was perspiring profusely, his tie was undone and his eyes were blinking. "Well," I said glumly, "it was rough. I got up this morning at 10 ... watched "General Hospital" and strolled over to the beach where I practiced my backstroke. Giggled with the female lifeguards..."

My friend sped off.

Sometimes, I actually do get frustrated that all my friends work during the day. I ring their doorbells and find there is no one

276 | Saul Schachter

home to come out and play tennis. I could ask the lady who lives behind me, but she's 85 and speaks only Russian. I could pester the 74-year-old woman down the street, but she's in excellent health and I'm afraid she'll beat me.

So, I've played tennis in the evenings when they return home and have gone to movie matinees where the average age of the audience is about 9.

I don't mind standing in line for a movie, but when you are surrounded by individuals who are 2 feet shorter than you, you feel like the kid who was left back three times in elementary school. In fact, on two occasions, I've run into former students in line who have wanted to know if we could all play stickball after the movie. I would love to, but at that rate, by the end of the summer I'd be looking for a prom date.

One summer, though, guilt overcame me and I applied for and was hired to do odd jobs at my synagogue. I didn't need the money, but my conscience told me I should do my part.

I moved tables, stacked books and, when my supervisor asked me to clean out all the weeds and poison ivy, I enthusiastically complied. After all, I had never gotten poison ivy before. I was immune.

I was wrong.

The next day, I was covered from head to toe. My temporary job was no longer temporary. I was confined to home. I had spent four days at the synagogue, two weeks scratching, and nearly my entire paycheck went to pay my doctor's bills.

I returned to my lounge chair, picked up my novel, poured a fresh glass of iced tea, wriggled into my slippers, and didn't once contemplate going out---even to mow the lawn.

87

Going Face To
Face With Facebook

Newsday, August 15, 2009

It all started innocently enough.

I received an invitation from a childhood acquaintance to join Facebook and be her "friend." A bit hesitant at first — I was, after all, involved in a very happy monogamous relationship with email — I complied. And, went off on vacation to explore Greenland.

When I returned a week later, I turned on the computer and discovered there were 127 individuals who wanted to be my "friend." My head glowed (and not because I'm bald). Look at all those people who want to be my friend. Suddenly I felt like Bill Gates at a pauper convention!

I wrote back to one person, Danielle Forbes, a delightful former student whom I hadn't seen in twenty years, apologizing for being tardy in my response. "I was in Greenland," I explained.

The next day, I awoke to find congratulatory messages ("Wow! Greenland!" "Send photos!") from 27 friends, 15 former students, and three total strangers who I think might have been from Azerbaijan.

Hmm... How did this all happen? It appears, unbeknownst to me, that my little personal message was read by Danielle.....and a lot of other people (I quickly learned how to send messages to one person).

Being on Facebook has been an amazing experience. Long-lost friends, parents of those long-lost friends, relatives, and students (some who never spoke in class) have "friended" me. It's refreshing to see them all, regardless of age, wanting to be a part of this new community. And, I've enjoyed the news they've shared: A job promotion, another who beat a serious illness, children's successes ("Ashley is having her first piano concert next week," "Justin spoke his first words today.")

In between announcements, I look over the list of my friends' friends — and am amazed at all the folks we have in common. I check out former student Anne-Marie Aulicino, now at the University of Madison-Wisconsin. The affable Anne-Marie has 897 "friends" and upon examining the names, it appears she's buddies with practically the whole state! Some, I must say, have more impressive "friends" than I do. Danny, who went into the entertainment business, lists Al Pacino, Mick Jagger, and Keith Olbermann, among his friends. Hmmm... I wonder if I could trade him my cousin, Harvey, for one Mick Jagger (And, I'll throw in my Aunt Beverly to sweeten the deal).

Alas, the problem with Facebook is that it can be addictive. I can sit literally for hours at the screen and every two minutes there is "news" from someone, somewhere.

I'm not sure if I will stay with Facebook. Some of the announcements I get: "I think I'll take a nap today" or "Wonder if it will rain" are time-consuming to read and draining. I might quit and go back to the easier world of e-mail.

But, first, I want to hear how Ashley did in her piano recital!

The Face
Looks Familiar, But...

Newsday, October, 2010

They say that life is a journey — but sometimes I want to pull off the road! At 20, I started losing my hair. When 30 came, I noticed some gray in the hair I had left. At 40, I needed bifocals. And, three years ago, at 50, I started forgetting the names of former students.

That's okay, said my friends. You've been teaching for over thirty years, you've had a few thousand students, it's understandable. But, no, I responded, I was doing fine until I hit 50. Yes, there are some students from say, 1986, whose names I can't recall. But, I'm having trouble remembering the names of students I had LAST year.

I teach 7th grade and in September when I see those former students in the hall as 8th graders and they say sweetly, "Hello, Mr. Schachter," I'm baffled. Is that Kira? Jennifer? Danielle? "Hi, girls," I smile lamely — and then go scurrying off to find the school yearbook.

Recently, I was in a local insurance office when a young woman come running in, eyes filled with glee. "Mr. Schachter!"

she cried, throwing her arms around me. I stepped back, looked at her, trying to find a clue, a hint, anything. Sensing my confusion, she said helpfully, "It's me, Lindsay!"

"Lindsay!" I cheered. "How are you, Lindsay Pegrum?"

"No, it's Lindsay SEIDER."

I was immediately deflated and embarrassed.

This Lindsay — whom I had had a few years earlier in class — was no anonymous, blended-into-the-woodwork student. She was one of the all-time most wonderful kids. I felt so bad I sent her a note of apology.

And, this obliviousness just doesn't occur with my students. I have the same problem with my colleagues. In the past three years, we've hired so many new teachers, I can barely keep up with their names. And, they are so young. (I think the average age of the faculty is now about 15).

But, fortunately, in that first year, most of them seemed to be named Jessica. The second year brought a wave of Michelles. It took me awhile, but I was able to learn their names.

But, then they did something that I really can't forgive them for: they went out and got married. And, took their husbands' names! Jessica Berner became Jessica McKinney (I think). Jessica Hoffman became Jessica McNeill (I think). Jessica Glass became Jessica Stime (I think). I was grateful for Jessica Donovan. She married Miguel Ortiz and... remained Jessica Donovan. Bless you, Jess!

And, what's going to happen when I hit 60? What malady will strike me then? Oh, I'm worrying too much. Maybe I'll go see our school psychologist Richard McKee. Or is it Roger McKee? Rex McKee?

Sigh. Life was easier when I was just losing my hair.

89

Bonding With My Niece

Newsday February 19, 2011

As a bonding experience, I decided to go to the movies with my niece, Jenny, for the first time. She's 5. She wanted to see "Ramona and Beezus." I preferred "Flickan Som Lekte Med Elden" (a Swedish thriller).

We were at an impasse.

Reluctantly — and to keep peace in the family — I gave in (I could see "Flickan Som Lekte Med Elden" on my own and Jenny, I reasoned, would probably have a tough time with the subtitles)

We had a good time, but I'm just not used to little, little kids. I'm 54, single, no children. Jenny, daughter of sister, Marjie, and brother-in-law, Rick, is the only grandchild and niece in the family.

I'm more comfortable with older ones. For over thirty years, I've taught 7th graders. I like them a lot. I can reason with them. They get my jokes. They can tie their own shoelaces.

My problems with the way-under 13 set, I guess, began during my childhood. When I was 5, and Marjie was 3, we were playing at a friend's house. I fell out of a tree and lay on the ground writhing in pain. "Go to Mommy and Daddy!" I cried to Marjie. And, off she went. I waited....and I waited. Perhaps I should have directed her to "Bring BACK Mommy and Daddy!" for I never saw Marjie again. I lay there for a long time. When it started getting dark and I gave up hoping a search party would find me, I struggled to my feet and staggered home. Walked in the front door and, to my dismay, discovered no one knew I was missing. Marjie had forgotten to tell my parents. (Turns out I had a broken wrist. It healed faster than my psyche).

I've since forgiven my sister and want to be of assistance to her and Rick. But, I'm all thumbs around Jenny. She doesn't seem to care about the Yankees and has little interest in politics. But, I have noticed Jenny likes to draw. And, she is helpful to my sister — always offering to carry the dishes to the sink. When she sees a crying child, she offers gentle support. Jenny, I can see, is turning out nicely — and I'd like to be there to help keep her on track.

So, maybe Jenny and I can duplicate the nice day we had. I wonder if there will be a "Ramona and Beezus" sequel. Perhaps Jenny would like to go with me.

And, this time, I'll pay.

90

Grade 7 More Fun
On Second Try

Newsday December 30, 2011

In 1969, I entered the North Shore Middle School in Glen Head as a 7th grader and in 1984, I re-entered North Shore Middle School as a seventh-grade teacher. And, I've discovered, I'm having more fun the second time around.

I have danced with dozens of girls, gone ice-skating, roller-skating, traveled to Boston, Washington, and Philadelphia, attended seven bar mitzvahs, six "Nutcrackers" and served as a skinny Santa Claus.

But, it wasn't this wonderful the first time around.

As I can testify, one of the most difficult things in life is to be 12-years old and in the seventh grade. I remember my first day in Middle School quite vividly. Most of my classmates were strangers. I was naive. When everyone started off to their first-period class after homeroom, I panicked: Where was everyone going? (I had come from a self-contained elementary school class and had never heard of switching classes). Getting only a 75 percent on my first Social Studies test was a traumatic experience. Occasionally an 8th grader would taunt me, and I didn't know how to fight back effectively. I didn't develop a sense of humor until, oh, about 10th grade. And talking to girls was a bit beyond the realm of possibilities.

284 | Saul Schachter

But, now, forty-two years later, things are a lot easier. I know where to go after homeroom. Most of my students might initially be strangers to me, but I get to know them by the end of the first week. No one picks on me in the hall. And girls find me more appealing at 55 than they did at 12 (when they ask me to dance at the 7th grade party, I graciously accept, rather than make a beeline for the bathroom).

These youngsters are on the cusp of becoming teenagers, but still maintain their adorableness. Once, in late January, when for some unknown reason, they decided to announce how much they weighed, the roly-polyish Sam Horowitz announced, "128 pounds." When his stunned, lighter classmates looked at him, he explained sheepishly, "I'm still carrying a little extra holiday weight."

Often the boys (who are half the size of the girls) stroll up to my desk for a chat. There we are, looking each other right in the eye (except they're standing and I'm sitting), discussing whatever is going on in their busy little minds.

But, I guess what I particularly enjoy hearing is what they do outside of school. Jenna Scott organizes fashion shows for autistic children. Aspiring singer Mac Ayres recently performed before 25,000 spectators at the U.S. Open. Nimmi Gandhi is studying her third language.

I, too, am making a name for myself after the 3 pm bell. Unbeknownst to me, I've become a hit on YouTube (During our study of the Roaring '20s, a student surreptitiously filmed me teaching my students the Charleston. At last check, "Mr. Schacter (sic) Dancing" has received over 1400 views). From the Charleston, it was on to the Hustle as I joined eleven other teachers (six couples) in our school's fundraiser, "Dancing with The Teachers." My partner and I spent hours perfecting our moves and had a lot of laughs in the process. Although we didn't win the competition (sigh), we hope to be back next year, perhaps doing a salsa.

I hope I never graduate!

91

Don't Overlook
This Great Name

Newsday, May 18, 2012

The Social Security Administration's survey of the most popular baby names for 2011 was announced on Monday and incredibly, amazingly, Saul didn't make No. 1 on the boys list. Saul didn't make the Top 10, either, and was nowhere in the Top 300. (Actually, it was 396.)

Things have to change. I think it's time for a new leader. It's time for Saul!

And, I'm confident it will happen. Of the Top 10 most popular names for boys, six — Jacob (No. 1 for the 13th straight year), Ethan, Noah, Daniel, Michael and Alexander — are found in the Bible. Saul, too, is in that august book. Admittedly obnoxious, Saul was a brave king in the Book of Samuel. In the New Testament, Saul of Tarsus had a vision and stopped persecuting Christians.

Other Sauls have made their mark. Saul Katz is a co-owner of the Mets. Saul Bellow was a great novelist. There were lots of TV comedy writers named Saul (decades ago, Saul Ilson wrote for the "The Smothers Brothers Comedy Hour" and Saul Turteltaub provided laughs for "Sanford and Son" and "The Carol Burnett Show").

Saul Rogovin pitched for the Baltimore Orioles in the 1950s. And in the movie "Ocean's Eleven," when George Clooney was assembling his team, he knew he needed one more talented person, an elderly con man played by Carl Reiner. "We need Saul!" he said triumphantly. "We need Saul!"

Checking ussearch.com, I happily discovered many Sauls — and, better yet, 13 Saul Schachters — in the United States. Of 12 with ages provided, all of them — except me — were listed as 86 or older. (Another reason to name your child "Saul." Many of us live a long time.)

My grandfather was my family's original Saul Schachter, and I'm proud to carry on his name. But as much as I like it, I'll grudgingly concede it's not easy being a Saul.

For one thing, no one believes it's your name. "What was that?" people say. "Did you say your name was Paul?"

And if they don't say Paul, they say something they prefer: "Nice meeting you, Sal," or, "It's a pleasure, Sol."

Even my beloved maternal grandmother had problems with the name. As luck would have it, I have a cousin Paul in Commack, and when Grandma was in her 70s, she'd call me Paul, and him Saul. Paul and I were bemused by this. My grandmother died in 1970 and at family reunions, in her honor, I address my cousin as Saul and he calls me Paul.

At any rate, although Saul's rank has slipped recently, in the long view, its popularity is rising. In the past century, according to the Social Security website, Saul ranked as low as 700th in 1944 (it was World War II and I'm embarrassed to say even Adolf and Benito ranked slightly higher). But 57 years later in 2001, Saul stood at a robust 278.

Seeing Saul atop the list of most popular boys names might take awhile. But there is reason for hope. Ava was No. 953 on the girls list in 1990, but is now No. 5! If Ava could jump 948 places in 22 years, Saul, too, can make a similar ascent.

I can be patient. After all, we Sauls live a long time!

92

The Italian Suit
I Found For $25

Newsday, October 2012

It was a Saturday afternoon, the third day of a four-day sale. The store advertisement had promised a "Spectacular" sale on suits: "50% off on regular prices; Then subtract another $50." After gulping down lunch, I was there, elbow to elbow, with grown men looking for bargains. Skinny guys, fat guys, guys with tattoos, sweating under the hot lights. Most of the suits cost $450, which made the final cost $175. I was looking for an American suit in gray or brown (I already had a blue suit). I wanted to avoid the tempting Italian suits. I had purchased one last spring. It was very stylish, but my friends pointed out that it really didn't fit me, and besides, I looked like a gangster. So, no Italian suits for me.

I looked through the 40s, interspersed with the 41s, 42s, 43s, and 44s. I saw one brown suit: 40 jacket, 33 pants. My size. And, then I looked at the price: $150."

There it was, printed on the label — not handwritten: $150. I ran the figures through my head: After knocking off 50%, plus another $50, my suit would cost $25!

I took a deep breath and looked furtively around, feeling like the person with the winning lottery ticket, but who doesn't want anyone to know. I shouldered my way up to the front of the counter and asked the clerk about the price. Glasses perched on his nose, he looked down at the price and then up at me: "Yes," he said almost solemnly. "It will cost $25." I couldn't believe it. I said, "Please ask him, too," motioning to the other clerk. Clerk #2 looked at the tag and nodded: "Twenty-five dollars."

Incredible. I looked at the label: 90% wool, 10% polyester. "This is real wool, right?" The clerks nodded in unison.

"Twenty-five dollars!" I said again. "I could pay for this suit in cash!"

And, yet I felt guilty about the whole thing (Not surprising, when you realize this is coming from the guy who returned to Waldbaum's supermarket after realizing he was never charged for a cucumber). I shook my head: $25 for this suit? I said to myself. Shouldn't I call the designer and alert him to this situation: "Mr. Alfini (yes, this was an Italian suit), you're going to lose money on this deal. I'll pay an extra $100 so you can stay in business."

But, I didn't.

My next step? I decided to try the suit on.

And, it fit. And, it looked good. It looked damn good! Saul Stud!

But, as I was examining the suit in the mirror, I started to sweat: I couldn't find the price tag. I checked the jacket, checked the sleeves. I couldn't find it! In a panic, I took off the suit, and there it was on the sleeve: $150. Whew!

There was no time to dally. I returned to the checkout counter and paid for the suit. I made sure the clerk removed all those tickets and gadget-like things from it. (I didn't want to be stopped at the door by the security guard, demanding to see my receipt. "$25 for an Alfini? Yeah, right. OK, buddy, up against the wall and spread those tapered legs").

I thanked the clerk profusely and said, "I'd like to look around for some more things." I made a cursory check of the remaining suits and then sidled over to the sports jackets, shirts, and ties. And, a funny thing happened. After paying $25 for a suit, everything else looked wildly expensive. Eighteen dollars for a tie? Ninety dollars for a sports jacket! You've got to be kidding!

I headed for the door. As I bid a final farewell to the clothes, I came upon Clerk #1. "Did you find anything else?" he smiled, almost conspiratorially. I shook my head. "Nope," I smiled and feigning a touch of disgust, added, "Looked all over and couldn't find a $4 sports jacket." And, with that, I marched out the door.

93

School Bells
Will Toll, But Not For Me

Newsday, August 29, 2014

I always thought I would teach forever. Or close to it. I figured that on my last day on the planet, I would have a class of seventh-graders on the edge of their seats listening intently to my spellbinding description of John Adams' Alien and Sedition Acts when I'd suddenly keel over and the custodial staff would be summoned to carry me out (which would be fitting because I've always liked dramatic exits). But it was not to be.

I remained upright (much to the relief of my family) and I retired on June 27 after 35 years of teaching, the last 30 at the North Shore Middle School in Glen Head. It was a wonderful ride, but it was time to go. It seems as if I was at North Shore forever. I grew up in the community, attended its schools, and after teaching two years elsewhere, I was hired by North Shore the day before school started — and never left. And I can't help but feel that many in the community have been cheering me on. I remember my first "back to school night" vividly.

After I outlined my plans for the year to parents, a 50ish woman approached me and said, "You gave a nice talk, Saul. I'll tell your mother."

In the beginning, I was often teaching the children of my

friends, and I quietly followed these youngsters' progress with interest (I felt like "Uncle Saul"). In recent years, I've taught the children of previous students. Over the decades, I've been happy to attend their bar mitzvahs, dance recitals, weddings, christenings and even a few brises.

I'm often asked how students have changed over the years. The interesting thing is, they really haven't. They are still innocent (most of them), generous, sometimes exasperating, but ultimately delightful. When I announced in late May that I was retiring, they all burst forth with suggestions. "Mr. Schachter," said one hopeful boy, "maybe next year you could be my bus driver." Another girl pointed out, "Now that you're retiring, you'll have more time to find a girlfriend." And a sea of 12-year-old heads nodded approvingly.

And now for the first new school year since 1979, I am not setting up a classroom, attending summer meetings or perusing student reports.

So, what will I do? Well, I will travel more. I just accompanied my mother, a vigorous 84, to Paris. In November, I am taking a cruise from Brisbane, Australia, to Papua New Guinea. And for six weeks over the winter I am renting an apartment in California where I will be among a dozen friends enjoying 60-degree (maybe 70!) temperatures away from the New York snow, sleet and ice.

And then what? I don't know. Perhaps, I will teach English in northern Thailand for a few weeks. A friend who teaches sick children has suggested I join her at Stanford Hospital near San Francisco. And I've considered working in a summer English program for refugee children in Dallas. Who knows? Maybe in my own quiet way — with time off for a good book and maybe some piano lessons (I've always wanted to learn) — I *will* teach forever.

Or perhaps I'll drive that school bus. The possibilities are endless!

94

I Fled Long Island
This Horrible Winter

Newsday, March 24, 2015

When I retired in June after 35 years of teaching on Long Island, I decided to spend the winter in sunny Carlsbad, California.

I was a little nervous about it because although I'd traveled extensively, I've never lived off Long Island. I grew up in Glen Head, and at 27, I bought a house in Sea Cliff, two miles away. Two addresses. That's it! Never had an apartment, lived in a dorm (I commuted to Hofstra University) or even slept in a tent.

Now I was taking a big step and renting an unseen apartment 3,000 miles away. Would I feel out of place? Would I survive? My fears were allayed my first day in Carlsbad when the real estate agent handed me the key to my studio apartment, a cute little place right on the beach, and said, "Welcome to Paradise!"

Indeed, it was — gorgeous magnolia and eucalyptus trees, pretty shops, tidy streets and what seems like a million bikers, joggers and surfers. I think I saw maybe three chubby people. Strangers smiled at me on the street, saying hello, as if they knew me. (In the beginning, I turned around to see whom they were talking to.)

And, I haven't even mentioned the weather — 68 degrees and sunny. Every day. (No need to get a weather app in Carlsbad). So, without hesitation, I became a Californian. I had a library card, I frequented the Mexican-run bagel shop, I read the local edition of the San Diego Union-Tribune and I shopped regularly at Albertson's supermarket, where I schmoozed with Miguel, Edna, Sumner and the rest of the staff.

Each night, I watched the local news, which always seemed to lead with a car chase. (Given that traffic in California is as bad as in New York and in some areas, worse, I couldn't figure out how any car could be involved in a chase.)

And I walked everywhere. People told me when I left Long Island that I would need to rent a car. They were wrong. I walked to the supermarket and the library. I walked to the weekly International Food Festival on State Street. I walked 3 1/2 miles twice to Trader Joe's. (It was, of course, 68 degrees, the sun was shining, the birds were chirping and I never noticed the distance.)

For day trips to Encinitas and Oceanside, I took the bus (only $1.75 each way). For downtown San Diego, I hopped aboard the Coaster train ($5.50 each way).

And in the evening? I was second on line at the Jewish Film Festival, where I think my presence doubled the Jewish population of Carlsbad, a predominantly Christian community.

I attended a play written by sportscaster Dick Enberg and posed for pictures with the author and with basketball great Bill Walton and football's John Brockington. I went to a lecture by author Joyce Carol Oates and took a selfie with her.

Other advantages: the Grammy Awards, the Super Bowl and the Academy Awards were all on TV three hours earlier than on the East Coast. When I was teaching on Long Island, the Oscars would end after midnight on Sunday night and I'd get only six hours of sleep. I require at least eight, so I'd be a mess all week. During my time in California — and I have re-booked for 2016 — I was fully aware of the snow and ice and cold back home on Long Island, and so I didn't post pictures on Facebook (didn't want to rub it in). But as I drifted off to sleep each night to the sound of the waves crashing on the beach, I thought maybe next year my family and friends can join me.

It would be nice to welcome them to Paradise!

95

Retirement?
Yes! But What Day Is It?

Newsday, June 6, 2015

When I began teaching at my alma mater in 1981, I was the "baby" of the North Shore High School faculty. Veteran teachers gently teased me that I should be taking classes, not teaching them. I liked the attention. And, then, in what seemed like the blink of an eye, as I neared retirement in June 2014, I was one of the oldest. New teachers called me Mr. Schachter instead of Saul. Wasn't crazy about that!

It's amazing how life comes full circle. Now that I am retired, I am back to being the baby.

I joined the Glen Head Gold Coast Library on a trip to the New York Botanical Gardens in the Bronx. I'm 59, but the average age of the participants seemed about 75 (I think even the bus driver was older than me). In November, I was the youngest at my first teachers' retiree luncheon. It was surreal. There was my fourth-grade teacher. At another table was my middle school football coach. Coming over to greet me, my sixth-grade math teacher. I felt like the clouds had parted and I was in North Shore Teacher Heaven.

Unlike some colleagues, I've adjusted well to retirement. I remember my dad happily proclaiming shortly after he retired from Grumman Aerospace, "Everyday is Sunday!" And, indeed, he is right. Not bound by the school calendar, in late November I took a cruise from Australia to Papua New Guinea. To avoid the brutal New York winter, I spent six weeks in sunny California. And, in April, to get my "teaching fix" (it never leaves those of us who loved the classroom), I taught English and math at the St. Constantine's International School in Tanzania to help prepare the students for their Cambridge International Exams.

Upon my return, I planted my first vegetable garden: tomatoes, green peppers, zucchini. (As of this Saturday, there was no sign of life, but I remain optimistic!)

So, how has my life changed? Well, now I shave only every other day — and if I don't anticipate seeing many people during the afternoon and evening, it's every third day. With no need to wear dress shirts and pants on a daily basis, my annual dry-cleaning bill went from more than $400 down to $12. I am now able to read the entire Sunday New York Times before the next Sunday's edition arrives. I take cooking classes and try out new recipes on my courageous family. I can accept invitations to parties and tickets to Giants football games on Sundays, when in the past I would wave them off with, "Sorry, I have school tomorrow. Have to prepare lessons!"

On the negative side, without the rhythm of the workweek and school year, I lose track of days — and sometimes months. I've missed friends' birthdays and anniversaries. Sigh.

But retirement is good. I recommend it. Although I miss teaching and the happy chaos of my classroom, I've discovered there is life after North Shore and beyond New York.

I am off to the Toronto Film Festival in the fall and hope to do some volunteer work, perhaps overseas, later on. I don't know the exact schedule yet, but it's OK, I'm flexible. As my father said, "Everyday is Sunday!"

96

Newly Retired, But Still A Creature Of Habit

Newsday, December, 2015

When I retired last year after 35 years as a schoolteacher, my friends and family encouraged me to make changes in my life.

"Stay up late!" urged my cousin.

"Get a cellphone!" cried a friend.

"Buy a new car!" crowed my mother.

Alas, I had always been a creature of habit. I would go to sleep at 10 pm and wake up at 6 (even in the summer). I didn't have a cellphone.

And, my Honda Civic — well, I bought it new in 1998.

So, I set out to change things, but it's hard.

It would be so nice not to wake up before sunrise. However, in order to sleep late, you have to go to bed late, and I just can't. In fact, things are getting worse. I watch "Jeopardy!" every night at 7 (yes, another habit), do some reading at 7:32, and by 7:34 I'm dozing off. It's a struggle to stay awake. If I make it to 9:30, it's an incredible accomplishment. I stagger off to bed, fall asleep before my head hits the pillow and sleep soundly until 6. When I wake up, I'm *wide* awake. Off I go to the YMCA in Glen Cove, where I swim, lift weights, cycle. After a shower, it's home for a hearty breakfast at 8:15. By 8:45, I'm ready for my nap. Not good.

Perhaps I'd have more luck with a cellphone. Since I spent much of last winter in California, I bought one to use just for sending and receiving phone messages. I made a few calls, but by the end of the first week, I hadn't received any (which was, admittedly, a little sad).

Then, one day, I was walking down the street and I heard a female voice purring from my hip pocket. A call! I whipped out the phone, but there was no one there. And, then it dawned on me — the sexy voice had come from a passing bus. Sigh. (I had never gotten a call before and only later did I realize that my phone should ring, not speak to me.)

As the months rolled along, I did receive some calls, and I was glad I made the purchase, if only to have a phone in case of emergency. Then one day, while removing socks, shirts, and underwear from the washing machine, I spotted a shiny object: my phone. My beautiful cellphone. My soaking wet, totally useless cellphone.

Moving on, maybe it is time to buy a new car. My Civic was 17 years old. The paint is peeling, but it only has 50,000 miles (I ride my bike a lot). We've had a happy marriage. And, then one day, the car wouldn't start until the third attempt. Oh, no. The problem persisted. Took three tries to get it going. On Day 4, I realized what was wrong: I was out of gas. Or nearly out. The needle had veered all the way to the bottom. I filled the tank and haven't had a problem since. But, perhaps this was a sign that it is time to get a new car.

Maybe I'll go to the dealership tonight. After "Jeopardy!" If I can stay awake.

97

Facebook Message
Shows How Small World Is

Newsday, May 2016

It was just after 9 p.m. I was messaging on Facebook with my friend, Dania, when Lisa, a friend of Dania, jumped in with her own message. Here is our unedited exchange. (Last names omitted.)

LISA: Saul — are you related to Henrietta ?

SAUL: Yes, I am. She is my aunt!

LISA: My aunt too!!!!
I'm her great niece!!!! Her sister was my grandmother!!!!!!!!!!

LISA: HI COUSIN!!!!!!!!!!!!!!!!!!!!!!!!

DANIA: This is absolutely amazing!

SAUL: Hey, Dania --- Can you please step aside for a second?!? This is a private conversation!

LISA: LOL ... We are cousins through Uncle Sam then!!

SAUL: So, Lisa, we are cousins?!? Yes, Uncle Sam! Sam Goldberg, right???

LISA: No .... Sam Schachter.

SAUL: Oops ... We've hit a bump.

LISA: LOL — Now what would be even funnier is if we WEREN'T cousins but had all the same names.

SAUL: It's very possible. Who was Henrietta married to?

LISA: Sam Schachter. He was a doctor. I feel sad now.

SAUL: Nope! My Aunt Henrietta was married to Herb. They lived in New Hyde Park. Herb was the brother of my father, Melvin. Both men are gone, but Aunt Henrietta is living, though with dementia.

LISA: Awww .... I'm sorry to hear that. My Aunt Hen passed away some years ago. She was fabulous. We are now ex-cousins .... LOL

SAUL: So, I won't be seeing you at Passover then???

LISA: Sadly, nope.

SAUL: Well, to paraphrase the line in "Casablanca,": "We'll always have Dania!"

LISA: That we will!!!

SAUL: It was nice meeting you!

LISA: Same here!

SAUL: Dania: You can come back in now.

DANIA: But now I must spend my night researching genealogy to see if you are distant cousins.

SAUL: Yes, there still is a chance! Never say never!

98

Frustration In
The Keyboard Of Life

Newsday, July 2016

Frustrated by the smudges, gook, and dirt on my computer keyboard, I finally said, "Enough!" and decided to clean it. I had put it off for too long.

Cognizant of my friend's directions — "Be careful!"— I turned off the keyboard, barely moistened a small piece of paper towel, and started cleaning each tile, gently, calmly, so that no water seeped in between.

When I was done, I resumed typing a letter to a friend, but then I noticed something odd: No "w" appeared on my screen. I tried other keys: The number 1 and the exclamation point didn't come up, either. I tried all of the others — and they worked!

So what to do? Initially, I decided to forge ahead. I wrote to my friend, Heather, who the week before happily informed me that she had earned her Black Belt in Krav Maga — despite coming down with the flu. I explained why I didn't get back to her earlier and then offered my sympathy and good wishes: "Tried ashing my keyboard — not ise. Sorry you got sick. Get ell soon. And, congrats again on inning your Black Belt. hen I ander into a back alley, I ill call you." Not the smoothest response, but I plunged on anyway. For other correspondences, I decided to avoid words that contained a "w" or "1" or "!" I substituted "terrific" for "wonderful"; "desire" for "want." Instead of "!," I pasted a smiley face.

And, I figured out a way to use an occasional "W." If I typed, "ashington," for example, spell-check would produce "Washington." I would then delete "ashington" to leave a "W" — a capital "W," however — and then finish the word. But, I couldn't get around "1." Intent on meeting a friend at 12:45, I wrote, "See you at a quarter of one." When he asked for my phone number, I began writing the area code, "5-One-6." Not good. Finally, I gave up. I called the Apple Store in Manhasset and spoke to Romaine, who I discovered later was actually living in Ontario, Canada. For forty-five minutes, Romaine, patiently and slowly guided me through a troubleshooting process. From Ontario, he would circle things on my screen. He drew arrows. It was like he was in the room with me — and that was scary (I had this feeling he was going to tell me I had a peach skin stuck in my teeth).

And, in the end....nothing worked.

I thanked Romaine for his help (resisted making a lettuce joke) and drove over to the Apple Store. There, a nice fellow named Brian, sat me down and heard my tale of woe. "Here's what we can do," he said finally. "Buy another keyboard, but keep trying to use the old one." He then removed the "w" tile and the "1" and "!" (same tile). "The keyboard might dry out after a couple of days and be functional again. If that happens, you can return the new one." I thanked Brian for his assistance and returned home.

But, after two days, the "w" and "1" and "!" failed to appear on the screen. I connected my new keyboard to the computer, made sure everything worked, and I was back in business.

I wrote to my friend, Heather, about my new keyboard, and I noticed a smudge. On the "B" tile. Instinctively — and without thinking — I got up to moisten a tissue. But, then I caught myself. I'll leave it alone. I like smudges.

99

Help Me, Honda

Newsday, November 2016

When my 1999 Honda Civic conked out earlier this year on Glen Cove Road---just turned itself off without warning---I felt it was time to get a new car. But, it wasn't easy. Just as people have a tough time saying goodbye to loyal pets, so it was with me and my once shiny-green automobile. We were together nearly 20 years and never had an argument. It had only 52,000 miles because I used it mostly locally, and I rode my bicycle to work each day. But its paint was peeling and everything else started to go. Unlocking the front door was frustrating. I'd twist the key and the lock would pop up, but then drop again. It would usually open on the third attempt. My battery died in 2014 and the radio petered out. The owner's manual told me to press a series of buttons to fix it, but I had no luck. I didn't want to spend $600 for a new radio so I drove without enjoying my oldies station.

I did research on new cars, talked to friends, and settled on two finalists, both of which were very impressive. It was like voting for Miss America: The runner-up looked pretty good, too. Then I decided the winner would be a new... Honda Civic!

Why? I was comfortable with that model, it had a good track record, they offered me $750 for my old car (I would have taken ten bucks) and I could drive it off the lot the day I bought it. The new car's "Modern Steel Metallic" (silver/gray) color drew raves from friends, but it took me awhile to get used to the vehicle, my first new car of the 21st century.

Looking at the accessories, I felt like I'm Rip Van Winkle awakening in an age of incredible technology — including a radio that not only worked, but identified the songs. My oldies sounded better than ever! However, the key fob that controls the door locks and pops open the trunk took getting used to. After buying the car, I unlocked the door, drove down the highway toward my house, gazed in the rearview mirror and saw that my trunk was open. Not a good start. I pulled over onto the shoulder and shut it.

After about five months, the vehicle still has that new-car smell, which ranks right up there with new-baby smell.

I hope I am not being overprotective. Before climbing in recently, I felt the urge to take off my shoes. At CVS, I parked next door in the Starbucks lot because I felt it had a smaller chance of getting hit. When I went to the supermarket, I left my place on the line to go out to the parking lot to make sure the other cars weren't picking on mine. When I mowed the lawn, I moved the car down the street first to avoid spraying it with clippings. I've done everything but burp it.

Then one day, my worst fears were realized: I emerged from the YMCA to discover a scratch on my door. Oh, no! I was crestfallen. Then, with the key fob, I tried opening the door. It didn't open. I tried opening the trunk. Nothing moved. Then I realized I was standing next to the wrong car. I looked around: Lots of silver cars in this parking lot!

I strolled up the aisle and found mine. It was easy to locate: It was the only car with its trunk open!

100

8 Ways We Can Improve Presidential Elections

Newsday, November 25, 2016

If there is one thing Republican and Democratic voters can agree on after this exhausting campaign, it's that our electoral system is broken. Our presidential election cycle is too long, moneyed interests control politicians, and nothing gets done in Washington.

So, here are eight ways we can clean things up:

1. Eliminate political parties. Before they came to dominate the process, George Washington could see that political parties were a disaster: "However [political parties] may now and then answer popular ends, they are likely in the course of time and things, to become potent engines, by which cunning, ambitious, and unprincipled men will be enabled to subvert the power of the people and to usurp for themselves the reins of government, destroying afterwards the very engines which have lifted them to unjust dominion." To which I add (and I think George would approve): Let everyone run as an independent, not beholden to political parties that often try to sabotage each other.

2. Shorten campaigns. Cut them from nearly two years to two months. If Australia, Britain and Canada can elect leaders in four to six weeks, we can, too.

3. Have one national primary. The current system is terrible and unfair. Why is New Hampshire's primary first? Why does New York go near the end, when my vote may be meaningless? I suggest Sept. 1 as the National Primary Day, with an Oct. 1 runoff vote to narrow the field to two candidates. Hold Election Weekend on the first Saturday and Sunday in November.

4. Ban public donations. Contributions — especially large ones from corporations and unions — can lead to corruption. Government-financed elections are the way to go. Give each candidate $5 to $10 million to run his or her campaign.

5. Ban TV political ads. England has done so because the ads tend to muddy political discourse. Today, the candidate with the most money can dominate the airwaves with no worries of rebuttals.

6. Limit presidential candidates to those who have served as vice president, in Congress or as a governor. Too many candidates are unqualified. You wouldn't hire your letter carrier — as nice as he may be — to perform heart surgery. While it's democratic to let anyone run for office, the presidency is serious.

7. Drop the Electoral College. Keep it simple and meaningful: One person, one vote.

8. Term limits. If we can limit a president to two terms, we can similarly curtail terms in the Senate (two) and House (four).

Last fall, I was in Toronto and watched Canada's campaign for prime minister. Three well-qualified men debated for 90 minutes on TV. They were respectful and didn't resort to name-calling. I hated to see it end! Shortly thereafter, Canada voted. We can emulate the Canadians, the Australians, and the British!

101

Teaching English
To Immigrants

Newsday, November 2017

After retiring from teaching thirty-five years in the North Shore Schools, I "downsized" and agreed to teach English to immigrants at the Glen Cove Library two nights a week. It's been a joy!

We started with three students, got as high as ten, but now we've settled on the "Fabulous Five." They range in age from 23 to 65, one young fellow from Peru among a sea of women. They've arrived from El Salvador, Honduras, Colombia, the Dominican Republic, and Peru.

With one exception, they are married, have children, and are working. Their responsibilities leave them with little free time, but they make an effort to come to our class. We talk about their hopes, their desires, their dreams. And, they always make me smile. I remember the first day when I asked them about the most surprising thing they discovered after coming to America. Isabelle, from Peru, thought for a moment and then said, "You Americans all stop at red lights!"

Another woman, sitting to my right, patted my hand recently, leaned in close and whispered, "You have great passion for me." Now, she was an attractive lady, but our relationship has been strictly business. I wasn't envisioning us running off to Paris together. Then, it hit me. She was saying, "You have great patience with me."

One student, Blanca, arrives with her three young children in tow. Actually, they arrive first, running in, waving to me as they dart to the children's section as an oft-exhausted Blanca comes trudging in behind. Blanca's kids are adorable. I keep forgetting their names so I call them Blanco, Blanki, and Blankette.

There's Nancy, who works at our local department store. I once mentioned my disappointment about a photo album I couldn't find there (I was told it was out of stock). The next time we met, Nancy came into class and presented me with my photo album — and wouldn't accept reimbursement from me. The next week she gave me a basket full of home-grown tomatoes.

Their lives are not easy. Over the past year, one woman got divorced and another's husband suffered a stroke. A third's husband, a truck driver, was in a horrific accident that left him home-bound for over nine months. But, they rarely miss a class.

And, they've, in turn, introduced me to others. I privately tutored one woman's niece, visiting for four months from Colombia, and then I was paired with Elena, 42, a divorced mother of three, who arrived from the Dominican Republic in December. She calls me, "Teach." When Elena told her daughter, the delightfully precocious Anna, 10- who has picked up English quite quickly, that I would be tutoring her mother, Anna looked at me, looked at her mother, and then back at me before declaring, "Good luck with that!" Elena and I laughed.

Elena is good-natured, ambitious, with plans to open her own perfume business (as she had before in the DR). In December, she is marrying a fellow who emigrated from Italy and I'm invited to the wedding. When we part after each session, the mothering Elena urges me, "Drive safely, Teach." I assure her, I will. After all, like a good American, I stop at red lights!

102

Taking My Students
To The Movies

Newsday, February 4, 2018

Recently schools across Long Island sent busloads of students to theatres to see "Wonder," a heartwarming story about a boy fighting to overcome a facial deformity. Hearing this news brought back wonderful memories of my years in the classroom when I would take my 7th grade Social Studies students to see inspirational films. Over the years, we saw, among others, "Gandhi" at Radio City Music Hall, "The Blind Side," "Invictus" (about Nelson Mandela), "Lincoln," and "42" (Jackie Robinson).

I \ enjoyed it for a number of reasons: First,I am a movie buff and I wanted my students to appreciate films; Second, it brought history alive; and lastly, it was a nice way for my students to bond with each other and with me.

All good memories that we still talk about years later.

Some of my colleagues, on the other hand, had less-than-wonderful experiences inside—and outside—the classroom. One teacher made the fatal mistake of not previewing a French movie when she took her kids to see it at nearby C.W. Post College. Beginning at 9 a.m., the opening scene contained explicit scenes of lesbian love-making. The teacher immediately hustled her childreen up and out the door and returned home by 9:25 a.m. in what some veterans said was the quickest field trip in our school's history.

Another colleague had a similar experience years earlier. Before the invention of DVDs or even videocassettes, teachers would project a film on a movie screen. Her movie about life in a small town was proceeding smoothly and without incident until a very well-endowed and thoroughly naked young lady frolicked across the screen. To shield her students from witnessing such a scene, the teacher stood in front of the projector only to realize that the naked young woman was now frolicking across her chest.

Thankfully, I had no such incidents, but there was one occasion when I was apprehensive about taking my students to the movies. It happened when I accompanied a small group of troubled students (purposely grouped together in my class to give them more individual attention) to see "Paper Clips," a documentary about a school in Tennessee where the students knew little or nothing about the Holocaust. (They couldn't fathom six million Jews murdered so the teacher had them collect paper clips.... six million of them. The class was featured on the evening news and soon celebrities were sending in paper clips. Steven Spielberg sent them a clip. Tom Brokaw did, too).

Despite my students' less-than-stellar reputations, I plunged ahead and we met on a Thursday night at the Roslyn Theatre. Walking in together, I could sense the apprehension of the mostly elderly movie-goers as my motley-looking crew entered the auditorium. Immediately, some of the patrons got up and went to the box office to get their money back. I grew fearful that maybe this wasn't a good idea.

But, unaware of the tumult their appearance caused, my students settled into their seats. And, before the lights dimmed, I witnessed a curious sight: Turning around in their seats, I could see them engaging the older folks in conversation. Wasn't sure what they were talking about, but there were abundant smiles and nods and... then "Paper Clips" started.

I watched my students. They were engaged in the movie. No one snuck out to get popcorn or soda.

When it was over, the crowd — students and local patrons — filed out. And, the older folks came over to me and offered compliments. One said, "You have very sweet students." One gentleman gave me the thumbs-up and said, "You must be proud of your children." I beamed at them and nodded.

I was.

103

Judging Girl Scout Bake-Off: A Piece Of Cake?

Newsday, February 18, 2018

It's Girl Scout Cookie time! From now through March, the girls (including my niece) will be selling their tasty treats to raise money for the organization. For me, it always brings back memories of the day when one of my students approached my desk, somewhat sheepishly, with this request: "Mr. Schachter, could you judge the Girl Scouts' baking competition this Friday after school?"

I looked down at that hopeful face and said, "Sure I will, Jennifer."

She beamed.

And, in the days leading up to the big event, I was beaming, too. Being required to eat cake was a task I could handle!

That Friday afternoon I strolled over to the Home Economics room. The Girl Scout leader made an effusive welcoming speech and I was given a score sheet, pencil, knife and a fork. I smiled at the girls around me and without much ado I dug into the first cake: Chocolate Chip. Mmm... delicious. Rich and creamy. Next, I plunged into the coconut. Another winner. The applesauce cake was waiting patiently on deck. I cut off a piece. Very tasty. I gave a hearty thumbs-up gesture as the girls looked on proudly.

"It's hard to decide," I said, "but I'll try to make a decision."

"Wait," implored the Girl Scout leader. "It's not over yet. You still have eleven more cakes to taste."

"Huh?"

Sure enough, she was right. There were eleven more.

I carved a piece from No. 4, a lemon-something or other. It was OK, but I soon found that I wasn't feeling just right. No. 5 impressed me less. No. 6 was even less appealing. I had trouble swallowing No. 7. At first, I couldn't figure it out, but then it hit me — I was growing sick of all this cake. But, as I looked from side to side at the eager faces in their matching green uniforms, I could see there was no way out. I smiled back weakly and plowed on. I don't remember what No.'s 8 and 9 tasted like, and by the time I got to No.'s 10 and 11, I couldn't remember what any of them tasted like.

I started cutting smaller and smaller pieces until it seemed I was sampling only crumbs. By the thirteenth cake, gritting my teeth, I felt like punching out every little Girl Scout in that room. Finally, I tasted, chewed, and swallowed a piece of cake No. 14. I had climbed Mt. Everest!

I had no idea which cake was best. After No. 6, they had all begun to taste the same.

Of course, I couldn't let on. I waddled over to the girls and congratulated them on a wonderful effort. I wiped off from my lips the crumbs from the chocolate, coconut, applesauce, lemon, and butterscotch cakes and considered a winner by gazing over the kinds of cake and saying softly to myself, "Eenie, meenie, minie, mo..."

Finally, I checked off No. 3 (Applesauce Cake) and the winner was announced.

That day marked the beginning of my illustrious pedagogical/judicial career. After judging the cake competition, I avoided the sweets and moved on to "Foods from Other Lands." I began to cross over into other disciplines, officiating at spelling bees, talent shows, sports field days, political debates, and history projects.

In looking back, however, I have to say that I'll always have a soft spot for that Girl Scout baking competition — but not necessarily in my stomach!

104

Facebook Still Gets A "Like" From Me

Newsday, June 2018

Facebook has been in the news recently — and for all the wrong reasons. Its founder, Mark Zuckerberg, faced an angry U.S. Congress delivering tough questions about the company's mishandling of data. As a result, some of my friends, worried that their privacy has been violated, are abandoning Facebook. But, not me. I'm sticking around!

Why? It's a great way to keep in touch with people. I love looking at pictures of new babies, trips abroad, and high school graduations. And I'm pleased that many of my friends' parents (most of them in their 80s and some in their 90s) have embraced Facebook. It's provided the folks — some of them homebound — with a link to the outside world. But I must admit, some are having trouble getting the hang of it.

"Richie," my friend's mother wrote, not realizing the whole world could see her message, "the toilet is clogged up again. Can you come over and fix it?"

Likewise, I am sometimes baffled at times by comments and responses. There were a slew of deaths they reported of famous people.

"RIP Harry Morgan" wrote one friend of the "M*A*S*H" star, whereupon a dozen others offered their condolences. What none of them realized was that Morgan had died seven years earlier, in 2011! The same thing happened with Bob Denver, the title character from "Gilligan's Island."

"Such a funny guy," wrote one, offering his condolences. "I'll miss him." These were followed by a flurry of sympathetic posts for the actor, yet no one seemed to know that he died in 2005.

Doesn't anyone read a newspaper? The reverse happened to John Amos, the star of "Good Times." On at least half a dozen occasions, I've seen friends post "RIP John Amos," with others chiming in with their memories of the actor, until someone (me!) pointed out that the guy is still very much alive.

Of course, being a former teacher, I sometimes want to get out my old red pencil and write across the screen: "Don't be vague!" "Be clear!" when they write cryptic messages such as:

"I can't even." I can't even touch my toes?

"Amazing what just happened." Did the Knicks win a game?

"You were so good. I just wish we had more time." Her husband? A long-lost love? Her hamster? (Indeed, many times it WAS the hamster.)

It is frustrating, but I will stay with Facebook, especially because I enjoy hearing from former students. I've loved watching them "grow up": college, careers, marriages, kids.

Nevertheless, I've set down some rules: I don't "friend" anyone. If former students want to "friend" me, they must be 24. (I figure at that age, they are finished with college, working, mature.)

It's amazing how many of them "friend" me and add: "I'm sorry I was such a jerk when I was in 7th grade." To which I would reply: "No apologies necessary. You were young. What matters is how you are now!"

My favorite request came from Sam Horowitz, a former seventh-grade student. When he was 21, he tried to "friend" me. I told him why I had to decline and concluded, "I'm honored to be asked, but if you want to be 'friends' with me, you have to wait until you're 24." Sam said he understood... and three years later, on his 24th birthday, he sent me a "friend" request. I happily accepted. I think I'll stick with Facebook!

105

Attention Must Be Paid

Newsday, July 8, 2018

When I was in college, I was smitten with a woman named Cathy. She was in my journalism class and was delightful, intelligent and gorgeous (she looked like the actress Lee Remick).

She seemed to like me, so one day, summoning all of my courage, I asked her out to dinner. She said yes, and before our first date, I was dreaming of her in a wedding dress. Off we went to a nice restaurant with hopes for a grand evening.

Well, it didn't turn out that way. Cathy treated the waiters with contempt. She was rude and condescending. Suddenly, Cathy didn't look so gorgeous to me. That was our first and last date.

I think about Cathy often because in these turbulent times, it seems we've made little progress when it comes to respect.

Recently, I was at an outdoor concert. A meek-looking older man struggled to direct traffic. He was clearly overwhelmed. Horns honked and one sharply dressed fellow in a sports car with a female companion, yelled, "Hey! What do you make? Two dollars an hour?"

The driver chortled, the woman laughed and the man cringed. So did I.

Why do we treat people in such a way? Even in death, we delegitimize their existence.

318 | Saul Schachter

When a school custodian who I worked with died recently, his obituary read that he "was a long-time employee at North Shore High School for over 20 years." It didn't say he was a custodian. But, when an elementary school teacher died, the obituary reported he was a "teacher." I see that often.

Was it a snub? I hope not. Funeral directors I spoke to said obituaries are written according to the wishes of the family.

I don't know about you, but I am in awe of our custodians. In fact, their job title is incomplete. They are electricians, carpenters and plumbers. I am amazed at their skills.

When I bought my house in 1983, the main stipulation was that it had to be in excellent shape because I couldn't repair a thing. Still can't. Indeed, when I screw in a light bulb, flick the switch, and the light goes on, I feel like Thomas Edison.

The author William Zinsser once took a job as a sanitation worker in Manhattan to write about life as a blue-collar worker. One night, a driver pulled up, asked him directions to the theater, but before Zinsser could reply (Zinsser knew the location), the driver yelled, "Oh, you wouldn't know. You're only a garbage man."

People deserve respect. I try to do my small part by writing thank-you notes to clerks, receptionists and sales representatives. (Macy's could paper an office wall with my letters.) And I contact their bosses, telling them how lucky they are to have such dedicated employees — and suggest triple raises in pay!

I'm always brought back to the scene at the end of Arthur Miller's "Death of a Salesman," when the wife of the beleaguered Willy Loman cries out in support of her late, much-abused, overworked husband: "Attention must be paid!"

"Death of a Salesman" was written in 1948. Seventy years later, those words of wisdom are still waiting to be heeded.

106

Helping Mom
Find Long-Lost Love Online

Newsday, November 25 2018

When I was vacationing in California a few winters ago, I received a call from my then-86-year-old mother in Glen Head. While we were catching up on the news, Mom suddenly interrupted: "I wonder whatever happened to Sid Dole."

Mom, a widow of four years since my father's passing at 88, was referring to one of her first boyfriends who accompanied her to my Aunt Bernice and Uncle Gerry's wedding in 1950. The Aunt Bernice-Uncle Gerry nuptials are famous in family lore because a movie exists of the happy occasion and Sid Dole's head can be spotted popping up in a couple of scenes.

"I don't know, Mom," I replied, "but I'll try to find him on the internet."

And, off I went! First thing I did was Google "Sid Dole" and "Sidney Dole." After several frustrating attempts, I found a "Sidney A. Dole" in Torrance, California. He was 87. Age sounded right. This could be the guy. There was a partial email address: s_____dole@_____.com. I figured the first part had to be sidneydole, but what could go before the ".com"?

I composed an email to Mr. Dole, preceding ".com" in the email address with "verizon," "gmail," "att" and four others. I introduced myself as the son of Vivian Sibener Schachter and told him how my mother was hoping he's had a happy and productive life. I also included my telephone number. I sent out the seven emails, six came back, which means — one made it through!

That night, the phone rang. It was Sidney Dole. We had a wonderful conversation. He had moved from New York to California more than 50 years ago. He had worked as an industrial psychologist/business manager. He'd been married twice, the second time over 28 years ago to a lovely woman named Beverly. He was content.

A few months later, Sidney called Mom and they reminisced for almost an hour. Mom was delighted.

A year later, I received an email from Beverly Dole. Sid had died. Her message read in part:

"I was with him when he spoke to you. That was nice of you to go to the trouble of contacting him. I know your mom was an important person in his life a long time ago. Sid died Friday morning from — I guess you would call — complications of old age. He was in hospice 1 1/2 days — maybe a record. We had a small service yesterday. I think it was nice. A few chuckles, which I think are pretty important. He had a good life, and I think that will help me.

"We were married for over 28 years, and July 17, 2016 would have been the 30th anniversary of our first date. Also — on 8/8 he would have been 88. Thanks again for contacting him. It's always fun to hear from your past!

Beverly Dole."

I went over to Mom's house to share the news with her. She cried. We talked about Dad and Sid and life. As I was leaving, she mused, "Why do all the good men die at 88?"

Then she poked me in the belly and said, "I'm going to make sure you live to 120!"

107

Seeing Beauty
With Limited Vision

Newsday, May 2019

Five days before Christmas, 2016, my then-87-year old vivacious, bubbly, loving mother, suddenly lost most of her vision. She had (CRVO) Central Retinal Vein Occlusion---"strokes in the eyes."

She was devastated, there were tears, and cries of "How could this happen to me?"

For years she has taken care of family and neighbors. Now she was a reluctant patient. Mom had limited vision, but could no longer drive or read the small print in newspapers. However, she didn't lose her spirit.

A couple of months later, we went to see a specialist in Manhattan. Clutching her newly-purchased cane and her pocketbook containing the peanut butter and jelly sandwiches that she made for us the night before, we took the Long Island Railroad into Manhattan, and then hopped on the subway up to the Lighthouse Guild at 65th St, right next to Lincoln Center. As soon as we entered the subway, everyone in the packed train seemed to smile when they saw Mom — as if they knew her. She started chattering away while I was gently nudging her towards a proffered seat. The train suddenly lurched forward for a second hurling Mom into the lap of a middle-aged woman. Undaunted, Mom kept chattering away. Five stops later, we were at our destination, found the Light-house, and after filling out the necessary paperwork, began eating our lunch as we waited for the doctor. When he emerged, Mom offered him half her sandwich, which for some reason, he declined.

We had a hopeful session with the good doctor (Mom's vision had gotten a bit better), bought magnifying glasses the doctor suggested — and started heading back. Mom loves New York City. It invigorates her. She often marvels, "How does everything work so smoothly?" We passed Lincoln Center and Mom smiled, "Wouldn't it be great to go to an opera here and then be able to walk home?" We got on the subway where a new group of passengers beamed at her. I think Mom could light up a prison.

Had a smooth ride back to Penn Station, but then upon exiting we made a wrong turn somewhere and ended up outside on 7th Avenue near the Madison Square Garden entrance. There was someone talking to a large crowd so Mom and I moseyed over. The Brooklyn Borough President was addressing the crowd complaining about how badly former Knicks' star, Charles Oakley, was treated a few nights earlier when he was arrested for disorderly conduct at a basketball game in the Garden. Then I lost Mom. Oh, no, I thought. Where is she? Then I spotted her. She had made her way to the front and was standing next to the Borough President (If the news conference had been extended a few more minutes, Mom probably would have given her two cents' worth about the incident).

I grabbed Mom and we went back inside and bought two tickets home on the Long Island Railroad. After we changed at Jamaica, I looked, with dismay, at the blighted areas outside our window. But Mom noticed something different. "Look at that wonderful architecture, look at those wonderful old buildings," she said. "This area will come back soon!"

She may have limited vision — and, sadly, it hasn't gotten any better — but I wish everyone could see the beauty that my mother sees.

END